Gay Mormons?

Gay Mormons?

Latter-day Saint Experiences of Same-Gender Attraction

Edited by BRENT KERBY

with Foreword by JUNE KERBY

April 14, 2011

The views expressed in this book belong to the individual authors, who do not represent The Church of Jesus Christ of Latter-day Saints.

Contents

Foreword

You may think it a bit unusual for the author's mother to write the foreword; but who knows Brent better or loves him more than I do?

It was Thursday evening, December 3, 2009, when my husband and I learned of Brent's same-gender attraction. We had just visited and eaten together and were enjoying some casual conversation, when I made a comment about how a wife could help him balance out his life. I will never forget the next few sentences in our conversation. He responded that while that would be nice, he just isn't attracted to girls. I then posed what seemed like a very logical question, "If you're not attracted to girls ... then ... do you like guys?"

I knew in an instant this was a life-changing conversation. It was the beginning of our understanding why Brent had never been able to fall in love with a woman, even though he had dated with that goal in mind. After several weeks of serious study, pondering, and reflection, it all began to make sense.

I cried a lot the first month. Not because I was ashamed or upset with Brent, but because I was sad for the life I feared it meant he would have. I worried about persecution and even physical abuse. I worried that he would live alone. I worried about AIDS. I especially worried about how he could possibly stay in the Church. But one thing I did not worry about was his standing before God. I knew he was a worthy, virtuous young man. It was a blessing to know that he was morally clean in every way, and that his honor and integrity were beyond reproach!

A lack of accurate information about homosexuality was part of the reason it took Brent so long to come to terms with his orientation. That was about to change. Throughout his life, Brent has followed a pattern of identifying an interest and then pursuing it with a passion. Computer programming, music, languages, Church history, juggling, and math are among the many interests he has pursued. So it was no surprise that after our conversation in December, he began scouring all available resources for information about the subject. Brent is very careful about details. When he was ten years old, he taught me a valuable lesson about speaking accurately and not exaggerating: when I used strong words like *always*, *never*, or *hate*, he would question me about it. Precise analysis and communication have been a high priority for him.

Over the next several months we talked often. We walked his path of discovery together, which was very helpful to both of us. I saw him grow and become more relaxed and outgoing as he came to understand himself better. He found that he was not alone, and he has reached out to lift others who are navigating the uncertain and sometimes unfriendly waters of being gay and Mormon. This book is part of his effort to lighten others' burdens.

We have supported Brent's efforts by hosting dinner parties in our home. Here I have had the opportunity to learn the stories of a number of LDS young adults. Their struggle often begins surprisingly young, and almost always painfully alone. Their anguish is obvious to me as they describe years of valiant attempts to become heterosexual. They did not choose to be gay. They pray that their family, friends, and fellow Church members will understand, but too few do. Ironically, those who ought to love them the most are often the ones who treat them the worst. Unkind words and actions make it even more difficult for them to reconcile their same-gender attraction with the gospel.

The Church teaches that the same standard of morality applies to everyone, yet many of us expect our gay brothers and sisters not only to be chaste but to live a life completely devoid of affection. We accept that an unmarried heterosexual couple can hold hands and hug, yet some of us can hardly tolerate a gay couple even sitting next to each other. Can that really be what the Lord wants?

I pray that those who read this book will seek the Spirit to soften their hearts, enlighten their minds, and give them true charity for all of God's children. Many of the stories are heart-wrenching, but if even one person is enlightened or encouraged by the words of this book, it will have been worth the effort of writing it. Keep up the good work, Brent. I'll be with you all the way!

JUNE KERBY
South Jordan, Utah
March 30, 2011

Preface

June 2010 is when I realized this book needed to be written. It was an exciting time to be at BYU, as the groundwork was being laid for Understanding Same-Gender Attraction (USGA), a now-thriving group of BYU students and friends who meet weekly on campus to discuss topics related to same-gender attraction, in an environment of respect for BYU, the Church, and the beliefs and experiences of others.[1]

Most of the stories in this book are contributed by personal acquaintances whom I met through USGA, North Star, and the Nicholson's monthly MoHo Parties. A few are from people I met through other venues such as the Sunstone Symposium, the Salt Lake City PFLAG, and Evergreen. One is a long-time friend of mine from BYU.

I am deeply grateful for the willingness of the contributors to share some of the most personal aspects of their lives. I have learned much from each of them. They represent a broad set of perspectives and experiences, and I have made no attempt to categorize their stories. Although this book focuses on aspects of their lives relating to their Mormon faith and same-gender attraction, the reader should keep in mind that each is a complex individual with diverse characteristics, interests, and accomplishments. Since they are still living, their stories are not yet complete, and their perspectives and choices may evolve after the publication of this book.

I want to give some detail about how this book developed and my method in editing it. There were about 160 people whom I individually invited to participate in this book, in addition to open invitations which I posted online through North Star and Facebook, to which two people responded (their stories are both included). In the initial information which I sent to potential contributors, I outlined the goals of the project:

---

[1] USGA is not sponsored, endorsed, or supported by BYU.

> Our goal is to reach out to same-gender-oriented Mormons, especially youth, and help them know that they are not alone, and that they don't have to be ashamed or feel isolated ... We also want to reach out to a larger Mormon and Christian audience to help them understand this issue better and be more compassionate.

> We want to take a positive, forward-looking approach. Although some contributors will have had some negative experiences — and these can and must be shared also — we want the overall tone to be positive; we don't want to include attacks on individuals or organizations.

Those who declined to participate often cited a lack of time. Some said that they would be unable to take a positive approach with the Church. Others indicated that they were unsure of their future and where they stood. One expressed concern about possible repercussions to his employment. Another worried it could affect her standing in the Church. One man indicated it would be too painful to go back and revisit his past. Two men said their wives were concerned about going public with their situation.

I asked each contributor to share a quote summing up their philosophy about life, and this appears at the beginning of each story. Most of the contributors share their experiences using their real names. The names of others have been changed to protect their privacy. The first occurrence of each pseudonym is enclosed in quotation marks.

Of the 37 narratives in this book, 24 are based on a written account by the contributor. In the remaining 13 cases, I interviewed the contributor either in person or by phone and recorded their words as they spoke. Either way, I edited the accounts by sequencing them chronologically, by removing grammatical stumbling blocks and redundant or less relevant material, by clarifying potentially confusing sentences, and by inserting section headings. In some cases where there was a gap or ambiguity I followed up with the contributor to obtain more information. Unless otherwise noted, quotations from journals, letters, and other documents are unedited: spelling and grammatical errors are retained without comment. A glossary of LDS terminology is included for the benefit of readers who may be less familiar with Mormon culture and doctrine.

In accordance with the principles of this project, I removed material expressing antagonism toward any person or group, such as the Church or the LGBT community. Objective recounting of negative experiences was allowed provided the privacy of others was appropriately respected. In stripping out antagonistic expressions, I attempted to leave the associated experiences intact.

In every case, I submitted the edited version back to the original contributors, asking them to carefully review it to ensure everything was accurate, and giving them an opportunity to make changes. Two accounts were withdrawn: in one case, the contributor indicated that he wanted to make changes but apologized that he did not have time to do so; in the other case, the author opted to withdraw the account rather than remove expressions which could come across as antagonistic. In a third case, I have been unable to make contact with the contributor to confirm his approval, so his story is also not included. With these three exceptions, every story which was submitted is published in this book.

The image of the temple on the front cover applies in several ways. Most of the contributors have spent many hours serving in the temple. Several of them have been married in the temple. Many have gone there seeking answers to difficult questions. For some it has been a place of comfort and revelation. For others it may be a painful reminder of eternal marriage and their inability to take part in it.

The question mark in the title likewise has several meanings. Some Church members question the existence of that which may be hard for them to understand. Also, many of the contributors have questioned their own feelings and beliefs and wondered why things are the way they are. Doctrinally, there are far more questions than answers.

I wish to express thanks to the ward members, bishops, and other friends and family who have shown interest in this project and supported me in it. I hope that its publication will contribute to a renewal of peace, love, and understanding in the Church. I have no doubt that there are many others whose stories are yet untold, and whose experiences may be different from any recounted in this book. I hope that this project may inspire others to open their hearts to their families, their wards, and their communities. I believe we may be transformed as we share our experiences with one another, our joys and pains. Whether those experiences have to do with same-gender attraction or something entirely different, I believe we will grow closer together as we take the risk of being "willing to bear one another's burdens, that they may be light" (Mosiah 18:8).

BRENT KERBY
Murray, Utah
April 13, 2011

Gay Mormons?

Introduction

> Now, we have gays in the church. Good people. We take no action against such people — provided they don't become involved in transgression, sexual transgression. If they do, we do with them exactly what we'd do with heterosexuals who transgress.
>
> We have a very strong moral teaching concerning abstinence before marriage and total fidelity following marriage. And, regardless of whether they're heterosexuals or otherwise, if they step over that line there are certain sanctions, certain penalties that are imposed.
>
> – President Gordon B. Hinckley[2]

Many ask, why are some people gay? Is it a choice? Can they change? And what exactly does it mean to be gay or same-gender-attracted? These are challenging questions which might not have simple answers.

Most of the people in this book describe being drawn to others of the same gender, loving them, and yearning for intimate companionship with them emotionally and physically. Many have never experienced attractions to the opposite gender, even after years of prayers and efforts. Others describe a degree of fluidity in their feelings, including at least a limited ability to connect romantically with the opposite gender.

Many have followed the Church's teachings from a young age but have experienced feelings of isolation and shame as they realized they were different. Some, feeling worthless and condemned by God, have taken steps to harm themselves or even end their own lives.

---

[2] Lattin, Don. "SUNDAY INTERVIEW – Musings of the Main Mormon", *San Francisco Chronicle* 13 April 1997.

Current Church viewpoints

In a 2004 interview with Larry King, when asked if being gay was something people were "born with", President Gordon B. Hinckley replied, "I don't know. I'm not an expert on these things. I don't pretend to be an expert on these things."[3]

In a 2006 interview with Church Public Affairs on same-gender attraction, Elder Dallin H. Oaks stated:

> The Church does not have a position on the causes of any of these susceptibilities or inclinations ... Those are scientific questions — whether nature or nurture — those are things the Church doesn't have a position on.[4]

In the same interview, Elder Lance B. Wickman acknowledged that "one's gender orientation is certainly a core characteristic of any person." At the same time, he encouraged people not to place undue emphasis on this one aspect of their personality: "Find fulfillment in the many other facets of your character and your personality and your nature that extend beyond that."

In a 2006 media interview, Elder Marlin K. Jensen stated:

> It has created a lot of pain for me just because I've known some of these wonderful people who have these feelings ... I've sat with those that have tried for years to transition to a more traditional way of life and who haven't been able to produce those feelings in themselves that would permit them honestly to marry ...

> [Their] choice has to be to live a celibate life. That is a very difficult choice for the parents, for the young man, the young woman, for whoever's making that choice, and my heart goes out to them. I think we're asking a tremendous amount of them ...

> We, again, as a church need to be, I think, even more charitable than we've been, more outreaching in a sense.[5]

[3] "A Conversation with Gordon B. Hinckley", 26 December 2004. http://transcripts.cnn.com/TRANSCRIPTS/0412/26/lkl.01.html
[4] "Same-Gender Attraction", 2006. http://newsroom.lds.org/official-statement/same-gender-attraction
[5] "The Mormons: Interviews, Marlin Jensen", 7 March 2006. http://www.pbs.org/mormons/interviews/jensen.html

In 2007 the Church released a pamphlet, "God Loveth His Children", addressed directly to members of the Church who experience same-gender attraction:

> You are a son or daughter of God ... God does indeed love all His children. Many questions, however, including some related to same-gender attractions, must await a future answer ...
>
> Same-gender attractions include deep emotional, social, and physical feelings. All of Heavenly Father's children desire to love and be loved ...
>
> Some people with same-gender attraction have felt rejected because members of the Church did not always show love. No member of the Church should ever be intolerant.[6]

This was followed by an Ensign article by Elder Jeffrey R. Holland:

> Although I believe members are eager to extend compassion to those different from themselves, it is human nature that when confronted with a situation we don't understand, we tend to withdraw. This is particularly true of same-gender attraction. We have so little reliable information about it that those wanting to help are left feeling a bit unsteady ...
>
> [R]ecognize that marriage is not an all-purpose solution. Same-gender attractions run deep, and trying to force a heterosexual relationship is not likely to change them. We are all thrilled when some who struggle with these feelings are able to marry, raise children, and achieve family happiness. But other attempts have resulted in broken hearts and broken homes ...
>
> [S]ome members exclude from their circle of fellowship those who are different. When our actions or words discourage someone from taking full advantage of Church membership, we fail them — and the Lord. The Church is made stronger as we include every member and strengthen one another in service and love.[7]

---

[6] "God Loveth His Children", pp. 1, 4, 9.
[7] "Helping Those Who Struggle with Same-Gender Attraction", *Ensign*, October 2007.

Controversy and clarification

In the October 2010 General Conference, President Boyd K. Packer stated:

> Some suppose that they were preset and cannot overcome what they feel are inborn tendencies toward the impure and unnatural. Not so! Why would our Heavenly Father do that to anyone?[8]

Many members interpreted this as saying that God would not allow someone to be born gay, that anyone could choose to be heterosexual. This seemed to run contrary to the official Church teaching that even faithful members "may not be free of this challenge in this life", as "same-gender attractions may continue".[9] Ten years earlier, even President Packer himself had acknowledged, "That may be a struggle from which you will not be free in this life."[10]

When the talk appeared on the Church website and in the *Ensign*, the word "tendencies" was replaced by "temptations", and the question "Why would our Heavenly Father do that to anyone?" was omitted.

President Packer's talk came at a particularly sensitive time, as the media had been extensively reporting on a nationwide string of suicides by bullied gay teenagers. Critics argued that President Packer's statements could feed into anti-gay bullying. The Human Rights Campaign delivered 150,000 petitions to the Church, claiming that the changes to the talk did not go far enough, and asking the Church to make a full correction. In response, the Church issued the following statement:

> My name is Michael Otterson. I am here representing the leadership of The Church of Jesus Christ of Latter-day Saints to address the matter of the petition presented today by the Human Rights Campaign.
>
> While we disagree with the Human Rights Campaign on many fundamentals, we also share some common ground. This past week we have all witnessed tragic deaths across the country as a result of bullying or intimidation of gay young men. We join our voice with others in unreserved condemnation of acts of cruelty or attempts to belittle or

---

[8] "Cleansing the Inner Vessel", 3 October 2010.
[9] "God Loveth His Children", pp. 4, 8.
[10] "Ye Are the Temple of God", *Ensign*, November 2000.

mock any group or individual that is different — whether those differences arise from race, religion, mental challenges, social status, sexual orientation or for any other reason. Such actions simply have no place in our society.

This Church has felt the bitter sting of persecution and marginalization early in our history, when we were too few in numbers to adequately protect ourselves and when society's leaders often seemed disinclined to help. Our parents, young adults, teens and children should therefore, of all people, be especially sensitive to the vulnerable in society and be willing to speak out against bullying or intimidation whenever it occurs, including unkindness toward those who are attracted to others of the same sex. This is particularly so in our own Latter-day Saint congregations. Each Latter-day Saint family and individual should carefully consider whether their attitudes and actions toward others properly reflect Jesus Christ's second great commandment — to love one another.

As a church, our doctrinal position is clear: any sexual activity outside of marriage is wrong, and we define marriage as between a man and a woman. However, that should never, ever be used as justification for unkindness. Jesus Christ, whom we follow, was clear in His condemnation of sexual immorality, but never cruel. His interest was always to lift the individual, never to tear down.

Further, while the Church is strongly on the record as opposing same-sex marriage, it has openly supported other rights for gays and lesbians such as protections in housing or employment.

The Church's doctrine is based on love. We believe that our purpose in life is to learn, grow and develop, and that God's unreserved love enables each of us to reach our potential. None of us is limited by our feelings or inclinations. Ultimately, we are free to act for ourselves.

The Church recognizes that those of its members who are attracted to others of the same sex experience deep emotional, social and physical feelings. The Church distinguishes between feelings or inclinations on the one hand and behavior on the other. It's not a sin to have feelings, only in yielding to temptation.

There is no question that this is difficult, but Church leaders and members are available to help lift, support and encourage fellow members who wish to follow Church doctrine. Their struggle is our struggle. Those in the Church who are attracted to someone of the same sex but stay faithful to the Church's teachings can be happy during this life and perform meaningful service in the Church. They can enjoy full fellowship with other Church members, including attending and serving in temples, and ultimately receive all the blessings afforded to those who live the commandments of God.

Obviously, some will disagree with us. We hope that any disagreement will be based on a full understanding of our position and not on distortion or selective interpretation. The Church will continue to speak out to ensure its position is accurately understood.

God's universal fatherhood and love charges each of us with an innate and reverent acknowledgement of our shared human dignity. We are to love one another. We are to treat each other with respect as brothers and sisters and fellow children of God, no matter how much we may differ from one another.

We hope and firmly believe that within this community, and in others, kindness, persuasion and goodwill can prevail.[11]

Terminology and labeling

In the past, some Church leaders discouraged using certain words to describe same-gender-oriented individuals:

We should note that the words *homosexual, lesbian,* and *gay* are adjectives to describe particular thoughts, feelings, or behaviors. We should refrain from using these words as nouns to identify particular conditions or specific persons. Our religious doctrine dictates this usage. It is wrong to use these words to denote a *condition,* because this implies that a person is consigned by birth to a circumstance in

---

[11] "Church Responds to HRC Petition: Statement on Same-Sex Attraction", 12 October 2010. http://newsroom.lds.org/article/church-mormon-responds-to-human-rights-campaign-petition-same-sex-attraction

which he or she has no choice in respect to the critically
important matter of sexual *behavior*.[12]

On the other hand, over the past two decades the meaning and
usage of these terms has evolved within the Church. The Church's
most authoritative and recent statement on same-gender attraction,
discussed in the previous section, refers to "gay young men" and "gays
and lesbians". Many faithful members of the Church use the term *gay*
simply as an objective description of their orientation. They retain
responsibility in the matter of sexual behavior, and many do not see
a need to make their "gayness" a major part of their identity; it may
form only a small part of their identity, or it may only be a descriptive
term having nothing to do with their identity at all.

Need for greater awareness

A recent national survey, based on a large representative sample,
found that 4.2% of men and 0.9% of women identified as gay or
lesbian, and an additional 2.6% of men and 3.6% of women identified as bisexual.[13] In a typical LDS congregation, there are several
members who are gay or bisexual. They may be your Sunday School
teacher, your organist, your elders quorum president, your Relief
Society president, your bishop.

The complexity of the conflict faced by gay Mormons is rarely
appreciated. Some outside the Church wonder, "Why would you
continue to be part of an institution which doesn't truly accept you
for who you are?" And some LDS members wonder, "If you believe in
the Church, then how can you not be committed to finding someone
to marry?"

For those who wish to adhere to Church teachings, their dilemma
is made more difficult by the hurtful or misinformed attitudes of
others. It can be alienating when members so often make statements
which assume that everyone in the room is attracted to the opposite
gender. Members may appear awkward or uncomfortable when they
learn of a fellow ward member's orientation. Some respond by judging
them and assuming they are unchaste or sinful. Others promise them

---

[12]Dallin H. Oaks, "Same-Gender Attraction", *Ensign*, October 1995.

[13]Herbenick, Debby, et al. "Sexual Behavior in the United States: Results from
a National Probability Sample of Men and Women Ages 14-94", *Journal of Sexual
Medicine*, 2010. Vol. 7, Supp. 5. p. 258. These figures are for the adults in the
sample. For adolescents, 1.8% of males and 0.2% of females identified as gay or
lesbian, and 1.5% of males and 8.4% of females identified as bisexual.

that they can change, through the Atonement, or try to console them that even if their life is lonely and rough, they'll get their blessings in the next life if they faithfully endure through their struggle.

But nobody wants to be pitied, to be told that their life will be a "struggle" or that they may have to wait until the next life to obtain full happiness. President Joseph F. Smith taught:

> It has always been a cardinal teaching with the Latter-day Saints that a religion that has not the power to save people temporally and make them prosperous and happy here cannot be depended upon to save them spiritually and exalt them in the life to come.[14]

Hope for the future

One sad fact is that a great many gay Mormons are concluding they cannot be happy in the Church. They are steadily streaming out of our midst. In this book, some individuals describe continuing to have a testimony of the Church but simply being unable to find a place in it. Others have experienced a loss of faith or belief. Some continue active in the Church but wrestle with doubts and uncertainties.

In the Church, we are sometimes uncomfortable with people who "leave the fold". There may be a tendency to lean on negative stereotypes, to look down on them as having selfish motives or lacking true faith. But what is the reality for these children of God? What is it like to experience the loss of one's spiritual home? The accounts in this book may help us approach these questions with greater sensitivity and compassion.

As people step forward and share their experiences, my hope is that others will feel less isolated. I hope they will feel that they *do* have a home in the Church, and that they don't have to hide who they are.

If unkind words are spoken among our friends or in our congregations, I hope we will have the courage to speak up and gently help others be more understanding. You may not know how much impact you will have, or whose life you might save. All of us have unique gifts and experiences. Sharing these may require making ourselves vulnerable, but it also opens the door to having our "hearts knit together in unity and in love one towards another" (Mosiah 18:21).

---

[14] "The Truth about Mormonism", *Out West*, 1905. Vol. 23, p. 242.

Brent Kerby

When I was five years old, my mother gave me a journal. The first entry, scrawled out in shaky letters, begins:

> BE NICE. TAKE TURNS ON COUPUTERS[.] SHARE.
> I AM 5 YEARS OLD. (Nov 10, 1988)

Each morning and evening our family would kneel together for prayer. My dad would wrestle with me, and we would jump on the trampoline together. From a young age, I loved the Church and its teachings and became immersed in the scriptures:

> I LOVE TO READ THE BOOK OF MORMON   IT IM-
> PORTANT READ THE BOOK OF MOR[MON] (Jan 22, 1989)

One Sunday at Primary someone noticed how I was sitting, with my legs crossed knee-over-knee. They gently explained to me that there was a difference between how girls sit and how boys sit. That came as a revelation to me! I made sure to sit "like a boy" after that.

I would love to see him again

Growing up, I enjoyed being around other boys and playing games together. When I was 12 years old, I began to feel a deep sense of fascination and spiritual connection with certain boys. One time while on a family trip away from home, I met a boy "Alvin" who made an amazing impression on me:

> Today was an awesome day! ... Today, in church, I met a boy ... He's a sharp kid ... When I first saw him, I had the feeling come over me that we'd known each other before this life. (Jun 23, 1996)

> I still remember the moment. We were on opposite sides of the classroom ... At that moment the Spirit was greater than any other moment in my life I can recall ... I think we may have had eye contact for a short time. Wow! I would love to see him again ... If I don't see him again in this life, I know I will in the next. (Jul 21, 1996)

On the same day that I met Alvin, I wrote:

> I really, truely want to live with Heavenly Father & Jesus again. They have loved me so much ... I am very anxious to go on a mission. I want to serve the Lord. I want to raise up a family unto him. I hope I will be given the chance to do so. (Jun 23, 1996)

A few years later, I had a friend "Ryan" who I felt a lot of affection for. I liked to sit next to him, and I often wanted to put my arm around him or massage his shoulders. I wasn't sure if it would be okay, though, so I held it in. Occasionally I would pat him on the back, and a few times we would "thumb wrestle", which created a way to hold his hand in a socially acceptable way. One time I stayed the night over at his house, and it felt so peaceful and sweet just being there with him sleeping in the same room.

I didn't see anything wrong with how I felt. I knew I felt more affectionate than other guys. But I understood this in terms of brotherly love, and I didn't perceive it as being sexual in any way.

Around this time, members of my family would occasionally ask me if I had started noticing girls yet. I would typically reply, "Not yet." I assumed I was a late bloomer, and that sooner or later the hormones would kick in. Year after year, I kept waiting for this anticipated transformation to occur.

Welcome to BYU

Following a tradition in my family, I decided to apply for and attend Brigham Young University (BYU). My first week at BYU, I was volunteered to perform a brief juggling act on stage at "Arise for Honor", an event which introduced new students to the Honor Code.

I lived on-campus in Heritage Halls. I liked the environment at BYU; it was a beautiful, clean campus with some of the friendliest people I had ever met. As I was making the transition to life away from home for the first time, I soon met "Nick", a nice returned missionary who befriended me. After church one Sunday, he set me apart to be a pianist for elders quorum:

> He blessed me to have agile fingers, and to be able to touch others with music; and he counseled me to seek the spirit. Then, we started to shake hands, but Nick gave [me] a big hug. I so love Nick; I've needed a hug bad for about a year. (Jul 15, 2001)

Later that same day I recorded:

> Something else odd is that I've been out here a month almost and gone on no dates. Sometimes I wonder if I have no horomones; I don't think I've ever really been attracted to a girl. Oh well.

I began visiting Nick frequently. We were in the same math class and would often work together. He would tell me about his problems with girls, and I would feel bad when things weren't going well for him. He would give me a tender hug each time I left his apartment in the evening. I was shy about it, but he could sense that I yearned for these hugs.

Near the end of the summer, one evening I went out jogging with him. We jogged around the Provo Temple, and on the way back I shyly asked him if he would like to be roommates next year. He hesitated but responded that he didn't think it would work out. I was painfully disappointed. At the same time, I was conflicted and confused about why I was feeling so emotional about it.

> I feel sometimes that my heart is somehow hibernating; I have feelings, but somehow it seems like I stifle them before they go anywhere because I don't want people to see them. (Aug 17, 2001)

I became involved in Y-Juggle, the BYU juggling club, and enjoyed teaching others how to juggle. There was a girl who sometimes visited our apartment. She and I played the piano and juggled together, and she made me a set of five homemade beanbags. She was very kind, and I wondered if she was interested in me, but I was also aware that I wasn't feeling any attraction to her or any other girls.

At the end of the school year, on the last day before I had to move out, I stayed up late packing my things. I visited the guys at the apartment next door and said my goodbyes to them. A friend "Mark" came up to me, I gave him a hug, and he hugged me back affectionately; he was such a kind, sweet guy, and I felt so happy to be loved by him like that. At the same time, after a couple seconds I felt a bit awkward because of what others in the room might think if we hugged for too long. I took a step or two back, but he held on and stepped with me and said he didn't want to let go, so we hugged for a few more seconds. It felt so tender; I loved him and didn't want to let him go either. I felt sad that I was leaving and might not see him again.

I hope they call me on a mission

By the time I was 19, I had put in my paperwork to apply to serve a mission for the Church. However, due to an oversight, the paperwork was delayed, so I returned to BYU for another year, which ended up being a blessing.

That year I took a weight-lifting class. A part of me was thinking that my lack of attraction to girls might be caused by some kind of incomplete development, and maybe it could be spurred to completion if I exercised and worked out? It seemed like a shaky theory, but I thought it was at least worth a try, and working out would be a healthy thing to do anyway. I wasn't really too worried. People often told me that I looked several years younger than I actually was, so it seemed plausible that I was still just a "late bloomer". I knew I didn't want to get married until after my mission anyway, so I didn't feel much pressure.

In the building where I lived, I met a guy "Tim" who shared my interest in computer science, and we quickly became friends. The next summer, we became roommates. For a while, we had a habit of giving each other a hug every day or two. Sometimes when I was sitting at my desk, he would stand behind me and massage my shoulders for a little bit, which I really appreciated. Soon I started reciprocating and would massage his shoulders when he was studying. However, one time just as I was starting he told me he was uncomfortable and asked me to stop. This hit me like a ton of bricks. I tried to figure out what I had done wrong; was there something bad about it, or was I doing it too frequently, or what? It came across to me as a deep rejection. On the other hand, I felt like I was making too big a deal out of it, and I was too embarrassed to ask him about it.

Throughout the summer, I had been hanging out with a girl that I met through church:

> It's funny; at times we've hung out enough together to be girlfriend/boyfriend, although that's not the way it is at all. In fact, I think I've never even touched her at all, so I guess you could say it's not a physical relationship.
>
> Hmm, being at BYU and all and seeing so many people flirting and getting married is kind of odd. Well, it makes me realize how nonflirtatious I am myself. I guess it probably goes back to hormone levels and stuff. Well I hope something changes someday (in about 2 years would be nice :-)), otherwise I can't see myself ever getting married, and that's kind of a scary thought. (Aug 9, 2003)

During the summer, I received my mission call to serve in Las Vegas, Nevada, which I was both nervous and excited about.

> Yesterday I watched the second half of "How Rare a Possession" [a film about the Book of Mormon]. That's really an amazing movie; it makes me psyched to get out in the mission. (Aug 9, 2003)

Called to serve

After a three-week training at the Missionary Training Center in Provo, Utah, I flew into Las Vegas. I found my mission stressful but also exciting and fulfilling.

> All right! First full day here in Las Vegas. Yesterday was pretty sweet. We flew in at 9:10 ...[W]e drove by the temple (Sep 10, 2003)
>
> We went tracting all afternoon yesterday; that was really fun. I learned a lot! Nobody let us in, except for a few

> members, but it was still a good experience. A few people
> let us schedule an appointment. (Sep 12, 2003)

> There's just not enough time to write everything. It's
> good. We're keeping busy. Our car overheated and started
> smoking yesterday. But we put some water in it and it's
> okay now. (Sep 13, 2003)

In my mission, companions were instructed to have "companionship inventory" once a week: this was an opportunity for companions
to evaluate their relationship and resolve any concerns. The mission
guidelines for companionship inventory included giving each other a
hug at the end.

> [W]hen I first came here, [my companion] seemed pretty
> unfriendly because he utterly refused to follow the pro-
> gram at the end of our companionship inventory by giv-
> ing me a hug ... I guess that kind of stuff makes him
> uncomfortable for some reason; it's kinda hard for me to
> understand. It's always just seemed like basic gestures of
> friendship, but I guess in these days with so many gay
> people, it can make you a little hesitant in sharing broth-
> erly love, for fear of being taken the wrong way. Maybe
> that's where he's coming from. I don't know. Anyhow, he
> found out it was making me pretty sad. Anyhow, things
> are pretty great now. (Oct 7, 2003)

In my mind, "gay people" were an abstract, foreign group that I
knew almost nothing about. Up to that point, I had never met anyone
that was gay, as far as I knew. Growing up, I was fairly insulated
culturally: I rarely watched television, and my close associations were
mostly limited to my Mormon friends.

There was one time on my mission, with a different companion,
when I patted him on the shoulder, and he told me that if I do that,
I should use the back of my hand, not the palm; otherwise, he said
guys might think I'm gay. I felt embarrassed and apologized. I had
felt like I was just expressing normal affection. But I didn't want to
make him uncomfortable, and it was scary to think that something
like this might make guys think I'm gay.

End of one mission, beginning of another

Near the end of my mission, with the permission of my mission
president I read the History of the Church. I was struck by a passage

from the journal of George A. Smith describing an interaction with
his cousin, the Prophet Joseph Smith:

> At the close of the conversation, Joseph wrapped his arms
> around me, and squeezed me to his bosom and said,
> "George A., I love you as I do my own life." I felt so af-
> fected, I could hardly speak, but replied, "I hope, Brother
> Joseph, that my whole life and actions will ever prove my
> feelings, and the depth of my affection towards you."[15]

Throughout my mission, I had difficulties adjusting to the stresses
of missionary life. I wished that I had invested more time in prepa-
ration before my mission. On the other hand, I felt that I was doing
my best.

> Things are changing real fast. It's making me get emo-
> tional, looking back at my mission ... But I have no
> regrets. It hasn't exactly gone the way I expected ... But
> who cares? The Lord's will has been done. I'm humbled
> that I've been able to be an instrument in his hands for
> this time, and am so grateful for the things I have been
> taught ... I feel very much at peace — the comfort of the
> Holy Ghost. When the great day of judgement comes, I
> hope that it feels like this. (Oct 22, 2004)

> I went to bed and prayed and sang hymns, and it just hit
> me: the sadness of leaving the mission. I don't think I've
> ever wept like that before. (Oct 24, 2004)

On the last day of my mission, my companion and I rode our bikes
to Deseret Book, and I purchased a set of scriptures for a girl "Anna"
who had recently been baptized; I wrote a note in the front:

> It's been wonderful teaching you! You're an awesome
> person! I pray you will always find the peace that comes
> from the Savior, as you study these sacred books. Best
> wishes ... throughout your life. Always remember you are
> a daughter of God. We love you! Please stay in contact.
> - ELDER BRENT LLOYD KERBY

I gave her the new copy of the scriptures, and she smiled and was
about to cry. She asked and I balanced a chair on my chin for her,
and we took some pictures. She gave me a tender letter in which she

---

[15] *History of the Church*, 5:391.

thanked me for teaching her the gospel and expressed her hope that I would never forget her. She said that she would miss me and that she really cared about me and liked me.

The next morning I flew home to Mississippi. I was honorably released and soon got a phone call from Anna:

> We talked for a while. She wants to come up to Utah and visit me in February or March. She asked what I thought of her letter ... I just said that it made me happy, especially that she expressed the gospel as the 'key to happiness'. But she wanted to know if I like her the way she likes me. Well, I was real honest and told her I was still in the missionary mindset and everything, that I liked her more as a friend. (Oct 27, 2004)

In my mind, the fact that I was "still in the missionary mind-set" was the explanation for why I had not yet adjusted into what I assumed would be my natural state of being attracted to girls. However, I did not intend to leave my mission behind just yet. I began vociferously reading books by Church scholars such as Hugh Nibley, about Church history and the scriptures. I also made a goal of reading the Book of Mormon in a different language each year, which I did in Spanish, German, and French, successively.

After my first semester back at BYU, I attended a Church broadcast:

> Dallin H. Oaks spoke to us ... He said that we need to date ... Looks like I need to repent :-) I could count my dates on one hand, and none since my mission. (May 2, 2005)

Soon after, I recorded:

> It was special time to me, my mission. It still feels like it never ended, like it's just beginning now. (May 4, 2005)

Everything is normal

One afternoon as I was studying on-campus in the Clyde building, I looked up at a guy sitting on the other side of the room. I felt a pang of disappointment as I realized I couldn't see him clearly — I had developed some minor near-sightedness, apparently as a result of so much reading. I thought to myself, "Darn! This makes it harder to check out guys." I immediately felt perplexed that I had thought of it that way. I was a bit embarrassed, and I put the thought out of my mind. Later I obtained a pair of reading glasses to avoid further strain on my eyes.

I was troubled that I still didn't feel any attractions to girls. At this point I was 22 years old, and the "late-bloomer" explanation was appearing less and less plausible. I wondered if something might be wrong with my hormones. My mother did some research and emailed me suggesting I see a urologist. I was feeling self-conscious about the whole issue and replied:

> Hey Mom ... I probably should have said this earlier: I'm hoping you haven't mentioned this to anyone (besides Dad), at least not until we find out for sure what, if anything, is wrong. I would rather you not email about it, because email isn't terribly secure, and I have no place to read it privately. (Sep 22, 2005)

In my journal, I recorded the urologist visit with a brief, discreet statement:

> Went to doctor appointment this afternoon (Oct 13, 2005)

After the test results came back, the doctor reported that everything was normal, and that in fact my testosterone level was "on the high end of normal". On the one hand, this was reassuring; but on the other hand, I had been hoping for a simple solution, and this information didn't provide any answers.

Dating and double-dating

I decided that I should try going out on dates more often; I thought this might be what I needed to do in order for an attraction to emerge. So I went out with a lot of different girls and attended dinners, plays, comedy shows, and movies. We went ice skating, watched the BYU planetarium show, played laser tag, went to dances, concerts, and so on. I developed some friendships but didn't feel any inkling of a romantic or physical interest. Sometimes a girl would start to be a little flirtatious with me, and that would make me uncomfortable. I was conflicted, because on the one hand I knew I felt nothing and didn't want to hurt a girl by leading her on, but on the other hand I wanted to give it a chance.

At different times there were a few girls who, in my mind, I was steadily dating. I would pick out a girl who seemed intelligent and happy, and I would ask her out and try to spend time with her on a regular basis. I didn't feel any sense of closeness or attachment, but I felt it was my priesthood duty to try. I assumed that when the time was right, things would work out.

One time I went on a double date, and as part of the activity the decision was made to split up until the end of the date, with me and my date going to my apartment and the other guy and his date going to another apartment. I remember feeling a bit disappointed, because I thought the other guy was nice and I really liked being around him.

On another occasion, I went on a group date with one of my roommates "Adam", and my natural inclination was to sit next to him rather than the girl I was dating; but I realized this wouldn't be polite. During our time as roommates, I had really grown to love and care about him.

One Sunday Adam disappeared. I noticed his car was gone but that he hadn't made it to church in the morning; in the afternoon he missed an appointment and didn't pick up his cell phone. Others didn't seem to think it was a big deal, but I was really worried and called the police so they could look for his car. That night, I went to bed but couldn't sleep. Finally, in the middle of the night he came home. I was so relieved to hear him come in! I got up and found out that everything was okay. I really wanted to hug him, and several times I almost did, but I decided not to because I thought it might be awkward.

That same month, our apartment received the October 2007 Ensign, which contained an article titled "Helping Those Who Struggle with Same-Gender Attraction". I read the entire article, being careful to make sure nobody saw me reading it. Then I put it aside, thinking it didn't really apply to me. And yet, deep down I sensed it had at least some relevance.

Disappointments and new beginnings

One time I was in the living room sitting on a couch next to Adam watching a movie. I was on his left, and a girl was on his right. I really wanted to put my arm around him, but it seemed like that might be weird. Instead, I put my hands behind my head and then let my elbow rest a little on his shoulder. He immediately turned, smiled, and asked, "Brent, what are you doing? Are you trying to hit on me or something?" I felt terribly embarrassed and said, "Sorry." I moved over to the other end of the couch. The sting of embarrassment and rejection persisted for several days, and I felt depressed; at the same time, I felt conflicted because I couldn't understand why I was so emotional about it.

This pattern was repeated over the years with many guys at BYU. I couldn't understand why I wasn't able to make a friend who cared about me the same way I cared about him. I assumed it must be because I just wasn't likable enough.

As summer approached and I wanted to make roommate arrangements, again and again I was turned down by guys who were my friends but who wanted to live elsewhere. One guy that I felt particularly close to left to go home for the summer without saying goodbye, which hurt a lot. At the same time, I was dealing with some health issues and other difficulties. And I felt worn down by my failure to develop even a spark of interest or attraction in all my attempts at dating girls over the past four years. For the first time in years, I slid into a low place emotionally for several weeks, feeling alone and discouraged. My parents were always there, but I wasn't able to verbalize what I felt.

I began to be uncomfortable at church, feeling that I didn't belong and that no one wanted to really be my friend. I also felt physically cold. I drove to church alone so that I could arrive early to play the organ for sacrament meeting. After sacrament meeting, sometimes I would go home rather than stay for the remaining two hours. I believe this was the first time in my life that I had ever skipped Church meetings. But I just felt terrible being there.

One Sunday in sacrament meeting, one of the speakers made some inspired comments which seemed to speak directly to me. He talked about how we needed to give our whole heart to the Lord. This led me to reflect on my life:

> I feel like I've been guilty of holding back for reasons which, in the end, are trivial, of having a "mental filter" by which I'm allowing a few negative events to blind me, to an extent, to the goodness and kindness of people all around.

That same day, in the evening I was visited by my home teachers:

> My home-teachers came by tonight ... They invited me to write down the things which bring me joy, and also what my life goals are. I think the things which bring me joy are 1) Just knowing I'm doing the best I can at living my life the way the Lord would have me, and

2) Having true friends. The life goal which seems most significant now is that I would like to marry and raise a family. This is sometimes frustrating because it seems like somehow I'm lacking the emotional ability to pursue a relationship which could lead to marriage, and I don't really understand why this is. But I feel like if I do my best, maybe someday this will change. (Jun 14, 2009)

That day marked a significant turning point. I still didn't quite understand what was going on in my life, but I felt a renewed sense of peace and happiness. Several months later I reflected:

There are some questions about my life that I don't know the answer to ... Should I be dating girls and pursuing a course leading to marriage? On the one hand, I love my family and feel some desire to raise a family; If this is what I am to do, then I should probably lose no time starting, because I'm 26 now and am not getting any younger. But on the other hand, I fear hurting girls, or at least wasting their time, in a pursuit that seems to have no prospect of success, for the strange but simple reason that I'm not attracted to girls and never have been ... I don't know why this is. Maybe there is a chance of this changing; I don't know. I want to live my life the best I can, and I ask the Lord for guidance. I hope I will be able to understand his will for me, and that I will be able to do it to the best of my ability. (Nov 15, 2009)

In the meantime, I had been continuing my study of Joseph Smith and Church history. I read Richard Lyman Bushman's biography *Joseph Smith: Rough Stone Rolling.* As I began to confront some of the harsh realities and also the beautiful complexities of history, I began to appreciate Joseph Smith more and more, as a person as well as a prophet. I started to understand that the world is not so black-and-white as I once thought. It brought me to a place where I was finally ready to confront what seemed to be my own harsh reality.

Maybe a little on the gay side

One evening I had dinner with my parents:

Mom & Dad came to Provo this evening and treated me to dinner at the Brick Oven ... On the way home, Mom remarked that she felt I could really use a companion (i.e., a wife), to help me in many ways in life. I told her I agreed ... but that the problem is just that I'm not attracted to girls ... I [have] prayed for many years that I might somehow learn to be attracted to women. I've tried spending more time with girls and going on dates, but in the end, nothing has changed. And so I'm wondering if maybe I'm praying for the wrong thing.

Mom asked something to the effect of was there an issue of being attracted to the same sex. I said, to me that was not so much an issue as rather an absence of attraction to the opposite sex. Said that if you represented sexual orientation 2-dimensionally, with four quadrants: straight, bisexual, gay, and asexual, I would probably fall into the asexual quadrant, maybe a little on the gay side. (Dec 3, 2009)

This is the first time that I had ever verbalized that I was attracted to the same gender, or that the term "gay" might apply to me even to a slight extent. I struggled to understand what it all meant: I knew that I had no attractions to girls, and that I was rather drawn to certain guys, and yet I didn't experience sexual attractions to either gender, and I was unsure of how to reconcile these facts.

This is the Lord's house

The following Sunday, early in the morning before I woke up to get ready for church, I had a dream:

I was riding a bicycle on some rough ground beside a street, on the right side. A couple times some youth appeared from the right and walked in front of me, so I had to slow and swerve a little to avoid hitting them, while they seemed unaware I was there; they seemed to be stepping onto the street to get onto a bus. It was just starting to get dark, with evening approaching. I found that I was riding through some tree-branches which I hadn't seen; I had my hat on, so I turned my head down to protect my face. To the right was an empty lot, filled only with gnarled, wild leafless trees ... Next on the right was [a] peculiar sort of building. It had no roof and no front wall, only back and side walls, like a movie set.

There were religious paintings on the walls, with spotlights on them. I believe I read a sign saying, "This is the Lord's house. Please don't despise it." I stood, looking for a few moments, a bit puzzled, when my alarm woke me up (Dec 6, 2009)

I thought about the people who had crossed in front of me; in my dream I had been frustrated, but I thought to myself, "Why should this frustrate me?" I felt there was a message that I should open my heart bigger and be more patient, and try to learn as much as possible from each person whose path crosses mine.

And then I thought about the house with its sign pleading for me not to despise it. I realized that it was the Church, and that, whatever faults may exist, it was my home. I knew that my path was not to just walk away from it, that there was a reason I was born in the Church, and that there was more I needed to learn from it.

Over the next two weeks, I reviewed my old journals and reflected on my life and recognized that if I was going to be honest, I had to admit that I had indeed been strongly attracted to guys from a young age. I also recognized that for years with all my heart I had yearned to be with a guy and have deep, lasting companionship with him.

I remembered the scripture, "It is not good that man should be alone," and I felt that it was true. And yet whenever I thought about marrying a girl, my heart would sink, because the prospect just seemed so hollow, so unhappy. It was a tremendous relief when I allowed myself to accept that this might not be what God wanted for me.

For the first time, I considered the possibility of someday spending my life with a guy. It was wonderful to think of being able to be together with someone who I could truly give my heart to; I had never even been able to imagine that before. But on the other hand, this idea also seemed to fall into conflict with my desire to stay in the Church. In any case, I determined to wait until I finished BYU before deciding what to do. I wanted there to be no question that I was keeping the commitments that I had made when I came to BYU.

I had to be honest with people

As I contemplated what I would do, I knew that living a "double life" was not an acceptable option to me. I felt I had to be honest with people when the topic came up, but I had no idea what that would be like at BYU.

I talked to my academic advisor, my bishop, my roommate Nathan, and a few other close friends. I gave each of them a fairly long explanation of my history and current situation. I felt this would be better than just saying "I'm gay" and risking being misunderstood. They were all very supportive, which was amazing to me.

One evening I talked with my roommate Daniel. At one point, I was talking about how I felt bad when a girl liked me and I couldn't reciprocate it. My newest roommate Andrew, who was just in the process of moving in, overheard part of the conversation:

> Andrew asked, "Are you breaking up with someone?" I was thinking for a moment about how to respond, when Daniel said, "We're talking about what to do when a girl likes you and you don't really like her back." ... Andrew said, "Oh, so you're a lady's man?". I just replied, "Well, not exactly."

A couple days later I got a chance to talk with Andrew. The next day I overheard him talking to his dad on the phone, saying how excited he was to have a gay roommate!

Bridging the gap

I searched on the Internet, trying to find BYU students who were gay. I found one, sent him a message, and we agreed to meet up for lunch on campus at the CougarEat. He was a returned missionary, had known he was gay ever since he was a kid, but had only talked to part of his family about it. He was taking dance classes and was frustrated that because of his mannerisms and interests, many people could identify him as "obviously" gay. He wrote on his blog:

> Ok, so two days ago I got a facebook message from another gay guy going to BYU. He wanted to meet at the CougarEat and talk. My gut reaction was, "You want to meet where?!" I worried that if people were to see us together, they would somehow know that we were gay and mistake our meeting for lunch as a date, and then would turn us into the Honor Code office and then I'd get kicked out of BYU ...
>
> After we finished our lunches and parted ways I felt really great (I was on a kind of high where I didn't care about who knew that I was gay, which dissipated when

I got home). I hope that he felt good too. Good in the sense of being open and bridging the gap that is, I would say unfortunately present between our gay selves and our BYU entities ...

An eye-opening experience

From the Internet, I found out that there was a monthly fireside for gay or same-gender-attracted Mormons held in a chapel in Utah Valley. I attended along with my roommate Andrew; he, of course, was straight but wanted to be supportive. I recognized the organist; he had been in my ward a couple years earlier. Everyone just seemed like nice, ordinary guys.

At the fireside, an emeritus general authority had been invited to speak:

> [He] said that same-sex attraction was an addiction, and compared it to alcoholism and also to smoking. He said that every one of us needs to get married, that having children is the purpose we came into the world. He related a story of a man who quit smoking by doing a 48-hour fast, from food, drink, and sex, and seemed to suggest the same would work for us. He recommended we spend time around children, that this would make our "problem" go away, and that it would be "easy".

I vividly remember him repeating three times in a row, "It's easy. It's easy. It's easy." I turned to the guy sitting next to me and whispered and asked if he believed what the speaker was saying. He said no.

Afterward there were refreshments in the cultural hall. I met some of the other guys, many of whom were BYU students. One guy mentioned that the talks were usually better, and he encouraged me to come again. It was an amazing, eye-opening experience meeting the people there. After the initial shock, I wasn't too bothered by the talk, because I figured it was well-intended. Afterward, I was informed that the talk did not represent the viewpoint of the fireside organizers, nor of the Church.

The organizers had invited people to bring a dessert if they wanted to help out. Someone brought a cake with a rainbow on it, which I thought was kind of funny.

Was that okay?

As I became more open, I learned that there had been over a dozen people who I had known from BYU who were gay, including two previous roommates at different times. It was funny to think that I had been at BYU so long without it ever entering my mind that anyone around me might be gay.

At the same time, I became apprehensive about expressing affection with guys. I had a close friend "Collin" who I used to hug when I would see him, but I stopped doing that. I even stopped giving high-fives to my friends. I was concerned that if I expressed affection, then they might think I was flirting with them.

During that time, I reconnected with many of my past roommates, some of whom I had been attracted to. I expressed my hope that I had never done anything to make them uncomfortable while we were roommates. In every case, they told me that I had never done anything inappropriate, that I had been a great roommate. This was a big relief.

Gradually I began to relax and realize that it wasn't some evil thing if I felt love for someone. Eventually I visited with a counselor at the BYU Counseling Center, and she helped me sort out some of my feelings. I talked to Collin, and he thought it was fine if I hugged him or scratched his back and things like that. He didn't really care one way or the other. He knew that I wasn't attracted to girls, and that I loved him a lot. He was fine with that; it wasn't an issue. I felt some disappointment because he didn't express the same affection for me. But I eventually came to accept that this was okay, that he was fine just how he was, and I was fine just how I was.

Questions about the Honor Code

For some time, I had been reviewing and thinking about the BYU Honor Code policy on homosexuality:

> One's stated same-gender attraction is not an Honor Code issue. However, the Honor Code requires all members of the university community to manifest a strict commitment to the law of chastity. Homosexual behavior and/or advocacy of homosexual behavior are inappropriate and violate the Honor Code. Homosexual behavior includes not only sexual relations between members of the same

sex, but all forms of physical intimacy that give expression to homosexual feelings. [16]

I was confused by what was meant by "physical intimacy". I had always understood the Church's law of chastity as referring to abstinence from sexual contact. But the interpretation of the law of chastity here made it seem like if I was intimate or affectionate in any way, like if I hugged my friend, or scratched his back, then someone might interpret that as breaking the rules.

I decided to go into the Honor Code office and try to get clarification about what was expected. I had a friendly chat with one of the counselors:

> I was wondering, what about giving a guy a hug: is that "physical intimacy"? He said, maybe, it depends on the type of hug. I said, "Well, I mean vertical, of course". He said, "You know, there are hugs, and then there are hugs. Just like there are kisses and then there are kisses." ... Then he went on, "Even handshakes; for example, sometimes a handshake means more than just a handshake". I said, "So a handshake might be against the Honor Code?" He laughed a bit and said no, he guessed that's not really what he meant. So he went back and forth on stuff like this for several minutes until I was fairly confused. He talked about holding hands: in some cultures it is normal for guys to hold hands and it's not considered homosexual, but in our culture it tends to "raise eyebrows"; he said the same applied to kissing ... (Jan 12, 2010)

At his suggestion, the next day I came back and had a nice visit with another Honor Code counselor. She attempted to clarify which types of physical intimacy would probably be considered against the Honor Code.

> I said it was a bit awkward in the Church, at BYU especially, where it seems like every other week I'm told I need to marry a girl, and I just feel kind of left out, because I know I'm not able to do this ... I understood the Church's teaching that I just needed to remain alone (single) the rest of my life ... I wasn't sure that was really the right thing, but that I was just trying to be careful and take things one step at a time, and try to listen to

---

[16]The wording on "advocacy of homosexual behavior" was removed in 2011.

God's guidance and do the right thing. She expressed
sympathy for my situation, and said, "Well, maybe the
day will come when the Church will say, 'Get married:
whether to a guy or a girl, it doesn't matter'. Sounds
weird, but who knows?" (Jan 13, 2010)

Her kindness meant a lot to me. Since then, I've learned that many
thoughtful Church members are wondering if the Church's teaching
could somehow be expanded to include gays who wish to be faithful
to someone who they can love, just like their straight brothers and sisters. In an interview with PBS in 2006, Elder Marlin K. Jensen, when
asked, indicated that he didn't see how this could happen, but said
that "through revelation, I suppose anything could be changed."[17]

Dear editor

A few days after my visits to the Honor Code office, I came across
a letter in the Daily Universe (the BYU newspaper) written by a
student the previous month:

I am a gay BYU student, and I know many gay BYU
students. We are good people. We are trying to do what
is right. My gay friends here behave no differently than
you do. They serve in the Church, hold callings, home
teach — some of them are married to wonderful members
of the opposite sex ...

The next day the Daily Universe carried a front-page story on a
novel about a gay Mormon teenager. I decided to write an appreciative letter to the editor:

I want to thank The Daily Universe for noticing Jonathan
Langford's new book "No Going Back" on Tuesday. I
hope that Langford's new approach to the subject may
generate discussion leading to improved understanding of
homosexuality ...

I feel grateful that, in my case, everyone I've talked to
has been kind and understanding. I've thanked the Honor
Code office for their clarification that they do not condemn
anyone for being gay, i.e., for having this orientation ...

[17] "The Mormons: Interviews, Marlin Jensen", 7 March 2006.
http://www.pbs.org/mormons/interviews/jensen.html

There's a misconception sometimes that this is all about sexual urges, when really it's an emotional issue more than anything else. A person in this situation wants to be able to have a companion they can love and share their life with, just as a straight person wants. They are faced with a difficult dilemma, because they have to decide whether they should sacrifice this in order to stay in the Church.

A purpose for the things that happen

Three days after that, I had a little get-together at my apartment with some guys from BYU. We had root beer floats and played some board games. My roommates, along with my roommate's girlfriend, participated with us. Later, when my roommates were gone, one of the guys asked me:

> "So are you 'out' to all your roommates then?" I said yes and explained my situation a bit. We started playing Quirkle, and I told about my visits to the Honor Code office ... Anyhow, we had a nice time ... As they were leaving, we were all telling each other what time our church was the next day. (Jan 23, 2010)

Afterward, one of my roommates said that he was kind of surprised, because to him most of my friends hadn't seemed obviously "gay" at all: they just seemed like nice, average, Mormon guys!

One day an impression came into my mind that I should say something in testimony meeting at church. I gave it considerable thought for several weeks, and planned precisely what I would say. When the time arrived, I walked up to the pulpit and said:

> Hi, I'm Brent. It's been several years since I stood up in a testimony meeting, but I wanted to share my belief that there is a loving God, that there is a purpose for the things that happen in our life, that we can receive spiritual guidance from God, who wants to bring us up to higher levels of compassion and understanding, so we can reach our full potential. I've felt this guidance in my life, especially during the last two months. I hope it's not inappropriate for me to take a moment to thank Bishop, and many of you, who have been so kind and understanding of me, even though I'm different. You've

made me feel like maybe there could be a place in the
Church for people like me, for people who love the Church,
who love the values of the Church, but who just aren't
straight. I just wanted to say how much I love this ward.
If there's ever anything I can do for any of you, or if you
need help with math or anything, just let me know, and
I'll be there. In the name of Jesus Christ, amen.

The congregation chuckled a bit when I mentioned helping out
with math. On my way to sit back down, someone sitting by the aisle
whispered to me, "Thanks." After the meeting, about ten people came
up to me and thanked me for my testimony.

An assumption I had never questioned

On June 27, 2010, a fireside was held at a church next to the
Idaho Falls temple. It was attended by more than 500 people and
was titled, "Finding Joy in the Journey: An evening of education
and hope for individuals who experience same-gender attraction, their
families, friends, and priesthood leaders". I drove up to the fireside
along with several friends from Utah.

On the way back, someone in the car asked how we would feel
about being in a celibate, lifelong relationship with someone of the
same gender. This was something I had never seriously considered
before. I had always thought that if two people were attracted to
each other, then they couldn't live together and not eventually have
a sexual relationship. It was just an assumption which I had never
questioned. But after a moment's thought, I responded that actually
I might be happy in a celibate relationship; and surprisingly, two
other guys in the car said the same thing.

This discussion forced me to reconsider what a loving relationship
means. I gained a renewed hope that maybe there was a way for me to
be happy and still stay in the Church. Maybe following the Church's
teachings on chastity didn't mean I would have to be alone? Maybe
it would be possible to have an affectionate, intimate relationship
without it having to be sexual?

I learned that in an earlier era, it was much more common for
people of the same gender to have intimate, non-sexual relationships:

> [M]ale friendships included much more physical contact
> and emotional intensity than most heterosexual men are
> comfortable with today. James Blake, for example, noted

from time to time in his diary that he and his friend, while roommates, shared a bed. "We retired early," he recorded one day in 1851, "and in each other's arms did friendship sink peacefully to sleep." Such behavior did not bother the fiancée of Blake's roommate a bit.[18]

Even Joseph Smith, in a sermon on the resurrection, briefly alluded to this common practice:

> [I]t is pleasing for friends to lie down together, locked in the arms of love, to sleep and wake in each other's embrace and renew their conversation.[19]

I came to understand that although love, intimacy, and sex may be closely packaged together in our present-day way of thinking, this has not always been the case, and it did not need to be the case for me. I realized that our culture had sexualized the concept of intimacy, to the extent that even the expression "sleep with" now means "have sex with".

We were comfortable with each other

In the fall of 2010 I entered the mathematics graduate program at the University of Utah and moved to Salt Lake City. I soon developed a close relationship with "Paul", a kind guy who I had met at the Sunstone Symposium that summer. Because we were both busy with school, and because he lived 30 miles north of Salt Lake City, we could only see each other once or twice a week, but we started texting and talking to each other almost every day.

> Later in the afternoon I met with Bishop in his office ... He said he hoped I had noticed the girls in the ward. He pointed out that there was about a 2.5:1 ratio of girls to guys, in my favor. I laughed and said that didn't really matter much to me. I explained I was one of a minority of guys who had never been able to be attracted to girls ... I added that, as of recently, there's a guy I'm dating. He didn't seem bothered by that, and commended [me] on my approach trying to stay inside the strictures of the Church. He indicated that as long as I was being chaste

---

[18]Coontz, Stephanie. *Marriage, a History.* Penguin Books, 2005.
[19]*History of the Church*, 5:361.

there was no ecclesiastical problem, that there was the same standard, regardless of orientation. He said if there was ever a problem with how people in the ward react, that he would be willing to help ... (Aug 29, 2010)

Paul and I had a lot in common, and we quickly connected; we were comfortable with each other and would often cuddle when we were together. After a couple weeks, we started holding hands.

One evening Paul came with me to a family gathering at my parents' home. We played on the piano a bit, and then he brought out his viola and we improvised on the hymn "If You Could Hie To Kolob". When he met my older sister, she said to him:

"You remind me a lot of Brent! You seem so similar, even have the same laugh." It seemed like a nice thing for her to say ... Paul felt that the family was very welcoming and warm to him, which made me happy. (Sep 4, 2010)

Later that night Paul and I went and watched the movie "Toy Story 3" in 3D. After that, he stayed the night at my parents' home; he slept in the guest bedroom upstairs, and I slept downstairs. The next morning, we went to church together at my singles ward, which was wonderful!

Paul's sister and her boyfriend were visiting Utah and staying at Paul's parents' house. I wanted to get to know them, so I suggested maybe we could hang out at the house. Paul talked to his parents about it and then told me some bad news:

Not only did they not want to meet me and not want me hanging out at their house, they didn't even want me to come with Paul to the house to pick [his sister and her boyfriend] up, even if I waited outside ...

He sounded pretty upbeat, like he was taking it well, but he mentioned that these kinds of conversations with his parents make him feel physically sick. I felt so bad for him and wished there was something I could do. (Sep 7, 2010)

We ended up meeting his sister and boyfriend outside at a nearby park. It caused me to reflect: even if parents do not approve of the sexual behavior which they assume a couple is practicing (whether heterosexual or homosexual), isn't it possible to acknowledge the positive aspects of their relationship, and to love and welcome the person their child loves? Of course, in this case the irony was that Paul and I were actually keeping Church standards.

Paul and I never really had a label for our relationship. All I know is that it was one of the most profoundly enriching things I have ever experienced. After a month, our feelings for each other became less intense, and we mutually decided that, although it had been great, we were ready for it to end. I had felt some nervousness about what a "break-up" might be like; I feared hurting someone or being hurt. But in our case, it was the most natural, drama-free thing ever, and we have continued to be good friends.

I'm very happy now

Since that time, I haven't been in a romantic relationship; instead, I've been enjoying developing friendships with all sorts of people, guys and girls, old and young. Sometimes I've gone on dates with girls; it's not really a big deal, as long as I know I'm not misleading her. Even though I've never been attracted to a girl, I don't feel like I have to defend a "gay identity" or anything.

I'm very happy now; I don't feel a need anymore to try to force myself to experience anything. On the other hand, I'm open to the possibility of experiencing love, affection, compassion, and under-standing in new and deeper ways, regardless of gender. I feel like that is something I want to cultivate, not suppress.

Over the past few months, I have wondered why we label ourselves based on the gender we're attracted to. If I were attracted only to blonds, or to people of a particular race, would I need to make up a label for myself to describe that? The whole labeling thing just seems like a strange concept to me, so I don't put much weight on it.

I see sexual abstinence as a logical choice for me, even aside from religious considerations. I consider it one way of taking a stand against HIV/AIDS and other sexually transmitted infections, which are out of control particularly among men who have sex with men.[20] Our culture puts sex on a pedestal, as though it were somehow the ultimate way of culminating a relationship. While I recognize there may be a biological basis to the sexual drive that many people experience, the glorification of sex is socially constructed. I actually believe that there are less messy, less risky ways of experiencing intimacy and love, and that at least for some of us, it may only be

---

[20] Recent CDC studies found that one in five MSM were infected with HIV, nearly half were unaware of their infection, and that MSM were 44 to 86 times as likely to be diagnosed with HIV compared with other men: "HIV among Gay, Bisexual and Other Men Who Have Sex with Men (MSM)", September 2010. http://www.cdc.gov/hiv/topics/msm/pdf/msm.pdf

our culture that leads us to assume that sex is inherently superior to other forms of intimacy.

Difficulties and misunderstandings

Sometimes I still have difficulty feeling I have a place in the Church. It is troubling when people put so much emphasis on marriage and say that it's our purpose here on Earth. One member of the Church, in a Facebook comment, questioned whether there was any point in me keeping myself temple-worthy if I wasn't going to get married:

> What is your purpose of being Temple worthy and not be eternally sealed and have a family? Is that not also in the scriptures as a requirement to gain an eternal glory and live in the presence of our father, and become Gods and Goddesses?

My response is that if this is true, then Jesus apparently didn't do a very good job on Earth. I believe that everyone has an individual mission to fulfill on Earth, and for some that might include marriage, and for others it might not. This is a private matter which individuals may determine through personal revelation. I feel it can be damaging when broad, sweeping assumptions are made which ignore the differences between individual situations. It is so much more uplifting when members stick with basic principles which apply to everyone; as an official Church statement reads:

> We believe that our purpose in life is to learn, grow and develop, and that God's unreserved love enables each of us to reach our potential.[21]

The unity which binds us together

Over the last year, I have had the chance to come to know some wonderful people with diverse backgrounds, perspectives, and beliefs. It has pained me to see the unfairness and unkindness which sometimes characterizes discussion on all sides of controversial subjects

---

[21] "Church Responds to HRC Petition: Statement on Same-Sex Attraction." 12 October 2010. http://newsroom.lds.org/article/church-mormon-responds-to-human-rights-campaign-petition-same-sex-attraction

such as this. I hope that we can all be a little more understanding, a little more careful, and a little more loving of all people.

The idea of an "other side", fundamentally opposed to us, is an illusion which leads to anger and conflict. We accept this illusion only by forgetting the unity which binds us together as humans, as children of God, and as living creatures.

If I have learned anything, it is that there is a reason for the experiences we have. No experience is a waste, if we choose to learn from it and channel it in positive ways.

Tiffany Demings

"To laugh often and much; To win the respect of intelligent people and the affection of children; To earn the appreciation of honest critics and endure the betrayal of false friends; To appreciate beauty, to find the best in others; To leave the world a bit better, whether by a healthy child, a garden patch or a redeemed social condition; To know even one life has breathed easier because you have lived. This is to have succeeded."
– Ralph Waldo Emerson

I've been Mormon all my life. My mother raised me by herself, but I visited my father on the weekends and every other holiday. I got twice the presents at Christmas time. My grandma lived next door to us.

In my childhood, I always knew I was different; I don't know if that difference had anything to do with my sexual orientation. I was just different from other kids in my neighborhood. In elementary school most of my friends were boys. I played soccer with them at recess. In middle school my best friend was a boy, until he kissed me, and then I started hanging out with a group of girls.

In high school there was a boy who still remembered my name after having left school for a year and coming back. I hadn't remembered his name, so I thought he was special and that I had a crush on him. Everyone else seemed to think he was the "rugged hunk" that one ought to have a crush on, so because my friends encouraged me I continued to profess a crush on him.

My freshman year is when I really began to feel an inkling of my attraction to girls. My friend was cute and funny and brilliant. I spent all my free time with her. I waited for her to get off work every night and often helped mop the floors after closing time. She was very kind and affectionate, and I felt like I could talk to her. But we were just friends. Since she was two years older than me, she moved away to college and I pretended to be interested in the rugged hunk my last two years of high school.

I couldn't admit it to myself

When I attended Brigham Young University, I was attracted to my dorm roommate. It was the first time I recognized my feelings for what they really were. Even though I knew that I was physically and emotionally attracted to her, I couldn't admit it to myself. I worried all the time that she would find out, that she would notice how much I liked her. I thought for sure she knew. One night we had been talking, and I sat on the floor next to her while she sat in a chair at her desk. I don't even remember what we had been talking about, but I got excited over something and put my hand on her knee to make sure she was paying attention to me. She pushed my hand away and said, "What, are you gay or something?" I panicked and thought that she had figured me out, but I hoped so much that she was just joking. So, I tried to impersonate the televised stereotypical gay man. I stuck one hand on my hip and flicked the other at the wrist, and I said, "Oh, yeah. Of course." I guess that ended our conversation, but I don't think I ever stopped worrying.

Another time, my roommate came into our room and announced that there was an article about homosexuality in the Ensign. I didn't know why she thought she had to announce that to me, and I didn't say anything about it to her. I read the article later. It was in the October 2007 issue. The article mentioned a man who told Elder Holland he didn't think he could be a member of the Church anymore because he was attracted to other men. Elder Holland asked if he violated the law of chastity, and the man said he did not. Elder Holland told him he was perfectly able to stay a member, and that he would be fine as long as he didn't transgress.

After reading the article I determined to never act on the feelings I had, and I thought that I would be able to continue living a normal life within the Church. For the most part, my freshman year at college was miserable. I was nervous about being found out; I had headaches almost every day; I still didn't want to admit anything to myself, though I did end up writing a fiction story for one of my classes, about the situation with my roommate where she asked if I was gay.

I tried not to think about it

My second year at college I lived with a friend from my freshman ward in an apartment off-campus. We had a blast doing crazy things like dancing in the street in the rain and making movies. I had wanted to serve a mission for the Church for several years, and I decided then that I only had a year to prepare. I woke up at 6:00 every morning to study my scriptures and exercise a little bit before school. For the most part, I felt happy and care-free and determined to be the best Mormon I could be.

That fall semester things were a little confusing. My roommates all talked about Proposition 8 in California. I found myself agreeing with what everyone around me said about it, and I was glad to know it had passed. I figured I would never personally want the opportunity to marry another woman, because I wanted to marry a man in the temple of God. At one point my roommate told me about one of her friends who told her he was gay. He had a boyfriend, and she said it made her sad that he had chosen that lifestyle.

The subject confused me, so I tried not to think about it. But when I received a letter from my brother I could no longer avoid the issue. My brother told me he was gay. It was nothing new to me; I had already known because I'm a snoopy little sister, but that didn't make it any easier to have him know that I knew. That was harder to deal with, because it meant I had to face my own feelings. I knew that whatever I would tell my brother would also have to apply to me, and I wasn't ready to face this aspect of my life yet. I wrote a letter back to him telling him I loved him and that I knew God loved him. I also included the article about homosexuality from the October 2007 issue of the Ensign. He wrote back expressing relief that I was so loving and accepting, and I thought I could now go back to how things were before.

I knew that it was true

In the spring of 2009 I flew to the United Kingdom for the BYU England and Literature study abroad program. My intention with the program was to experience religion in a different context, to find

God and to learn to understand myself in a different setting. As I became friends with others in my program, and as I took the time to think about my true feelings I knew that I could no longer deny my attractions for women.

There was a distinct moment when I knew that it was true, that it was a part of me that would not go away. We were gathered for a group meeting, and my friend and I sat on the floor together by the window. She offered to massage my legs and knees because they hurt from hiking around. It was an innocent and friendly thing to do, and it meant nothing more than a kind gesture. But when her hands touched my thigh my body betrayed me by feeling what I did not want to feel. I cried that night. I wish I could explain how much it hurt — how evil, disgusting, and vile I felt. The rest of the program was miserable for me. I hated myself. And I began to wonder if it was possible for anyone — even God — to love me.

While in England I had to face my true self. I didn't handle it very well. I treated myself worse than anyone has ever treated me. If my intention was to discover myself and God for who we really are then I failed. God did not cease to love me. But I thought that He did, and the more I hated myself the more I began to hate God.

I didn't understand why I had to feel this way. I didn't understand why God would make me a lesbian but then say that it is wrong. I didn't understand why the Church I had loved all my life now made me feel evil and wrong just because I had different feelings than most people. I felt alone. I didn't think that anyone would understand me. I didn't think that anyone could love me or like me if they knew this terrible thing.

We spent the last ten days in London and I decided to finish the book we had been assigned: *Mrs. Dalloway* by Virginia Woolf. I identified most with Septimus, the character who feels "nothing" through the whole book until he kills himself. I finished the book and couldn't shake the fact that I could feel nothing, just the way Septimus was described. A friend of mine asked what I was thinking about, and I said, "Suicide." She got a worried look on her face, and I tried to reassure her that I wasn't contemplating my own suicide. But I don't know how much of that was true. I didn't want to kill myself, but I didn't feel like there was much to live for, if everything I had thought I was and thought I wanted wasn't real or possible.

I'm not alone

The summer after my England program, I was a nomad. I spent two months couch-surfing at my mom's and friends' houses in Provo and various cities in Arizona, and I camped a few days in Bryce Canyon. I think four months of not having a solid place to hang my clothes and call home wore me out more than I ever thought it would. I had no job, and I wasn't in school. I had nothing to do with myself except bum around. All I had were my thoughts. And thinking was a dangerous pastime.

At the end of the summer I started cutting myself with a sewing needle. As time went on I used pocket knives and box-cutter razors. Cutting seemed to be the only way I could cope with my feelings, because I didn't think I could talk to anyone. I didn't think that anyone would understand that this wasn't going away. I suppose I didn't think others would understand because I didn't even understand. Why would I be this way? How could God love me? How could anyone love me? There were many days that I did not want to get out of bed, and a few days when I didn't get out of bed. I hated myself. I didn't want to stand in front of the mirror, and I didn't want to face anyone else either. I closed myself off from a lot of people. Most of the time I wouldn't talk to my roommates at all. Not even when they greeted and welcomed me with enthusiasm and love. They loved me, but I thought if they knew the real me they could never love me.

One Sunday night I decided to go to my ward prayer. That night there was a girl there who I had met a week or two before. She beckoned me to sit next to her, so I did. The small room heated up as it filled with people. At one point I pushed my sleeves up because it was so hot, but I pushed them back down to conceal the cuts on my arms. The girl noticed, and at the end of the meeting she asked if we could talk.

I started seeing a therapist every week in the BYU Counseling Center. For the first couple months I didn't think the counseling was doing me any good. I wasn't sure how open and honest I could be with my therapist. When I finally said out loud that I am attracted to women, nothing happened. My counselor didn't make a big deal out of it. She wasn't surprised or disgusted like I thought she might be. The next day one of my friends asked me if I was bisexual. I told her, "Not exactly. I only like girls." After talking with that particular friend, I realized that I'm okay. That it is okay to be who I am and maybe people will accept me. Around the same time another friend opened up to me about being attracted to men and women. That was when I started to understand that I'm not alone. After a few months of going to therapy and coming out to a few more friends, I was able to look back and see how much progress I had made with accepting myself. I still experienced depression, but I stopped cutting myself.

I believe in love

My greatest challenge was overcoming my emotional dependence on one of my close friends. I spent most of my time with her and felt that we connected very well on an emotional level — so well that I didn't want to lose that connection. I found her very attractive in a lot of different ways. She was smart, sarcastic, outdoorsy, and beautiful. Overall, I thought she was a great friend. I dreaded telling her how I felt about her, but I also felt like she was the only one who I absolutely needed to tell. Once I felt like I was stable and okay with myself I decided to tell her that I loved her and that I was attracted to her. I had convinced myself that she already knew everything and so nothing about our relationship would have to change.

I was wrong. When I saw her after that, she was distant, and she wouldn't hug me anymore. I have always been very physically affectionate. I love to hug everyone. After my friend's reaction, I stopped hugging people altogether. I was scared to touch anyone because I didn't want it to seem like it meant anything more. I still probably don't hug people as much as I used to.

But because my friend avoided me, it forced me to break my dependence on her. It took several more months of therapy for me to get to another point where I felt okay being myself and being open with my friends about my feelings.

Now I feel good. I like who I am. I'm still studying at BYU, and I'm getting ready to graduate soon. I serve on a Relief Society committee in my singles ward, and I volunteer as a developmental editor for BYU student journal Leading Edge. One of my goals is to help others understand people who have experiences like mine. I attend the weekly discussion group Understanding Same-Gender Attraction at BYU and have organized community discussion panels which address these issues, in an attempt to raise awareness and provide greater understanding. I believe in love, and I believe that to achieve love, there must be understanding. My hope is that I can make someone's life better by being an active voice in my community.

Richard Draper

"Life is the classroom.
Love is the lesson."

When I was about nine years old, my family and I took our annual trip to Canada to visit my father's best friend. While we were there, he asked his sixteen-year-old son to take me and my brothers swimming at the local pool. In the dressing room, I found myself standing within inches of him. As he undressed, I felt something inside of me that I did not and could not understand. This is the first time I remember experiencing any sort of sexual attraction.

About a year later, I was visiting with some friends from church. One of them invited us to follow him outside to his fort. Once inside, he began to dig in the soil, and brought out a large plastic garbage bag filled with "girly" magazines. As he pulled them out, I could not understand the appeal of these pictures. I was completely indifferent while my friends were completely taken in. This was the extent of my exposure to porn, ten minutes of watching my friends go crazy while I sat there bewildered.

Numerous times I listened as family and friends referred to men who liked other men as "fags". Even though I did not fully understand what it meant, I knew that they were talking about me. I began to see that what I was feeling was not "normal". About this time, I attended a General Priesthood meeting where they played a video of Elder Boyd K. Packer giving a talk about morality. This was the first time I realized how bad same-sex attraction was considered to be. After listening to what was said in this video I felt I must truly be disgusting in the eyes of the Lord.

By the age of fourteen, my soul felt damned, worthless, unlovable, and hideous in the eyes of God. I felt that if I was good enough, righteous enough, then God would change me and make me so that I liked girls instead of guys. Yet the change wasn't happening. One day as I was sitting in a seminary class on eternal marriage, I wrote a poem expressing the thoughts that were going through my mind:

ALONE

Have you ever felt alone
Like the silence in the night
There was only one alone
Who would listen with loving care.

Have you ever felt alone
Did you ever wish for a true friend
Why aren't your brothers ever alone
While you always are

I know there's hope for me
Somewhere in this dark and cruel world
There's got to be hope for me
Somewhere in this dark old world

I wish I had a home with parents to hold me tight
Every step I take seems out of place
Everything I do never seems right
But yet I've got to, just got to win this race.

When I think of all the joy and fun
I can't end life with a knife
I'll never be anything if I run from life
So for now I'll try to just have fun

I've got this emptiness deep inside of me
I've tried but it just won't let go
This emptiness will not always be
I can't let it stay I've got to fight it.

I've never wanted to be alone
It just seems to be that way

Someday I'll have a family of my own
And then I'll never be alone again

No I'll never be alone again.

At this time I was becoming a master at hiding what was going on inside me. There were times when I would rather have died than for anyone to have known that I was attracted to males. It didn't matter whether I was in a crowd or sitting home alone, I always felt alone. At this early age I saw suicide as a way out. While in high school, after having experienced one of the worst dates of my life, I wrote the following poem:

Behind The Mask

I wear the mask each day
I put it on when I awake
And face the day anew.

As long as the mask is in its place
Then none shall see the inner face
The hurt, the pain, the inner hell.

Sometimes the mask is heavy
It seems impossible
To lift it into place.

On days like those I hide and wait
until the mask feels lighter
or at least I get it to my face.

The Pain it hides
Keeps my soul on fire
Unseen unto the world

The thing becomes too real
Forget I sometimes do
What lies behind the mask?

The pain it hides lies deep
Please, do not let others see
No matter, others must not see.

I may not survive
If others see what lies behind
The mask I wear today

So on it goes
It hurts
No hope

If others saw what lie behind
They would turn and run
Turn and run would they

If I saw myself what lie behind
Would I turn and run?
Turn and run I would

Now when I try to take it off
The pain becomes severe
For stuck in place it is

This mask I wear
To hide the pain and tears
Works no more for me

The pain it creates
Is far worse
Than the horror it hides

Without the mask I cannot survive
With the mask I die inside
What is a soul to do?

Can't someone see my mask
And take it from my face
To see what lies beneath

Will they scream and run
from what they see?
Death, sorrow, emptiness

One day it will end
It is written in the plan
It is the only way

There is only one way
To remove the mask
For good

One way!

Serving with honor

During my senior year of high school, a girl I had met in gym class asked me to a dance. I accepted, and we ended up dating for the next two years. One evening her mother approached me as I was leaving her house. She handed me a note, and whispered for me to read it when I was alone. On my way home I stopped at a park and read the note. It said that I needed to show her daughter more affection and actually kiss her. We had dated exclusively for over a year and I had never once kissed her. The next day, I took her out to dinner for her birthday and told her I loved her, but that I didn't believe in kissing until after my mission. I told myself I didn't want to kiss because I was "saving" that part of myself. Truth be known, I was terrified of having to kiss this young daughter of God; I cared a lot for her but felt no physical attraction.

At age 19, I left on my mission. I worked hard, served in many leadership positions, and never did anything I would regret. There was, however, one companion who I had strong feelings for. Each day as I would work closely with him, thoughts and feelings would arise which I would constantly fight. I never acted upon them and buried the feelings deep to hide them, but I often felt like scum merely for having them. I asked God to take these feelings away, and promised him many things in return, but the feelings remained. Even though I did not act on these feelings, I condemned myself for my thoughts.

After I returned from my mission, I attended BYU and worked as a teacher at the Missionary Training Center. I spent my summers working with the Especially For Youth program. During my third year of teaching, I signed up as a substitute teacher with the Church Educational System and taught seminary classes several days each month. I also served weekly as a baptizer in the temple, worked as a tour guide on Temple Square, and served in several church callings. During this time, I was convinced that if I was righteous enough, served enough, read enough, and prayed enough, the Lord would change me and I would eventually find that special young woman I was meant to be with. I would fall in love, marry, and live happily with her for all eternity. When change didn't happen, I was convinced it was because I was not righteous enough and the Lord was displeased with me and my efforts.

The biggest mistake of my life

I decided I wanted to teach seminary full time. I was accepted into a new program where I was to teach my own seminary class four hours per day, during my last year of college. Around this time, I began dating a young woman I knew as a child, and who was also in my singles ward. We got along pretty well, and dated for about four months before I had to leave for a job I had accepted in Hawaii. I was in Hawaii for 11 months, but we maintained the relationship through letters and phone calls.

While in Hawaii, it was brought to my attention that if I was not married by the time I turned 28, then I would not be permitted to teach seminary. The Church has a policy that full-time male seminary teachers must be married. My coworkers were also constantly hounding me about why I was not married. My branch president constantly told me I needed to ask my girlfriend to marry me. He told me the Lord wanted me to marry and I just needed to trust Him and take the plunge. I was so confused, but I felt the Lord would bless me if I followed through with this advice.

I honestly felt I was doing the right thing, the thing God wanted me to do. So I bought a ticket home, bought a ring, and asked her to marry me. I was only in Utah for two days before I had to fly back to Maui; I had still never kissed my new fiancée. Once back in Hawaii, my heart kept telling me I had made a mistake, but everyone around me, especially my Church leaders and my parents, kept telling me I was doing what the Lord wanted me to do.

I was due to return home December 11th and our wedding was scheduled for December 20th. During this two-week period, I felt dead inside. I would take her out and make up some excuse to drop her off at her parents' house by 9:00 every night. I was trying so hard to keep myself together inside, but my soul was screaming that this was wrong. I tried to talk to my bishop and to my father but both assured me that I was merely experiencing "cold feet" and that if I followed through all would be well. I decided to follow their advice instead of my heart.

I can only remember bits and pieces of that day. I was a walking zombie. One thing I do remember is that after having sealed us and given us permission to kiss over the altar, the officiator looked at me, puzzled, after I had laid my first-ever "peck" upon her. He said, "Is that all this beautiful daughter of God gets? You give her a real kiss and show her how much you love her." My heart sank as I leaned over and gave her another "peck".

After the reception was over, the wedding night began, and before the day ended I knew without a doubt that I had made a terrible mistake. I would never be able to fill the needs of this daughter of God. The next day, I made some excuse and left her for a couple of hours to go talk with my mission president. I didn't know whom else to go to, so I called him and drove to his house. After I told him of my feelings, he looked me in the eye and said, "Elder, have you ever had homosexual feelings?" to which I replied, "Come on, Pres., you know me better than that!" He came so close to discovering my secret, and it scared the heck out of me! I was so frightened that he somehow knew. I had never acted upon these feelings even though I knew they were present, but I refused to admit to myself that I was gay.

I left my mission president's home knowing that I had to talk to my new bride and end this marriage. We were due to leave on our honeymoon the next morning and I knew I had to end things before we left. It was the hardest thing I had ever done, but I told her I feared we had made a mistake and I needed time to figure things out. I wish I had had the guts to tell her the truth, that I was not attracted to women. I know I broke her heart, but I didn't know what else to do or how else to handle the situation. She went on to remarry and have children with her new husband, but I will forever be sorry for the pain and grief I brought into her life.

There was no hope for me

After the wedding incident, a part of me died inside, and the next few years were filled with self-loathing and a constant desire to die. I spent a full decade of my life literally running from myself. I took a job that kept me traveling constantly, and I had very few connections with people. One day when I could bear it no longer, I went to my parents' home, pulled out my pistol, loaded it, put it in my mouth with the barrel on my palate and positioned my finger on the trigger. Just as I was about to pull the trigger, the phone rang. I looked down at the caller ID and noticed that it was my twin brother's number. Immediately I thought of my niece who was the love of my life and thought of what this would do to her. I took the gun out of my mouth and answered the phone to discover it was this very niece calling with a question for "Uncle Richie". I wanted out of this life so bad, and yet I couldn't do it in a way that would scar this sweet little girl. I was dead inside, but I kept on living.

A year later, I found myself in Parley's Canyon standing on the outside edge of a freeway overpass, preparing to jump in front of the next passing semi-truck. It was about 11:00 p.m. and as the first truck began to approach I readied myself. I was literally hanging over the edge when I noticed a minivan pulling up alongside the truck. All I could think of was that the truck would swerve to miss me and kill everyone in the van. So I let the truck pass and waited for the next.

While waiting, a county sheriff pulled onto the on-ramp and turned his vehicle so that it was facing my direction. He was parked about three hundred feet away and sat there in his Bronco watching me. Each time a truck drove by there was a car nearby. I stood hanging over the edge of that railing from 11:00 p.m. until 2:30 a.m. with this sheriff sitting there the entire time. I am sure he must have feared that if he approached me I would jump, so he waited. Finally I realized that this wasn't going to work. I climbed back onto the bridge, walked to my car, and drove home. I wanted so badly to die. It felt like the only answer to my dilemma. I felt damned anyway, so why not just end it now rather than wait and be sent to hell? Twice more I found myself with a pistol in my mouth, but each time something would happen to stop me.

I still traveled for work and would spend many hours a week waiting in airports. I would sit and watch people walk by, and before I knew it I was checking out all the cute guys. I would catch myself and try to make myself watch the women instead. This would last for a minute or two before a cute guy would walk by and I was right back to watching the guys. One day a man walked by who instantly stole my heart. I thought to myself, if this man approached me I would go anywhere with him. For all these years I had been able to bury the feelings deep, but now here they were at the surface, ripping at my heart. The thought came into my mind that if I was fat he wouldn't like me.

I didn't consciously begin to eat but within two years I had gained well over one hundred pounds. Eventually I reached almost 380 pounds. I had found my safety net, since if I was this big then no one would have me, so there was no chance of giving in to temptation. Besides, if I continued to gain weight, then I wouldn't have to worry about taking my own life.

My life took a turn for the better

At a time when I was near giving up, a caring bishop came into my life. He spent quite a bit of time trying to help me. One day he asked me if I would visit a particular counselor he knew. I had no faith in anyone's ability to help me, but I agreed. As I met with this dear sweet lady, she began to help me turn my life around. We worked together until we had accomplished all that we could. Yet I had never been able to tell her that I was gay. There were a number of times that I had come close, but I was always unable to speak the words.

When my bishop was released, a new bishop took his place. And after some friendly coercion from the caring, new bishop, I finally agreed to meet with a psychologist that he was recommending. It was during my second visit with this counselor that I blurted out the words, "I am gay," for the first time in my life. I had thought them numerous times, but I had never once said them out loud, let alone to another person. It was this evening in October of 2008 that my life took a turn for the better. It was this night that the reality hit my soul with such fervor that I could never deny it: this gay son of God was a good person who was fully accepted by the Lord. This was the beginning of a transformation where I no longer condemned myself, because I was beginning to understand that my soul was indeed good and that my Father in Heaven loved me just as I was.

Coming out

The second person I came out to was one of my best friends of over two decades. We spent the morning working on my brother's boat and decided to take it out for a test run. All afternoon I dropped hints to see whether or not he would pick up on them. Finally, he looked at me and blurted the question, "Are you trying to tell me you are gay?" I was afraid he would be mortified, but he was so accepting and kind. He looked at me and said, "I was wondering if you were ever going to figure it out." He asked me if I remembered him asking over a decade earlier if I was gay. He said I was so adamant he was wrong that he left it alone, and assumed I was not ready to deal with it. Besides, he figured there was always the possibility he was wrong and I was not gay. I laughed so hard! It felt peaceful to actually say the words, "I am gay," to a friend. I couldn't believe how peaceful it felt; I had not felt peace like this for more years than I could remember!

I was surprised that three of my best friends had this same reaction when I told them. My best female friend in Texas replied, "Well it's about time, I was wondering when you were going to figure it out!" My next friend told me she and her daughter had discussed it and tried to figure out how to approach me on the subject without offending me. I was stunned! Even though I had tried hard to hide it, so many people already knew.

In 2009, I attended an LGBT-affirming interfaith service at the Capitol Rotunda in Salt Lake City. There were a number of television cameras present, and I later found out that one of them aired footage in which my face could be seen. I decided I didn't want my family to hear the news from someone who saw me on television, so I called my twin brother and told him I had something I needed to talk to him about. He was unable to meet with me but pushed quite hard for me to tell him over the phone, so I did. Many painful words were exchanged. I was preparing to share the news with my parents the next day when I got a call that my father's brother had just passed away.

A week after the funeral, I called and made arrangements to talk to my mom and dad the next evening. The next day I was shopping when I got a call from my older brother late in the afternoon telling me Dad had just died. At first, I thought he was joking, but after a minute I realized he was not. I decided not to share the news with anyone else in the family for the time being. However, during the next two weeks word got out to some, and I ended up sharing it with others, wanting them to hear it from me. In the end this was the loneliest Christmas I ever remember. The pain went deep, but I sit back today and thank God that with the help of some good friends I was able to make it through those darkest of days.

Opening eyes

In 2010, I moved to Kansas City, not far from where my younger brother and his family lived. For Mother's Day, I sent my mother two books: *In Quiet Desperation*, by Fred and Marilyn Matis and Ty Mansfield, and *No More Goodbyes*, by Carol Lynn Pearson. Three months later, I found out she had not read the books and had no intentions of doing so. I asked my older brother's wife if she would pick up the two books and return them to me. She in turn asked my brother to pick them up on his way home from work one day. Mom gave them to him and he walked to his car before looking to see what they were. I feared he would throw the books away if he knew what they were. Instead, he walked back into the house, handed them to Mom, and said he couldn't take them. He couldn't get rid of the feeling that she needed to read them and that she needed to start now. Wow! It blew my mind when I heard this.

One afternoon, Mom called and informed me she had been reading *No More Goodbyes*. She apologized for how she, the family, and the world had treated me. She said what she read really opened her eyes to what gay men go through, especially gay men within the Church. She said she felt sick that we had suffered so much.

Recently, I attended an activity with my brother and his wife here in Kansas. Before I had even moved to Kansas, my brother had told those in attendance that I was gay. While there, the hostess approached me and let me know that I was invited to be a permanent guest at their gatherings. She told me most people came with their spouse, but some came with their date or "partner". I laughed and said, "I can only imagine how everyone would act if I ever showed up with a guy!" She became serious, looked at me, and said, "You are welcome here anytime with anyone: boyfriend, girlfriend, you're welcome!" Wow, another first for me. It was so different from what I had experienced before.

Not long after this, my brother and some of his friends from church were going skeet shooting, and he invited me to tag along. At first, I was uncomfortable with the idea of being there with men who I thought did not like me because I was gay. But it didn't take long before we were all friends, equal human beings out having fun. As we were getting ready to go, one of the men came up to me, shook my hand, looked me in the eyes and said, "I am really glad you were able to come and I was able to get to know you." It felt like he was saying, "After getting to know you, I realize you are just a normal, decent guy!"

A growing experience

I feel deep compassion for those who choose death over life. They just don't understand that things can get better. I hope that anyone reading this will see that even some of the worst scenarios have the possibility of turning out good in the end. I thank God I am alive today, because if I had ended things when they were at their worst I never would have known the love and joy I now experience. I never would have met some of the best people I have ever known. I never would have opened myself up to the possibility of knowing what true love is.

It is still a day-to-day roller coaster ride, but the lows are not so low and the highs are great! After finally accepting who I am, I have experienced fantastic changes in my body as well as my soul. A year and a half ago I was approaching 380 pounds. After accepting that this gay soul was good in God's eyes, the need for the weight was gone. Not only did I no longer desire to die, but I no longer needed to hold on to the safety net of the weight. It took about six months after I first said the words, "I am gay," for me to be ready to start shedding the weight, and once I got started, there was no looking back. As 2010 is nearing its end, I am nearing the 200 pound mark, and I am enjoying life more than I ever thought possible.

Through years of denying who I was and constantly trying to change my core, I discovered confusion, unrest, and self-loathing. Through accepting myself as a gay child of God, I found the opposite. Absolute Peace: these are two simple words that completely describe how I often feel since I accepted the fact that I am gay. The scriptures teach us what the fruits of the Spirit are, and with this in mind I can no longer deny the being my Father in Heaven created. When people choose to tell me I have been deceived, I look to the feelings of peace within and smile with knowledge that my Father in Heaven loves me just as I am.

There have been many difficult moments since I first came out of hiding in the closet. My family is still having a difficult time with the fact that I am gay. There are times when I have felt lonely, but I can also honestly say I am truly happy for the first time in my life. I have gone through different stages, from self-loathing and hatred of life, to self-acceptance and a deep-rooted love of life. I have gone from loving the Church and thinking it is fault-free, to being angry and feeling I was duped, and then back to the middle where I realize the Church is not perfect, the prophet and apostles make mistakes, that they are human like the rest of us. The Lord has no choice but to use imperfect men to run His earthly organizations. I still haven't decided exactly how I feel about the Church, but I can at least attend without being bitter and angry. As each new day presents itself, this journey of mine continues to be a changing, growing experience. I pray that someday I will have all the answers, but until that day comes I will continue to live the best life I know how, as a gay man.

Carlos A. Arciniegas

"Gratitude bestows reverence, allowing us to encounter everyday epiphanies, those transcendent moments of awe that change forever how we experience life and the world."
– John Milton

It was a day like any other. My bishop pointed to a pamphlet on a shelf in the corner. I could see its title shining in the weak light filtering through the window.

"Have you read this pamphlet?" he kindly asked.

"I have not," I responded quickly. "What is it about?"

"It's about helping those who struggle with homosexuality," he responded candidly. "It will do well for you to read it before you go on a mission."

We were in an LDS Distribution Center, and I looked nervously over my shoulder to check if anybody was walking by. The pamphlet, called *To the One*, by President Boyd K. Packer, suddenly grew bigger and bigger in my mind. I was sixteen at the moment, and I had never discussed homosexuality with my bishop before. Ever. The word *homosexual* resounded through my ears and felt like ice cubes sliding down my throat.

A lot to be grateful and happy about

I was born in the beautiful city of Bucaramanga, Colombia. My parents converted to the Church of Jesus Christ of Latter-day Saints in the early seventies, when the Church was barely established there. As we struggled to live the gospel in a place where Latter-day Saints were a minority, we were challenged but also blessed. Being the youngest of four children, I had the opportunity to learn from my parents and siblings. My mom went out of her way to help the poor and the needy and has been an unwavering example of faith. My dad instilled in me an insatiable desire to acquire knowledge. As I've grown older, I've been grateful for their spiritual and moral guidance.

Now here I am, twenty-three years old, sitting in front of a computer in the school library. For a long time I've felt the impression to share the struggles and joys related to my same-gender attraction. When I was offered the opportunity to write this, I understood that it was time to finally draw courage and share my experience. I hope to help someone out there who may be facing the challenges of reconciling this part of themselves with what they believe and hold dear. I want them to know that they are not alone, and that they are loved. I've found joy as I've tried to learn from my life experiences. There is heartache, but there is also a lot to be grateful and happy about.

It just didn't make sense to me

Growing up I always felt a bit different. I was more quiet and contemplative than my peers; I enjoyed reading and creating fantasy stories in my mind, while other boys enjoyed sports and more physical activities. I made a few close friends in my early years. Like other children, I enjoyed playing outside, killing insects, drawing, and playing pranks (such as putting worms in the girls' backpacks in elementary school!)

When I was about six years old I had a friend "Daniel". He and I became very good friends and would hang out a lot. I remember feeling very excited when he came over to play. When he moved to another neighborhood a few years later, I felt a deep longing and sadness. I missed him terribly.

In elementary school all my friends were boys. For some reason, I found many of the girls in my grade annoying, and that's probably why I enjoyed playing jokes on them. Around the same time, I remember one day I was playing hide-and-seek with a few friends and for some reason I felt the strong impulse to kiss one of the boys on the cheek. And so I did. The other boys and girls were astounded. Fortunately after a few minutes they all just laughed about it. The boy I had kissed said nothing, but after this there was always a certain awkwardness when we interacted with each other.

When I was about seven or eight, something interesting happened. One of my friends got a girlfriend! I was confused and didn't know what a girlfriend was. My friend and this girl even made rings with paper that they put on each other's fingers. Even when I had read fairy tales about princes and princesses I found it weird that a boy would like a girl. It just didn't make sense to me.

A spiritual transition

As the years passed, my friends became more and more interested in two things: sports, and girls. A feeling of isolation and loneliness started to develop and persisted for a few years. I felt that those two things, more than anything, were taking my friends away from me.

As I entered junior high, the attraction of my peers towards the opposite sex became more apparent. They would talk about their first kiss, about dating, and about having sex. I always found those ideas repulsive and usually justified my rejection of those behaviors with religion: I would think, "We are not supposed to do that," or "That's wrong," and soon I became a little Mr. Scrooge. As the years progressed I started questioning why I didn't feel the same way, why I wasn't interested in girls at all. But I could never find the answer.

Then it came time for high school. I was fortunate to go to one of the most prestigious high schools in the city. It was an all-male, Catholic school. Friendships with people at my school were scarce because I couldn't relate to their interests: video games, girls, sex, and soccer. Instead, I found excitement in reading, particularly the books by Jules Verne. I wrote stories and narrated them to my nephews. I loved going to the movies with my dad, painting, and going to church.

Those days, from age fourteen to eighteen, were lonely years. This was also the time when I started noticing guys more, at least unconsciously; I especially admired the athletes, those whose lives I perceived as easier: they were loved and they were popular. And that was what I wanted the most: to be respected, to be recognized, and to be loved.

Around the time when I was to become a priest in the LDS

Church, about sixteen years old, I experienced what I call a "spiritual transition". This was when my testimony started to sink in and my commitment and devotion to the Church emerged. I told people that I would wait to date girls until after my mission. I immersed myself in books and spiritual activities. Members of my ward admired me for my dedication, but in reality it was a way of compensating to hide the internal turmoil and emptiness of my soul.

I often found myself checking out guys, but I rationalized this by telling myself that my attention to them was some sort of admiration, that I just wished I was as strong or as ripped as they were. In my mind, I could never think that I was attracted to them. And if I ever thought so, those feelings were deeply ignored and buried under layers and layers of self-hatred and shame.

What I had always waited for

As the time approached to serve a mission, I felt my heart filling with excitement. I remember the day I received my call. I was surrounded by loved ones, and a rush ran through my whole body as I opened the envelope. It was one of the happiest days of my life. As I read the letter calling me to the Chile Vina del Mar mission, I felt that I had touched heaven. This was what I had long waited for.

The days immediately before leaving home for the mission, I experienced what I understood to be opposition from the adversary. This was what my leaders and seminary teachers had warned me about. I was walking with my mom doing mission shopping and it was as if a veil had been lifted from my eyes: everywhere I looked I saw gay people, I saw guys checking me out, I saw good-looking guys. I disliked it very much.

Happily, the day to leave came soon enough. I was sad to leave my family, but this was what I had always waited for: to go to another country and preach about Jesus Christ, change lives, and make everlasting friendships. I wanted to serve with honor and not fail. I remember the last words my dad told me before I left, that I would face adversity, that the mission would not be all that I was expecting, and that I should be careful and beware of the closeted gays that went on missions.

How blessed I was

The mission was an amazing experience. I worked hard and found joy in it. I made my goal to be a strict missionary and obey all the rules.

One day my companion, who I was close to, revealed to me that he was attracted to men as well as women. He told me about his past experiences, his past transgressions, and how he had dealt with it. Soon a connection started to develop between us that turned into physical attraction. This was the first time that I confronted my homosexual feelings, as I seriously questioned my sexuality.

My companion recognized what I was feeling, and this scared me. I felt that the defenses that I had built so long ago were collapsing, as deep feelings of shame overcame me. I thought I was not worthy anymore. How could I serve the Lord if I was like this? I remember sitting next to a window every night and crying. For the first time in my life I desired to be dead.

I packed my suitcases and decided to escape during the night. My companion saw me and stopped me, telling me to be strong and stay. As we sat down in the living room that night to read the scriptures, I found a passage that reached my heart:

> Behold, canst thou read this without rejoicing and lifting up thy heart for gladness? Or canst thou run about longer as a blind guide? Or canst thou be humble and meek, and conduct thyself wisely before me? Yea, come unto me thy Savior. Amen. (D&C 19:39–41)

After I read this, the gospel took on a new meaning: God was calling me to rejoice. He was not an ethereal angry creature ready to punish his children. We were not machines working to increase our chances for felicity and avoid misery. We were indeed His children, with the potential to love and be loved, with mercy and redemption and the Atonement available to us. God's invitation to me that night was to come unto Him, to rely on His love and grace.

Things got better. I was focused in the work and served with honor. The last day of my mission I was exhausted, both physically and emotionally. But I offered a personal prayer of gratitude and thanked God for the opportunity He had given me to serve. And I felt accepted. I was tremendously scared to go back home and cried copiously that night, but I was blessed with a feeling that everything would work out.

I thought that I was in love

As I went back home, my goal was to live the greatest of the spiritual ideals of Mormonism: marriage and family. I continued living the missionary code of daily scripture study and daily prayer, and I was continuously looking. I found some girls pretty, but I didn't have a strong desire to date. My hormones were certainly not the box of dynamite that I expected.

A few weeks after getting home, though, I met a girl that I became interested in. I asked her out, and the date went well even if it was awkward at times. I found her harmonious and mysterious and found myself thinking about her, so I thought that I was in love. When I disclosed my feelings to her, she replied that she wasn't ready for a relationship, so I moved on.

Meanwhile, the good-looking guys were everywhere. I started to question my lack of interest in girls and started to read about gay issues. I became continuously preoccupied with the "causes" and "cures" for homosexuality, and I spent hours in front of my computer reading coming out stories. I could relate to the despair that those men had experienced, the conflict between what they believed and what they were.

The feelings were not going away

One day in October 2008, something happened inside, and the pain and the fear that I had buried deep in my soul could no longer be hidden. That day as I walked home from school, I admitted to myself that I had same-gender attraction. I just could not deny it anymore.

The uninvited realization of what I was feeling quickly turned into fear and hopelessness. Now that I knew, how could I deal with this? And most important, how could I get rid of this? I tried to dominate my feelings with willpower, but it was not working. The attractions were only increasing. I started to feel hopeless. I supposed that either I was weak or that I didn't have enough faith to overcome it. This failure to overcome it automatically implied the failure of my life. My mind became crowded with suicidal thoughts.

I realized that I had to make a radical change in my life if I wanted to succeed. The thought came to mind that I should move to the United States. Following a spiritual impression, I applied to

BYU-Idaho. This required a great deal of faith not only from me but from all my family because our financial situation was not the best.

I wanted a fresh start, and I believed that being in a spiritual environment surrounded by thousands of beautiful Mormon girls would cure me, and I would be able to live my heterosexual ideal. This hope provided me with the spiritual stamina to come here and face many trials. But soon after I hit campus I realized how naive I was. The feelings were not going away.

What is love?

I started going to counseling. It helped me overcome the shame that I felt, but in some ways it only increased my pain. One of my counselors told me that my same-gender attraction originated from an intense fear of girls and that I needed to date more. I strongly disagreed with his diagnosis, and from that point on I became more and more discontent with this kind of therapy.

One particularly frustrating day, I went to see my counselor. I told him how my week was going, how I was trying to deal with the anti-gay comments from some of my roommates, how I was still scared to tell my parents about my situation, how lonely and depressed I felt, and how much I craved companionship and love. He proceeded to give me some advice on how to infuse hope into my life. But his words seemed to have no effect on me. I decided to ask a question that had been in my mind for quite a while: "What is love?"

Silence ensued. He looked me straight in the eye. "That's an interesting question," he answered calmly. He stood up, grabbed a few books and started reading a few psychological definitions on the theory of love. Then, my real question burst out, "Can gay people feel true love for each other, or are their feelings simply something evil, twisted, and unnatural?"

He scratched his head, moved closer to me and then said something that I will always remember: True love is a feeling of connection with another person. These feelings are not only physical but also emotional and spiritual. Since God has forbidden these kinds of relationships, that implies that it's not possible for a gay couple to connect spiritually, and therefore they cannot feel real, true love.

Pray and search for guidance

His response was stuck in my mind for a few days. I had started to feel curious about what it would be like to experience a relationship, to love and be loved. I have been blessed with an inquiring mind, and easy answers to complex problems did not satisfy me. I decided that if I wanted to find the truth, then I had to experience it for myself.

But I was conflicted. It was as if I was in a terribly hot desert, with an insatiable thirst and at the edge of collapse, with an oasis right in front of me, inviting me to go and drink and satisfy my long-awaited need. But next to the oasis there was a sign that read in abominable big letters, "Don't drink." No further information was given. And here I was, dying of dehydration, yet waiting for a miraculous event to satisfy my thirst, an event that I was no longer sure would ever come. This was indeed a trial of my faith: it was not just a matter of learning to subdue the carnal desires, but what was being required was to avoid satisfying one of the most basic of human needs and desires: to experience love.

That was when I met "James". We had been pen pals for a while. His was one of the first blogs that I had found. We came from similar backgrounds and shared the same beliefs, yet we were in different positions in our lives. When I went down to Utah for Christmas that year and met him in person, I found him to be not only physically attractive but also extremely witty, charming, and sweet. Nervously, I asked him to hang out, which he accepted. We enjoyed each other's company and had good conversations, about life, our past spiritual experiences, and our challenges in dealing with our attractions. At one point I asked him if we could pray. And so we prayed together, and I was blessed with a feeling of peace.

As the weeks passed, I found myself thinking constantly about him. I desired his happiness and he desired mine. We both committed to a strict code of no physical involvement. I started having romantic feelings for him, but I didn't feel bad for that. That kind of surprised me because this was something I had so strongly been preached against. But what surprised me the most was that I could connect with him not only emotionally but also spiritually. We had deep conversations about many topics.

But I was still conflicted and confused. How could something that had been so poignantly described as evil, perverse, and wrong produce such feelings of comfort, joy, and contentment? James saw the conundrum I was in and suggested that I should pray and search for guidance from God on the matter.

All things which are good cometh of God

One day in December 2009, I attended a temple session in the Jordan River Utah Temple. In the celestial room that morning I asked God directly what I should do with my life, and I specifically asked if gay relationships were wrong. I really wanted to know, and I believed that by the power of the Holy Ghost I could receive an answer to any serious, sincere inquiry. That day God didn't shut the door; He listened and answered. The scripture came to my mind:

> For behold, a bitter fountain cannot bring forth good water; neither can a good fountain bring forth bitter water
> ...
>
> Wherefore, take heed, my beloved brethren, that ye do not judge that which is evil to be of God, or that which is good and of God to be of the devil ...
>
> For behold, the Spirit of Christ is given to every man, that he may know good from evil; wherefore, I show unto you the way to judge; for every thing which inviteth to do good, and to persuade to believe in Christ, is sent forth by the power and gift of Christ; wherefore ye may know with a perfect knowledge it is of God. (Moroni 7:11–16)

I found this scripture very touching, not only because it applied perfectly to my situation but also because I discovered some important concepts that I had long forgotten. That day I didn't receive an absolute answer to my question, but another invitation: to judge for myself. God trusted me enough to do this because I was His child, not a machine that simply followed directions. He wanted me to ponder, reflect, and then make my decision with the knowledge I obtained. That's why I decided to do as Moroni suggested: to test the waters and see if what I was doing increased my desires to follow Christ, to do good, and to serve God and follow Him, or if it actually led me to despair, to do evil and serve the devil. I expected to receive further revelation from God when the time was right.

So, I decided to keep visiting with James, and although we had agreed not to do anything that two brothers wouldn't do, romantic feelings for each other continued to increase. Thinking back on it, we were both testing the waters: he was trying to decide if a future relationship with me would be possible, and I was trying to get out of my confusion, believing that God would give me further direction.

That direction came while I read my patriarchal blessing. As I read it, I felt an impression that I should stay in the Church, that somehow I had a mission to accomplish in it. I shared this with James. We had always been very honest with each other. I told him that I had to choose the Church. He was very understanding, and we stayed friends.

Tears fall on this paper

After "breaking up" with James, I found the coming days unusually challenging: not only did I have to deal with the sadness and depression of a "break-up", but I also needed to reconcile the principles of the Church, some of which I found intellectually troublesome and difficult to accept. The process was further complicated as I faced the challenge of dealing with other people's lack of understanding and compassion. That was indeed a tough time, and I often questioned if God's love was real. But through it all came a refining fire. One of those days, in deep contemplation and melancholy, I wrote to James:

> Dear Friend:
>
> I have already told you how grateful I am because of my association with you. Since I met you I knew you would be a major influence in my life. In my darkest hour you have been a crutch when I was too tired to keep walking. Our lives have been similar in many respects, but at the same time our paths have to be so different. However, because of your influence I have lived, and have begun to bloom, even when I thought that was impossible.
>
> Today was one of those days. I just wanted to walk and walk and walk. Again I felt depressed. I looked around and didn't see a single soul. The clouds were breaking in white tears. All was silent. I crossed a street and then another and another. And I kept walking. I saw a factory in the distance. I was on the outskirts of the city. And I kept walking. Here, the snow had accumulated and [it] was difficult to walk. On my left there was a gloomy old house. Here and there on the walls there were traces of paint tile. Next to the shack was a small barn. The doors were open and I could see that they had piled wood inside. A skinny dog kept the barn and looked at me sadly through the bars. The house's windows were opaque and

in the door hung a small U.S. flag. An African American man was shoveling snow in the entrance. When he saw me pass by, he smiled and greeted me.

This brief [encounter] transported my mind to a different location, a year or so before, to a day like this when [I] questioned if God really loved me and if my life would have some value for him; a time when I cried along with David: "How long wilt thou forget me, O Lord? for ever? how long wilt thou hide thy face from me? How long shall I take counsel in my soul, having sorrow in my heart daily?" (Psalm 13:1-2). After going to that place in the mountains where I used to retire and meditate, I walked and walked and walked. When I reached the park, I ran into some evangelical women who were sharing pamphlets. They started talking to me and told me about Christ and how I was a special child of God. Although familiar, their message resonated in my mind. Then I kept walking. When I was close [to] home, I noticed a little boy looking at me through the rolled window of his mom's car. The boy had Down syndrome. He smiled and waved his hand at me and I smiled back.

This, I believe, was by far the answer I needed. I think the most conclusive way in which God has shown His love for me is that I can feel His love through me. This has been a challenge for me lately. Although there are many logical evidences of His love for me, one thing is to know that one is loved and another is to feel loved. But I'm trying. Once again, for some strange reason, I feel that my life has direction and purpose. I want to serve others and love them. And you know that ours can sometimes be a lonely and gloomy road, but as I saw recently, by helping others to flourish, we flourish too ...

Perhaps that is our role in life. To be Christ's hands to those who are in need and be ambassadors for Him to all the world. God is a God even for the smallest. Gandhi once taught that "it is easy enough to be friendly to one's friends. But to befriend the one who regards himself as your enemy is the quintessence of true religion. The other is mere business."

In recent months, more than ever I've sought the Lord's guidance. You've been a great example to me, of someone who seeks the guidance of the Father, and strives to know His will. I appreciate you for motivating me to get the answers I needed. Now more than ever I'm grateful for being a child of God and a member of the Church of Jesus Christ of Latter-day Saints. You are also an example of what the Mormon historian B.H. Roberts described:

"[Mormonism] calls for thoughtful disciples who will not be content with merely repeating some of the truths, but will develop its truths; and enlarge [them] by that development ... The disciples of 'Mormonism,' growing discontented with the necessarily primitive methods which have hitherto prevailed in sustaining the doctrine, will yet take profounder and broader views of the great doctrines committed to the Church; and, departing from mere repetition, will cast them in new formulas; cooperating in the works of the Spirit, until they help to give to the truths received a more forceful expression and carry it beyond the earlier and cruder states of its development."

Thank you so much for your help and example for me. Thanks for being there when I've needed you the most. Tears fall on this paper as I write. I hope that you soon find the peace and fulfillment that you so dearly desire. Love you, same as always.

– Carlos

A burden was lifted off my shoulders

The next step for me was talking to my parents. When I talked to them they were at first shocked and didn't know how to help me. Their response was to invite me to exercise faith in the Atonement and through diligence and prayer the Lord would take the "trial" away. I tried not to contradict their views, but in my life I have gradually come to understand that this aspect of me is so intrinsically connected with my spirit that I will most probably live with it for the rest of my life and even for all eternity.

I decided to talk to my bishop. He told me that the reason I was on this Earth was to marry a woman and procreate and if I didn't do that then I was wasting my time here. I left his office feeling horrible. I just wanted to cry and cry. Even though I knew the things he had said were not true, I felt deeply hurt.

All I wanted was to move to another ward. Nevertheless, following a spiritual impression I decided to stay. I shared with my bishop the "God Loveth His Children" pamphlet and prayed for him. After a while he called me back to his office and almost crying told me that he was grateful I had helped him understand a bit better about same-gender attraction. He recognized that he didn't know how to help me but encouraged me to trust in the Atonement.

I started disclosing my feelings to good friends. As I shared with them my trials and my feelings, they expressed love and encouragement, and I felt as if a burden was lifted off my shoulders. I started to see that there were a lot of people who accepted me for who I was. Then I started to meet other people on campus who were in the same boat. They were actively trying to live good and moral lives, and they extended me their love and welcomed me into their support group and circle of friends. I value their friendship very much.

Deep gratitude now fills my soul

One particular night, worried about the problem of pain in the world, I was particularly frustrated. No matter how righteous I tried to be, I felt like I was missing something. I was mad at God for letting me down, for punishing me in such a cruel way. I yelled at him, asking, "Why?" There was no answer, but a complete and devastating silence.

A few weeks later I had the chance to visit with Fred and Marilyn Matis. Some of you may be familiar with their story and the story of their son Stuart. During those days, I had identified myself as a Christian agnostic because I had found it hard to reconcile the belief of a benevolent, loving God with the inequality and pain of the world, but then being at the Matis' home that afternoon, and listening to them as they shared some of their experiences, I felt like something clicked: my same-gender attraction wasn't something I had been punished with. This was a gift, like a package deal, and I had accepted it with joy in premortality, not only because it would be a challenge but because along with it came certain unique talents that I could not have in any other way. As this realization came to my heart that day, healing finally started to occur.

As the weeks of summer progressed, I was blessed with further knowledge and understanding and the assurance of God's involvement in my life. I felt that I had a mission to accomplish. As I was unique, God's plan for me was also unique. I had to live the best way I could and rejoice in the fact that I was one of the lucky ones. I believed that little by little the Lord was talking to me and giving me knowledge about the spiritual significance of being a gay Mormon.

Of course, since then life hasn't always been easy, and I expect it will never be, and sometimes I still struggle with the uncertainties of the future. But I rejoice in the beauty that has been added to my life. I rejoice in how much my heart has been enlarged in its capacity for love. I rejoice even in the sad things. Being rejected has helped me better sympathize with those who are left behind or aren't accepted. I have learned how to put my trust in God. My same-gender attraction is no longer a burden but a blessing; and my life is no longer the one that I have been given but the one that I have accepted and the one that I'm working to build upon.

Deep gratitude now fills my soul. Gratitude to God for his tender mercies. Gratitude to my family for their support. Gratitude to my friends for being there when I've needed them the most. And above all, gratitude to Life for teaching me so much. As John Milton once wrote: "Gratitude bestows reverence, allowing us to encounter everyday epiphanies, those transcendent moments of awe that change forever how we experience life and the world." This I firmly believe.

Chris Taylor

"*The Lord did not people the earth with a vibrant orchestra of personalities only to value the piccolos of the world. Every instrument is precious and adds to the complex beauty of the symphony.*"
– Joseph B. Wirthlin

As I sat nervously in the bishop's office, I wondered what the next few minutes would be like. I had kept so much from everyone that knew me, from my parents, siblings, priesthood leaders, and even my wife. Now, as I sat, my leg bouncing up and down in anticipation of what was about to unfold, I couldn't help but feel a little sense of relief that the weight that I had carried for so long was about to be released.

In reality the relief had begun a couple of weeks previous. As creative and elusive as I was, there really was no way to hide such a tremendous secret from the person I had chosen to spend my life with, the person I had committed to across the altar of the temple. Little clues along the way should have given away my secret: the way I couldn't look her in the eyes, the way I was so uncomfortable showing affection to her, and most of all the electronic evidence of my attraction left here and there. On December 23, 2008 the walls of my deception came tumbling down. When she confronted me this time, there was nowhere left to hide, no excuses left to make, to myself or to her. The truth had to be told, and so I told it from the beginning.

Unworthy of God's love

I was about nine or ten when I had my first crush. I didn't understand what it was. All I knew was that there was a boy I really liked being around, and when he moved away from our neighborhood I felt a loss that I hadn't ever experienced before. I wrote him a letter, telling him how lonely I had been since he left, and how much I had missed being around him. It was an innocent expression of something that I was unable to comprehend at the time.

As I grew and changed, so did my attractions and my desire to hide them from everyone, including myself. From every source I trusted, I knew that my attractions weren't something that I could ever admit to the ones I loved. From an early age I knew that what I was feeling was wrong and unacceptable. I read in *The Miracle of Forgiveness*:

> This perversion is defined as "sexual desire for those of the same sex or sexual relations between individuals of the same sex," whether men or women. It is a sin of the ages.

Those who felt powerless to change their feelings were called "weaklings." I placed all my trust in my Church leaders. Hearing myself described in such language, I could not help but feel unworthy of God's love. I created a wall within myself. On the one side I was what everyone expected me to be. I fulfilled my callings the best I could. I attended church faithfully. I did what I could to make sure that no one would ever know how wrong I felt. On the other side I would steal glances here and there at cute guys, and I would flip through my mom's clothing catalog to see the handsome guys and dream.

She made me feel comfortable

As the time approached for me to serve a mission, I found myself at a crossroads. I prayed to know what direction my life should take, and I felt that the Church was true. I served an honorable mission in France and Belgium and then returned home more persuaded than ever that all I needed to do to overcome my attraction to men was find the right woman and get married.

I began dating slowing and deliberately. I went on many first dates but very few second dates. Eventually I decided to try seriously dating a girl that I had grown up with. It was a disaster from the beginning.

I felt so uncomfortable with physical contact; she probably thought I had some terrible disease that I was afraid she might catch. In reality, I couldn't be close; I couldn't be intimate because it felt dishonest. It felt as though I was lying to her and to myself about what I was feeling.

It wasn't long after this that Camilla came back into my life. We had first met at school in the ninth grade. During my mission I had received a letter from her informing me that we would be mission neighbors, as she had been called to the mission just south of mine. As luck or fate would have it, I was transferred to her mission, and I ended up serving three months as her zone leader.

Soon after Camilla arrived home she contacted me to arrange a carpool to a mission reunion. Camilla always made me feel comfortable. As we began to see more of each other I started to realize how much I cared for her. I don't know if I've ever had a strong physical attraction to her, but I do know that I developed a strong emotional and spiritual attraction. I thought that if there ever was a woman that I could be married to, it was Camilla.

Living as a divided person

I thought of my attractions to men as a thorn in my side. I knew that if I did what I had learned in church, the Lord would bless me and remove it. Many nights I bargained with God. I placed my demands at his feet, and what I was willing to offer in return for His help. It was a prayer offered in sincerity and hope, but to my dismay and often my great disappointment, He continually refused my request.

It wasn't long after Camilla and I started dating that we decided to be married. I shopped for the ring by myself, asked her father for permission, and tried to make sure it was a total surprise for her. Two and a half months later we were married.

Months turned into years and I still hid much from Camilla. Living as a divided person I created habits that were unhealthy and destructive. I deceived myself and my best friend. I had been taught to value honesty and integrity, but I was failing to live up to those standards in the most intimate of my relationships.

It wasn't until that day in December that I finally began the process of destroying the walls of my deception. As I told her the extent of my attractions and the depth of my deception, I could see the pain and hurt in her eyes. It was a terrible moment, one that

I don't ever want to repeat, but at the same time it was the most liberating and cathartic experience I have ever had.

So good to be free

At the urging of Camilla I went to see the bishop. It was here that I sat in his office, nervously waiting to tell him my secrets. While he was compassionate, I believe he was totally unprepared for the revelation on my sexuality. We spoke for nearly two hours. I explained our situation and tried the best I could to help him understand. He gave me the current Church pamphlet "God Loveth His Children" and referred me to a therapist.

The therapist was a member of our high council. The first session we spoke briefly of what my goals were. The second session we spoke of my background and began to talk about therapy options. By the third session we were speaking of reparative therapy. At this point I decided to do some research into what that type of therapy involved. As I read and began to understand the premise and purported results of the therapy, I became less and less inclined to believe that it was right for me. The therapist was asking to meet weekly, for an indeterminate amount of time. Considering my lack of trust in the type of therapy he wanted to pursue, and our precarious financial situation at the time, I chose to discontinue the sessions and embark on my own journey.

I discovered that many of the answers I was looking for were found in the inner parts of my own heart and mind. As I began to shed the guilt and shame that had accompanied me for so long, I began to feel a sense of freedom. It was truly an enlightening experience. I no longer fear part of who I am. I no longer carry around a weight of guilt and shame that pulls me down. I no longer try to live a life divided between who I think everyone wants me to be and who I feel like I am on the inside. It feels so good to be free.

What the future holds

Soon after this, I decided it would be beneficial for me to tell my family about our situation. I wrote them a letter, and the next day Camilla and I went to their house to discuss and answer any questions. Their response was amazing. I have never appreciated a hug from my dad as much as I did on that day. I only wish I would have had the courage to speak with them years earlier.

Since then I have come to know and love many other gay Mormons, mostly through online venues. For many years I felt so alone, so isolated in my pain. I have been so amazed to find wonderful, good, honest men and women who have shared in my struggles. It has been their love and kindness that has gotten us through many rough spots.

Going forward I often try to see what the future holds for our family. I wish I could know what will happen to us, what our choices will be down the road. As I've learned from the past, it's nearly impossible to predict the future. There will certainly be speed bumps, twists and turns, dead ends and accidents along the way. What I do know is that if I live up to the values that I have committed to — honesty, compassion, integrity, love, kindness, and charity — then regardless of where we end up, I will be confident that I've walked a path that I can be proud of.

Camilla Taylor

"The only way to get through life is to laugh your way through it. You either have to laugh or cry. I prefer to laugh. Crying gives me a headache."
– Marjorie Pay Hinckley

Chris and I met in the ninth grade; it was 1996 when he moved to my part of town. Throughout our high school years, we hung out with the same crowd. A couple years later we both served LDS missions, and as fate would have it, we served not only in the same mission, but also in the same little branch, where he served as my zone leader for several months. It seemed that God kept making our paths cross, so we took the hint.

Six weeks after I returned home from my mission, Chris and I went on our first date. I felt so comfortable around him; dating Chris felt completely natural and right. The physical aspect of my relationship with Chris moved slowly, but I was appreciative of that. Before my mission I had seriously dated another guy who enjoyed kissing a lot. Although I knew "Paul" loved me, I frequently wondered if he wanted to date me just because I was a girl to kiss. Many times I told him that I wanted to be sure our relationship was based on friendship and not just the physical part. Paul would respect my wishes temporarily, and then he would fall back to his old ways of kissing me more than I felt comfortable with.

While dating Chris, I did not have to question whether or not he liked me for me. We were friends first before anything, and I knew that his love was based on that before anything physical. During our courtship, we would give each other a short kiss goodnight at the end of a date. Although it should have been a warning flag, I thought this respect he was showing me was refreshing; he was the perfect gentleman throughout our entire courtship. I had no question that his love was sincere.

He was hiding something

After knowing each other for seven years and dating for about nine months, in October 2004 I married the man of my dreams. Chris was near perfection in my eyes, and I felt so lucky that he had chosen me to be his wife. I had known since before our first date that I wanted to marry someone just like him, and I was ecstatic to become his wife. He was kind and funny and was a hard worker. We had so much in common, and we loved spending time together. My sister-in-law used to jokingly call us "The Celestial Couple" because we both served honorable full-time missions, were married in the temple, and generally did everything that a righteous couple should do. We were blissfully happy in our tiny basement apartment with no oven or dishwasher. We were poor students trying to work our way through college, but we had each other, and that was all that mattered to us.

Although we were happy, deep down I felt there was some intangible, indescribable block that kept a distance between us that I could not understand. I always thought it was a little strange that he would avoid looking directly into my eyes; it was like he was hiding something from me. We have never fought in our marriage. It really isn't in our natures or personalities to do so. Instead we have "discussions". Throughout our marriage, whenever such "discussions" arose about our marriage and family life, somehow I usually ended up feeling like it was my fault. I always felt like that invisible distance between us was because I wasn't good enough, smart enough, funny enough, pretty enough. I felt that my inadequacy was the reason I could not make Chris completely happy and fulfilled.

It didn't make any sense

In the spring of 2008, we were moving out of state, and because of my work obligations, Chris had to move ten weeks before me and our son. It just about killed me to be away from him for such a long time. About half way through, my parents surprised me with an early birthday present: a plane ticket for me and our son to go see Chris for the weekend. I was ecstatic to see him again and wanted our time together to be nothing but happy. Chris still had to work his early morning shift, so I decided to go there and hang out for awhile. Earlier I had noticed that our cell phone bill had been higher than normal, so while sitting in his office, I picked up his cell phone and started looking through his text messages. I assumed this was the reason for the recent expensive bill since texting was not included in our plan. I was shocked to find sexually explicit messages and pictures from people. It made my heart hurt and my stomach sick.

He walked in on me holding his phone, took it from my hands, and put it in his pocket. I didn't tell him what I saw; I tried to pretend I was just checking the time on his phone. I went home to our little apartment, sat down on the floor with my head in my hands and sobbed. Our sweet little son, who was almost two years old at the time, sat down beside me and asked, "Mommy sad? Mommy cry? I get you a blanket." It didn't make any sense to me at all. The Chris I knew and loved did not match the Chris I was discovering through internet chats, emails, and text messages. Later that day I checked his phone while he was in the shower, and each and every sexually explicit text message had been deleted.

My head could not deny the facts I had found, but my heart could not accept the truth. I felt like I was going crazy. All these things were adding up to something I didn't want in my life; at the same time, I knew that Chris was a good person and everything seemed so out of character for him. I decided against confronting him about the text messages at that time, so as not to ruin the few precious days I had to spend with him before flying home for the remaining five weeks apart. I put on a happy face, but inside I was hurting badly.

He still loved me very much

Life continued on, and through the following months I would occasionally find more inappropriate pictures and videos on our computer. It all came to a head two days before Christmas, December 23, 2008.

I confronted Chris about everything. There was no explaining his way out any longer. He finally broke down and told me the truth. It should have been obvious to me what was going on — my husband was gay. Because I loved him so much, I had a difficult time admitting it to myself.

We were at a crossroads. We loved each other very much, had a happy home and a sweet little boy to raise and nurture; but combined with all that, my husband's ability to lie straight to my face terrified me. I could have kicked him out. I could have left him to go our separate ways, but I didn't; I couldn't. I still loved him too much to let him go. Although I could never in a million years be the person to fulfill him 100%, he still loved me very much and wanted to try to make our marriage work.

For the first few days post disclosure, I went through stages of shock, sadness, anger, and fear, and somehow I always ended up in his arms and felt safe. Over and over I would repeat, "I don't want to lose you," and he would reply, "I'm not going anywhere."

After getting over my anger, I went through a period of mourning. I mourned the loss of the marriage, family, and life I thought we had. My dream of having more kids, my expectation of having a faithful priesthood leader as my husband — all gone.

I began to question the authenticity of our courtship. I relived and reevaluated all the magical moments we had had together. Were those a lie too? He had made the first move to kiss me; he was the first to say, "I love you." When he held my hand for the first time, it sent sparks and electricity through my entire body. It was 100% real to me. It scared me to think it might have all been a fabrication. It took me time to believe him, but I was happy to discover that it was, indeed, real for Chris too. He genuinely loved me. His love for me was just different than my love for him. Not less, just different.

Together we make a great team

For the next several weeks and months we had many long conversations about our curious little situation — what it meant for us and for the future of our little family. We would stay up late talking everything out, sorting everything out, crying everything out. It was incredibly refreshing to have open and complete honesty after having been lied to for so long. After years of me blaming myself for not being able to make him happy, I finally came to know the real Chris and the true reason for our marital issues.

We eventually felt the need to reach out to others in our same situation. Making those connections with others in mixed-orientation marriages helped me feel less alone and was pivotal in helping us move forward. We have also told both our families who in turn have been incredibly supportive and loving.

As is life, we have our highs and lows. We go through periods of time when one of us feels discouraged or lonely. During these times we may question why we continue in our marriage, and begin dreaming about how life could be if I were with a straight husband or if Chris were with a gay partner. I have found that it is not helpful to dwell on the "what-if's" in life. During these times, I try to count my blessings and make myself realize that I really do have a great life: my husband is my best friend, and together we make a great team raising a sweet little boy who brings us so much joy. Getting through these times also just takes patience. After several days of feeling down, a good cathartic crying session helps. I also like to talk out my feelings with Chris. If none of that helps, the most helpful thing is just being held in my husband's arms knowing that although his love for me is different, it is pure.

We are so blessed

Chris and I have come a long way since that December evening when he told me everything. Our relationship is much stronger and we are able to talk without holding back any secrets. It's a pretty serious thing to realize that your spouse is not exactly the person you thought you were marrying. What I have learned is that in life there will always be unexpected disappointments, twists and turns. So rather than dwell on the negative, I try to remember all the good in life. Chris and I often make light of our situation. We enjoy comparing notes on our Hollywood boyfriends and are very open to pointing out who each of us thinks is cute. Instead of always feeling sorry for ourselves, we are able to laugh and have fun with it.

When I start to become discouraged about my life, I pull out a quote which helps me gain perspective:

> Anyone who imagines that bliss is normal is going to waste a lot of time running around shouting that he's been robbed. The fact is that most putts don't drop. Most beef is tough ... life is like an old-time rail journey — delays,

> sidetracks, smoke, dust, cinders and jolts, interspersed only occasionally by beautiful vistas and thrilling bursts of speed. The trick is to thank the Lord for letting you have the ride.[22]

Through my experiences, I have learned and grown a lot. I have learned that although I do not understand everything, God does, so I keep my faith in him and try to understand his plan for me.

Another lesson I have learned is that of repentance and forgiveness. We all have temptation and weakness; none of us is perfect. God sees the intents of our heart and knows our effort and commitment to overcome those shortcomings. If we expect God to forgive our shortcomings, we should never withhold forgiveness from anyone. God will be the final judge.

Since that awful day when my suspicions were confirmed, December 23 has now become a second anniversary for us. It is a day to celebrate our openness and honesty with each other. It is a day to celebrate our love and devotion to sticking through it together even during the really hard times. I do not know what the future holds for us. What I do know is that in the end it will only be good if we keep that line of communication open and be completely honest with ourselves and with each other. Our marriage is a work-in-progress, but we're doing the best we can. Our son is lucky to have such a fantastic dad, and I am blessed to have Chris as my best friend. Our home is truly a happy place. We are so blessed.

---

[22]Gordon B. Hinckley, BYU devotional address, December 1973.

David Dinger

"We must realize that all of God's children wear the same jersey. Our team is the brotherhood of man. This mortal life is our playing field. Our goal is to learn to love God and to extend that same love toward our fellowman. We are here to build, uplift, treat fairly, and encourage all of Heavenly Father's children."
– Dieter F. Uchtdorf

I was born in Utah and grew up in the Church. I was the oldest, and I wanted to be a good example to my younger brothers and sisters, so I tried to do everything I was supposed to do. I went to seminary all four years, earned my Eagle Scout, and served a mission.

In junior high, I started really noticing the guys in the locker room. I really liked what I saw, although I didn't do anything to act on my feelings. I didn't know any gay people. I knew I was expected to have crushes on girls, although I didn't really know what that meant. I thought I had crushes on girls, but I kind of knew that I didn't really.

In high school, there was a guy in my same drama and music classes, and I liked his personality. We were good friends, and I enjoyed hanging out with him and talking with him. I wanted to spend most of my time with him. He was physically attractive, and I enjoyed it when he would be touchy-feely with me. Nothing inappropriate ever happened, but sometimes he would put his head on my shoulder, and I would think, "This feels so good!"

When I was about 17, I went to the magazine shops downtown a couple of times and looked at the gay adult magazines. One time the clerk asked to see my ID, and I just left. Another time there was a guy who was looking at me, smiling and trying to make eye contact, and it kind of creeped me out, so I left. He followed me out, so I started walking really fast and got in my car and drove off as fast as I could. After that I didn't go back anymore.

I didn't think it was right

Next I went to BYU. A whole bunch of people from my high school went to BYU, but I didn't really see them much. I felt really isolated, and it was kind of a depressing time. Then I got my mission call to the Dominican Republic and left in January after one semester.

I was a good missionary. I loved the mission and loved the people. I got out there and did what I was supposed to do, but I hated focusing on numbers and authority.

Before my mission, although my feelings were always there, I didn't think much about them. But on my mission, I started to be bothered by them. I was attracted to some of the members, and I thought, "This isn't right. These aren't the thoughts I'm supposed to be having. Heavenly Father, please take them away from me." I never really felt guilty about it; I didn't feel like I was a bad person for having them, but I just didn't think it was right.

Near the end of my mission, I did some stuff with another missionary that we shouldn't have done. He was pretty forward about it. I don't want to put the blame on him, but it happened, and I didn't say anything about it or confess it to anyone. That was the first time I had done anything intimate with a guy, and I felt pretty guilty about it. I was thinking, "What just happened? What did I do?"

I didn't feel much of anything

After I came home, I went back to BYU the following fall. I was thinking, "I need to do whatever it takes to not have those feelings anymore." So I prayed and fasted, went to church, went to the temple, and all those kinds of things. I figured if I did what I was supposed to be doing, then everything would be okay and God would take those feelings away.

I met "Lisa" through a friend from my mission. I could tell that she liked me. I had actually never kissed a girl at that point. But I could tell she wanted to be more than friends, so I went with it.

When we made out for the first time, my first thought was, "This felt so much better when I was doing it with the missionary." But I quickly put that to the back of my mind and tried to convince myself that I liked it. We ended up being boyfriend and girlfriend. I figured that since she liked me, she was probably the one I should marry.

We dated for about six months, got engaged, and were married in the Salt Lake Temple in September 2000. The day we got married, I was just thinking, "This is supposed to be the happiest day of my life, but really I don't feel much of anything." I kind of just wanted to get it over with.

That night, I was nervous. I was thinking, "What the heck do I do?" I tried to get into it, thinking that since now we're married, that it was okay and what was expected. But the clothes never came off and we just fell asleep.

I needed to make a choice

I felt like I was leading a double life. On the one hand, I was supposedly a straight married guy, active in church, praying, going to the temple, doing everything I was supposed to be doing, thinking that if I kept going, everything would work out and I wouldn't be gay anymore. On the other hand, I was talking to guys on the Internet, just getting to know them and trying to understand what it meant to be gay. I was too scared to ever meet anybody in real life. I really wanted to not be gay and not have those feelings. I wanted to be a good husband to my wife.

I kind of went through phases with pornography. I wouldn't say I was ever addicted to it or that kind of thing. It started right after I was married. When I knew my wife and I were going to be intimate, I would look at porn to get myself aroused so that I could perform. When we were intimate, I would have to think about other guys. This was usually the only way I found that worked. Looking back, I feel terrible about that.

My wife became pregnant, and as the years passed, in all we had three kids. We moved to Seattle for my master's program in social work. I started chatting online with a guy "Gabriel" who lived in New Mexico. We started talking on the phone too, and I fell for him pretty hard. My wife knew I was talking with him. If I didn't get to talk with him, I would tend to be mopey and sad. This was the first time I had ever really felt like this. It was the first time I had ever really loved another guy. It made me think, "This is what love is supposed to be! This is how I'm supposed to feel when I love somebody."

It made me think, "I need to make a choice here. I need to get this figured out." I was thinking in pretty black-and-white terms: if I was gay, then I would have to leave my family behind, I would never see my kids again, and I would never be in the Church, because I would be living a "gay lifestyle". So I got pretty depressed. I didn't want to leave my family behind or abandon the Church, but I wanted to love somebody and be loved, and I couldn't do that the way things were going.

I couldn't keep this inside anymore

I was pretty depressed, and I didn't know what I was going to do. I just wanted everything to go away. One time my wife asked me, "Are you gay?" I denied it and said, "No. Why would you think that?" I don't think she said much, but she asked me again a week or so later, and I finally said in my mind, "I can't keep this inside anymore, or I'm going to go crazy or do something stupid," and out loud I said, "What if I am?" She said, "What?" And I said, "Yeah, I am gay." So I admitted it, and it was very emotional for both of us. She cried without stopping for about two days.

Once we got through the initial shock, we tried to figure out together what we were going to do. She was saying I needed to stop talking to Gabriel and just focus on us and figuring out how we were going to do this. In my mind I knew she was right, but at the same time, I knew that if I didn't confront and experience the gay side of myself, I would never be able to make a decision.

So I flew to New Mexico and met Gabriel in person. It actually turned out horribly. It just wasn't good. It was wrong, and it wasn't what I wanted. So I went back home, and my wife and I talked to the bishop. He had no idea how to react, but he set us up with LDS Family Services, and we did a few sessions there. I didn't like it, though; I felt like the counselor didn't understand me at all and was putting me down. So we ended it after two or three sessions.

It was a really emotional time

After that, we just kept going with the flow. Neither of us really wanted to be intimate with each other after that. But we knew we wanted what was best for the kids, so we didn't split up.

Neither of us had any family or really close friends in Washington that we could talk with. I loved my job at the time, but we decided to move back to Utah where we could have family support and closer friends. My mom and dad flew up and talked to us. They encouraged me to pray harder and do more Church stuff. I don't think they were rejecting me or trying to use the Church against me or anything like that. It was just a shock for them, and they didn't know how to react either. I tried to explain that I've been dealing with this for years, trying to get Heavenly Father to take these feelings away from me. It was a really emotional time.

After we moved to Utah, my parents wanted me to go to LDS Family Services again, so I did. But all I could really think about while I was there was, "I'm paying $75 an hour for this?" The guy was nice, but he didn't really know what to say to me either. I only went two or three times.

We're still a family

Eventually my wife and I both came to the conclusion that this wasn't really what either of us wanted. It was not working for either of us. I was still pretty depressed at the time. I would spend the evening by myself because I didn't want to deal with everybody. Even though we were trying to do what was best for the kids, we realized that it wasn't what was best for the kids, because neither of us were happy and that affected the kids too. We decided it would be better if we split up. So we got divorced.

It's an interesting relationship, because we still see each other every day. She works graveyards, and when she does, I sleep over there with the kids. We still do a lot together. We go out to eat together, or go to the movies together as a family. She lives in her house and I live in mine, but even though we're not together anymore, we're still a family.

Through all of this, I have always been active in the Church. I haven't ever quit going. I have skipped every so often, but I've never gone for a period of time where I would say that I'm inactive. I go to the same ward as my wife and kids. We have a good relationship. I don't really know what the other ward members think.

Listen to your heart

As far as my relationship with the Church goes, I attend because I believe most of what the Church teaches. I like the focus on family and being good and helping others. I know I'm His son and that He loves me just the way I am. My testimony of that is as strong as it's ever been. In other things, it's not as strong as it once was. As far as Joseph Smith and the Book of Mormon, I don't think I believe everything happened the way the Church tells us it happened. For me there are too many questions and doubts from studying Church history. It could have happened that way, or it could have happened another way. But there are good things to be found in the Book of Mormon and the Joseph Smith story, whether or not it 100% happened that way.

I'm definitely not bitter toward the Church. I do believe that it is God's church, that it's where He wants me and what He wants me to be doing. I believe that He loves me just the way I am. I prayed for a long time for Him to take these feelings away from me, and He didn't. So what that tells me is that it doesn't matter to Him if I'm gay. It's not that big of a deal to Him.

I'm a dad and have my own three kids and know that no matter what, I'll always love them. And if I feel that way toward my kids, then Heavenly Father, being so much more perfect and all-knowing, must feel the same way and even more. So even if Boyd K. Packer gets up and says what he said, it doesn't really affect me that much. I know that God loves me.

I hope someday to find my prince charming. I don't want to live celibately forever. I want to find a partner and live the law of chastity with him for the rest of my life.

To someone trying to figure this issue out for themselves, I would say, listen to your heart. It's between you and God, no matter what others say. If God doesn't take away those feelings, then He may have His reasons. Don't beat yourself up or convince yourself you're worthless, because that's not what God is going to tell you. Always know that He loves you.

Blake Hoopes

"Have you ever noticed how easy it is to look back on events that happened a year or more in the past and see the perfection in them? For most of us this is true even for situations which seemed tragic, horrible or even devastating at the time. Now, if it is possible to see the perfection in those things a year later, doesn't it make sense that the perfection must be there in the moment it happens, too?"
– Kurt Wright

I grew up in Star Valley, Wyoming and was raised as a devout member of the Church of Jesus Christ of Latter-day Saints.

There was never a time I recall not feeling attracted to males. The first crush I remember was on a child actor in a movie I had seen when I was five. Every time I played "house" with my sisters, I took on his character's name. I didn't recognize my feelings as being a crush; I assumed my feelings were the same as everyone else.

I loved my sisters' toys, especially Barbies! I knew that if I was playing with my sisters, or any other girl, I was mostly safe from ridicule. However, whenever anyone caught me playing with them by myself, I would quickly tear their heads off to demonstrate to whoever saw that I wasn't actually "playing" with them. I hated having to do this! My heart yearned to be able to play without interruption, without having to risk any sudden and tragic executions by decapitation.

I overheard a conversation once between my mother and a female friend she had; my mother said something about how she admired this woman for her beauty. Hearing this allowed me to feel okay about "admiring" boys for their looks. After all, my mother had expressed these feelings outright. It must be completely normal to recognize that someone is attractive and admire them for that attribute. Needless to say, I spent a lot of time "admiring" boys at school as time went on, though I didn't vocalize these thoughts. I knew that boys were supposed to "like" girls, and I was friends with girls, so I thought that meant I had a crush on them.

I was a faithful young man

Gradually I began to recognize that I wasn't merely admiring boys, nor was I crushing on girls. The topic of homosexuality had been touched on enough in church for me to know that any "inclination" toward it was awful. I turned to God, praying to be more normal. I slowly went from feeling abnormal to feeling worthless, shameful, hollow, alone, lost, scared, and unlovable. At the age of 12, I knelt down and prayed that I would get cancer or some other illness that would end everything. That way no one would ever have to know how I truly felt inside. It was so appalling to know that I was attracted to men.

By the time I was 14 or 15, I had accepted that I was bisexual. I was attracted to guys, but I could look at women and recognize which ones were attractive. I had no intention of ever succumbing to the temptation of dating men. That would be a sin beyond imagination! I was a strong, faithful young man. I wanted to serve a full-time mission for the Church and return with honor to marry a wonderful young woman.

Even though I knew I would never act on my feelings, it didn't stop me from feeling awful merely for experiencing them. By this time, I had given up on the idea of cancer from God and had begun making considerations to take things into my own hands. Suicide would be my fallback plan in case I couldn't fight any longer. It was about this time that I discovered cutting. The self-mutilation provided a temporary release from reality, but it wasn't enough and soon led to an actual suicide attempt.

A weight off my shoulders

Prior to the suicide attempt, I had sought counseling with my bishop. After the attempt on my life, my parents took me to a couple of psychologists in town. I didn't click well with either of the therapists I was seeing. I found out later that one of them told my mother that I was a spoiled brat begging for attention, and that a bit more discipline would solve everything.

Eventually, at the recommendation of my bishop, I went to a counselor with LDS Family Services in Salt Lake City. This therapist specifically dealt with the "Same-Sex Attraction" (SSA) issues. It was incredibly comforting to learn that I was not alone. Other people within my own faith group were experiencing this too! Perhaps I wasn't the evil sinner I had believed myself to be. The therapist recommended my parents purchase a book designed for LDS men struggling with SSA. I stayed up late into the night, spending hours crying while reading this book. It was such a weight off my shoulders to read a firsthand account of someone dealing with the same feelings which had plagued me for years. The therapist tried to teach me how to stop these thoughts of SSA. One of the exercises was for me to envision an actual stop sign anytime I saw a male and felt attracted to him.

During this time, I had a steady girlfriend in high school. She didn't know anything about the SSA, but she did know about the cutting and the suicide attempt. She was incredibly supportive of me and wanted me to be happy. She told me about other girls in her ward who were jealous of our relationship because I never pressured her to do anything immoral. We went on dates and cuddled while we watched movies and even spent quite a bit of time kissing, but I had no desire to do anything sexually with her.

The hope of normalcy

Around this time, I was an honor-roll student involved in multiple extracurricular activities at school; I attended church regularly and had become quite a social butterfly. But inwardly I was screaming. My teenage hormones may not have been raging when I was with my girlfriend, but they certainly were whenever I spent time by myself looking at guys on the Internet. It was a way to release some of the frustration I felt from hiding my true self, without actually having to act on my attractions with another human being. As time went on, I spent more and more time looking at pornographic images and covering my tracks. I hated myself for allowing myself to succumb to the temptation. My grades started slipping and the cutting became a nightly ritual.

Things were getting worse and worse. Finally, my therapist suggested that my parents place me in an intensive treatment center for troubled youth. My bishop got the approval for the Church to pay it.

While my parents were making plans for me to enter treatment, I was busy being a teenager. Toward the end of my junior year of high school, I changed the word that I internally identified with, from "bisexual" to "gay". I was still planning on fighting it with everything I had; I wanted to be able to have a temple marriage and an eternal family. I thought I would be able to overcome it through the methods I was being taught at LDS Family Services. I held tight to the hope of normalcy, or at least the appearance of normalcy.

"He told me himself."

At school there was a guy "Lewis" who was obviously gay. People talked about it frequently, myself included. Whenever I would see the bullies, I would deflect their negativity away from me toward him, since he was more flamboyant than I was. I still regret allowing someone else to go through more torment just to spare my own feelings. The more I began to accept myself though, the less I talked about him, and the less the bullies picked on me. It's funny how that worked out. As I internally became okay with who I was, the other people in school stopped picking on me for it.

One night at a school dance, one of my good friends mentioned Lewis and stated out right, "He's gay!" I could see that she was being serious and not trying to poke fun at him for his feminine demeanor. I asked her how she knew he was gay. She quickly responded, "He told me himself." This sent a chill through my soul. He had mustered up the courage to actually vocalize how he felt. Not only that, but this girl, and the other girl he had told his secret to, were still friends with him.

A few weeks later, I was sitting around late one night with these same two girls, talking and laughing, and I brought up Lewis. Then I just said, "I am too." They didn't know what I meant, so I explained, "I'm gay too." They laughed and thought I was joking.

I was rewarded with a candy bar

A few weeks later I entered the treatment center. I spent just over five months there. I was taught new tools for fighting my homosexual desires. Toward the end of my stay, I saw a new doctor at an offsite location who gave me a set of personality profile tests and sexual arousal tests. They hooked me up to heart rate monitors and strapped an inhalation monitor around my chest in addition to a device called a penile plethysmograph which was attached to my genitals.

The initial test consisted of me listening to scenarios while images were displayed on a screen. All the while, the machines I was tethered to were gathering data based on my physiological responses to the images and audio situations being read to me. The results came back about a week later, confirming that I was in fact suffering from a "deviant attraction" to males my own age.

Subsequent treatment was scheduled to follow. The way I was going to move past this deviant attraction to men and develop a healthy attraction to women was first to write out two scenarios of my own. In the first essay, I was to write about a future sexual experience with a female, more specifically, my wife. It had to include all the feelings of love and companionship we would share together as eternally sealed husband and wife. Then I was to write out another situation featuring a sexual encounter with a male.

Once I had written my stories and they were approved by the doctor's staff, the next step was that I was hooked up to the same monitors as before and read through the scenarios I had written. Anytime any of the machines indicated I was becoming aroused by the story involving a male, a container was placed in front of my nose and opened. It contained a rotting moose liver. The odor would trigger a negative response in my brain which would be associated with becoming aroused by men. The smell was enough to make you want to snort battery acid to find refuge! Alternatively, after reading the story involving my wife, I was rewarded with a candy bar. The process was much like Pavlov's famous experiment on dogs.

I knocked on the door

I'll be the first to admit that the treatment center did provide me with alternative ways to deal with my depression and helped me to cope with those types of issues better. However, after beginning aversion therapy with this new doctor, I began spiraling back into the depression again. I felt trapped and didn't know how to regain control. I made a decision to run away.

During the five months I was in treatment, my parents had moved to Draper, Utah. I planned to stay missing for a minimum of a month without any contact with my family. I knew that if I were to return home, I would immediately be driven back to the treatment center, and that was not an option I was willing to make available.

I arrived home at night and crept into the backyard. I was planning on going in quietly to get better supplies for my stint as a homeless teenager. But I noticed the lights were still on. I took the opportunity to peak in through a crack in the blinds. Inside my house sat my grandmother with tears in her eyes. Her house was over four hours away in Wyoming. It meant she had come to be with my family and help search for me. I knew that the tears she shed were a direct result of my actions and the pain I had forced her to bear. At that moment, I knew I couldn't remain missing any longer, so I knocked on the door and proceeded inside.

At first, my parents planned to bring me back to treatment, but the therapist said he would only allow me to come back if I would stand up in front of everyone else in treatment and apologize for running away and ask them if they would allow me back. I knew that the treatment was not the right place for me anymore and refused his offer.

I was finally ready

I was enrolled back in high school, and life continued on. I was still in the mindset that I could be straight, so I reconnected with an ex-girlfriend from Wyoming for a long-distance relationship. Over the next few months, I started contemplating all that had happened in my life. I nearly didn't survive as a result of the hatred I had developed for myself, due to the guidance I had received that being gay was immoral, wicked, sinful, and evil. Finally, just before I turned 18, a thought occurred to me that I should kneel down and ask Heavenly Father himself if being gay was so wrong. I had always been taught these things, but I had never actually asked for myself.

I have to tell you, the overwhelming feeling of comfort I received was more powerful than anything I can possibly describe. I was forced from my knees into a weeping slump on the floor. I wept with joy that I wasn't evil after all. I wept in grief for all the wasted years spent hating myself. I wept at the confirmation that not only was being gay okay, but it was part of God's plan for me. I wept with bliss at the knowledge that I had a future with a loving husband and adoring children. I had finally come to terms with my sexuality and fully embraced the fact that I am gay. I was finally ready to come out to the world and live honestly. I was sick of the shame I felt in hiding all these years.

Now came the daunting task of informing my parents. I didn't know quite how to approach them with the news. I wanted to plan some way to tell them, but I was so afraid of their reaction that I couldn't just come out and say it. My thoughts were to just go on a date and on my way out the door say, "Bye Mom, I'm going on a date ... his name is Cameron!" and then run out the door. The problem was that not only did I not have a Cameron, I didn't have a gay boy by any other name either. I was the only gay person I had ever known aside from the one guy in high school, and he had never actually confessed his secret to me.

"It's exactly what it looks like"

I got online and quickly found Gay.com, a social networking website. I started staying up late to chat online with guys while the rest of my family slept. In order to help myself keep track of things, I wrote down the names of a few guys I had chatted with, along with some details about our conversations. I labeled the note "Gay.com" and folded it up and hid it in my room between two DVDs.

One day my younger sister came and borrowed one of the two DVDs I was using to hide my note. This resulted in my note landing on the floor. She opened it, read it, and took it to my parents. This was a blessing in disguise, because it forced the issue out of the bottle I had shoved it into.

That night when I got home from work, my parents pulled me into their bedroom for a meeting. I had no idea what it could be about, but I was incredibly nervous. My mom unfolded the paper and held it out to me, asking what it was. My initial instinct was to lie. I opened my mouth to spout out the best cover-up I could come up with, but I hesitated, thought better of it, and said, "It's exactly what it looks like." She acknowledged that it meant I was gay. Then she got a disgusted, horrified look on her face; it had made her think of a sexual act, which she described and said, "Doesn't that gross you out?" I was mortified! I explained that love was not about sex; it's about companionship. Sex is just one aspect of a loving relationship. I explained that the reason I'm attracted to men isn't about sexual desire; it has everything to do with longing for a connection with another human being to share my life with.

He looked completely shocked

My parents later admitted to me that they both cried over this turn of events, though neither of them shed any tears in front of me, and for that I am grateful. My mom did some research and let me know about a group called GLYA which stood for Gay LDS Young Adults and consisted of young gay LDS men ages 18 to 30 who met weekly for activities. I went to a few of their activities and made a few friends. It was nice to meet other men who were from LDS backgrounds and yet could accept their sexual orientation.

Next came the overwhelming task of outing myself to the rest of my close friends. A few months back, I had won tickets to the theme park Lagoon, so I invited my best friend to come up from Wyoming and go to Lagoon with me. The entire day, I was trying to come up with the courage to say what was on my mind. As we were getting ready to leave, we walked out to his car so he could play me some songs from the "Chicago" musical soundtrack. After he was finished, I told him that I had something important to say. After hesitating for a moment, the words "I'm gay" slipped out of my mouth. He looked completely shocked. He spent the next several minutes telling me that it was the worst mistake I would ever make in my life. It was an abominable sin against God, and he desperately wished I would reconsider.

Years later, after he returned from his mission, we were all together at a friend's house playing board games, and when he got up to leave, he said that he felt like he should go around and shake everyone's hand. He proceeded around the circle, starting to my left, shaking everyone's hand, but ending with the person to my right. He had deliberately skipped my hand while making his rounds. When he got married, I was the only one in our group of friends to not get an invitation to the reception. It hurts to know that he feels so uncomfortable with me, but at the same time, I realize that there's nothing I can do.

I became a new man

After the negative response of my best friend, I wrote an e-mail to my other close friends, explaining that I am gay, that I wasn't going to change, and that they could either accept me as I am, or we could agree to move on from the relationship. To my utter surprise and delight, every single one of my remaining friends responded with love and kindness. A few felt the need to explain their feelings a bit further by letting me know that they may not agree with my "choice", as they called it, but that they loved me no matter what and we would always be friends. One girl said she still enjoys me as a person and feels that I'm a great friend and one worth keeping around. She has been an example of true unconditional love and I'll be grateful to her for that as long as I live.

Once I was open and honest about who I truly was and why I had been so incredibly depressed, I became a new man. I wasn't sad at all anymore. I had never experienced fulfillment in life like that before. The light was back behind my eyes and the gleam in my smile was dazzling once again.

That was when I quit going to church. I wasn't angry with the LDS Church; I just couldn't attend any longer. When the Church started helping with Proposition 8, though, I felt betrayed. They were supporting organizations which were spreading untruths and half-truths about me and my future family. I still didn't feel it would be appropriate to attend any of the protests held near LDS property. They had their beliefs, and I couldn't change that, nor did I have a desire to change them; but I did attend the demonstrations held at the City-County building and Capitol buildings in Salt Lake City.

One final goodbye

When news broke that the Church and others had succeeded in removing the freedom to marry from thousands of Californians, it was devastating. That same summer, I had fallen in love with a guy who ended up breaking my heart. These things together with other day-to-day stressors sent me into a spiral of despair. Before I knew it, at age 23, I was standing on the edge once more, with thoughts of suicide continuously crossing my mind.

November 22 was the one-year anniversary of a close friend's passing away. He enjoyed going out dancing a lot, so as a way of holding a memorial, a friend of mine held a small party at a local dance club. My cousin had agreed to attend the party as my designated driver. I ended up consuming too much alcohol. My cousin drove me safely to my friend's house where I had made plans to spend the night. I don't remember that drive, but I remember being at the dance club and the next thing I knew, I was completing field sobriety tests with a police officer. Needless to say, it was a very sobering experience and I remember everything after that. Due to my cooperation, the officer allowed me to go home rather than to jail if I could find a sober friend to drive me. While I was sitting in the back of the police car waiting for my friend to arrive, I had time to evaluate my life. My depression along with the shame of being arrested and charged with DUI was more than I knew how to cope with. I made a decision to end my life.

As soon as my friend dropped me off at my apartment, I got on my computer and jotted a few quick lines vaguely explaining that I was depressed about the Church's involvement in Proposition 8 and had an overall dissatisfaction with my life. I then proceeded to take every pill I had in my medicine cabinet. I decided to call my sisters and mother to tell them goodbye. None of them answered, but I left voicemails for each one of them explaining through sobs that I was sorry for leaving them, that I loved them dearly, and ending with one final goodbye. I also left a voicemail for my ex-boyfriend explaining that I still cared for him, and I knew that my actions would affect him too, but I wanted him to know that my decision was not a result of anything he had done.

After that, my phone started to ring. It was my sister. Although it was around 2:00 a.m., my call woke her up, and after listening to the voicemail I left, she was completely alert and scrambling to obtain more detail about the situation. I was sobbing quite hard by this point, and I'm sure it was difficult for her to understand me. I explained my feelings and informed her that it was already too late.

The thought crossed my mind that my sister might come to my apartment to try and take me to the hospital. So while I was talking with her, I left the comfort of my apartment and started winding aimlessly through the Avenues of Salt Lake City, turning random corners so as not to be easily found. Just then I remembered that my cell phone could be tracked by GPS. At that, I informed my sister that I couldn't talk anymore, and I removed the battery from my phone.

I continued walking aimlessly for a time before deciding to try again to get in touch with my ex-boyfriend. I felt a need to hear his voice one last time. When his phone went immediately to voicemail, I called his mother and asked her if she would wake him up for me. As soon as he was on the line, he could tell something was wrong and started asking questions. I was honest with him about the situation, and I heard him drop his mom's phone as he used his to dial the police. At that, I took the battery out of my phone again.

By this time, it had been nearly an hour since I had taken the pills, and I didn't feel like they were having an effect on me. I decided to walk to the 24-hour Smith's on the corner of 8th South and 9th East. By the time I got there, I was really feeling the effects of the medication, but I wanted to take more pills for good measure. I sought out a specific brand of cough medicine which I had heard had caused some cases of accidental overdose. I took all the pills inside two boxes of the medication to guarantee I would not survive.

She wrapped her coat around me

During the summer months, I had often enjoyed spending time at Liberty Park feeding the ducks and geese at the pond. I had often come to this same Smith's for the purpose of buying bread for the birds, because the park was just down the block. It seemed like a nice place to spend the final minutes of my life. By the time I made it to the park, the sun was starting to rise. Suddenly, one of my best friends was there wrapping her coat around me and forcing me to put on her gloves. By that time, I was having an out-of-body experience. I could feel her touching me and trying to warm me up, but I was watching the interaction from a raised position to the west of both of us and watched the scene unfold in a third-person perspective. She told me that I needed to go to the hospital, but I refused to allow her to take me.

The next thing I knew, I was coming back to consciousness in a hospital room and asking why it hadn't worked. It turned out that after calling my ex-boyfriend, he had given the police my best friend's name and they woke her up. She had been driving around the Avenues looking for me. At the same time, my ex-boyfriend had driven to my apartment and broken in, to see if I was still inside. He was able to provide the police with the names of the empty medication containers I had left on the kitchen counter. Meanwhile, my family was all awake thinking about possible places I may have gone. They told the police that I had used my phone, and the police obtained an address by way of GPS. My best friend recognized it as the park and knew that was exactly where I had gone to die.

While I was in the hospital recovering, it was discovered that the medications I had taken at home were enough to complete the job, but that the medication I had taken at Smith's counteracted them and extended my life just a little. However, if I had agreed to go to the hospital with my friend instead of refusing, which forced her to call an ambulance to come and get me, I wouldn't have survived. The timing was crucial, and my expedited entrance into the emergency room via the ambulance enabled me to receive the necessary treatment to save my life.

Things are much better now

As soon as I became fully conscious, I realized what a horrible mistake I had made and was grateful to be alive. I spent a few weeks recovering and several more months going through therapy to help put things back in perspective.

I have since made a full recovery. Things are much better for me now and are constantly looking up. I've successfully graduated from college and love working in my field. I'm currently in a loving, fulfilling relationship. Ironically, my relationship is with a charming young man by the name of Cameron. Yes, I finally did find my Cameron. The connection we've formed is more powerful than anything I have ever experienced.

My entire experience has changed how I view life. Shortly after coming out, I still viewed the LDS Church as being true, regardless of how misguided they may have been on the issue of homosexuality. Over the course of time, my thoughts and feelings toward religion in general have adapted. I feel that religion can be a great blessing to people, but my view is just that there are multiple laws which make up the Universe and govern our activities. I use the term "God" to describe these laws, but I don't think that human brains are capable of interpreting all the laws which govern us. I do believe in an afterlife as well as a preexistence; I just don't feel that organized religion has the right idea with regard to what's actually going on.

One of the biggest turning points in my life was when I finally had the epiphany to kneel down and ask about homosexuality for myself. If you or someone you know are struggling with similar questions, my advice would be to learn as much as you can about it, and then kneel down and pray for the truth to be revealed unto you. My story is one of thousands. Unfortunately, some aren't as lucky as me, and their stories are cut tragically short. Too many precious lives are lost as a result of the sometimes unbearable torment experienced. I extend a challenge to love with all your heart unconditionally. Love is the best way to move forward.

John Gustav-Wrathall

"Wherefore, ye must press forward with a steadfastness in Christ, having a perfect brightness of hope, and a love of God and of all men. Wherefore, if ye shall press forward, feasting upon the word of Christ, and endure to the end, behold, thus saith the Father: Ye shall have eternal life."
– 2 Nephi 31:20

I grew up a fifth generation Latter-day Saint in a faithful, loving home. When I came home from school, Mom was always there to greet me, listen to me, and comfort me if I'd had a bad day. As I grew up, Dad took time out with each of us for one-on-one activities and talks. My parents told us every day how much they loved us, and they frequently shared their testimonies of the gospel. Shortly before I was baptized at about the age of eight, I obtained my own testimony through the witness of the Holy Spirit that the Church was true. That testimony has continued to grow since then through countless experiences.

I first became aware of my sexual attraction to other boys at the age of eleven. As I got older, other guys my age started showing interest in the opposite sex, but I only felt interest for my male peers. When I was fourteen years old, intense feelings for my best friend caused me to wonder if I might be homosexual.

One time at Church, a priesthood leader gave a lesson in which he compared homosexuals to murderers. He told us that homosexuality was so despicable that a homosexual orientation alone was grounds for automatic excommunication. I believed him, and responded by doing what Church leaders had always taught me to do in response to temptation: to seek to master my thoughts, to pray, to fast, to study the scriptures, to devote myself more fully to my Church callings, to share my testimony often, and in every way to be as faithful as I could. I truly believed that if I did all these things, these temptations would pass.

I loved the Church with my whole heart, and my highest priority as a youth was preparing for missionary service. In high school I gave personally engraved copies of the Book of Mormon to all my friends and teachers. I spoke openly about my faith and my testimony. My senior health class voted to give me an award for "standing up for my beliefs" because of my outspoken positions on moral issues such as abortion and pre-marital sex. I invited my best friend to receive the missionary discussions, and he agreed. He eventually gained a testimony of his own, and I had the privilege of baptizing him. My friend later served a mission in Chicago, is married with children of his own, and is faithful and active in the Church to this day.

If they only knew ...

I was called to serve in the Swiss Geneva Mission. My first night in the mission field, before bed my companion stripped down to his undergarments and invited me to join him in scripture study and prayer at the kitchen table. I found him very attractive and couldn't control my reaction of arousal. That night I could not sleep. I lay in my bunk and prayed, "Lord, what am I doing here? How can I serve You when I have these kinds of feelings?"

The challenge of managing my feelings for my companions continued throughout my mission, and my response was just to pray harder, study harder, and work harder. If the mission president wanted us to get up at 6:00 a.m. to study our scriptures, I got up at 5:00. If the mission president wanted us to tract at least six hours a day, I tracted seven. I developed a reputation for being one of the hardest working, most serious missionaries in the mission, and finished my mission as a branch president in Béziers, France. But the more I was praised by my peers, the worse I felt. I thought, "If they only knew ..."

In spite of these feelings, I served honorably and feel blessed to have been the means by which two families were brought into the Church. Two of the souls I baptized in France eventually served their own missions for the Church, and in reflecting on this I am awed by the way our lives touch other lives, and ripple outward in ever greater circles.

Utterly worthless

When my mission ended, I attended BYU. The first thing my BYU bishop said to me when he welcomed me into the ward was, "You've completed a successful mission, so now your primary responsibility is to get married." I wasn't quite sure how to do that. I went on some group dates, but was never attracted to the women I dated, even though I recognized them to be lovely women. Meanwhile my feelings of attraction to my male peers only intensified. I also began to experience a crisis of faith related to the fact that the version of Church history I had been taught as a youth did not seem to square with what I was learning as a history major at BYU.

In my junior year I moved and was assigned to a new ward with a new bishop. When my bishop interviewed me for a calling to be a ward clerk, I confessed to him that I was struggling with masturbation. He withdrew the ward clerk calling he had extended to me, took away my temple recommend, and told me to stop taking the sacrament for at least three months. I explained the things I had been doing to overcome the habit, including fasting, prayer, scripture study, and trying to channel my thoughts in uplifting directions through inspirational music. I said I didn't know what more I could do, and I asked him for advice. He told me that I needed to get married as soon as possible.

I left the bishop's office feeling utterly worthless. I felt I needed things like temple attendance, the sacrament, and a ward calling to feel connected to the Lord, and to feel that it was worthwhile to keep struggling. I felt not the slightest attraction to women, and was generally very uncomfortable being physical with women in any way. Marriage made no sense to me; it seemed unreal and impossible. This left me feeling like I would never, ever be worthy again in my life. It was at that point that I began to think often about dying.

I believed that if anyone knew of my sexual orientation, it would lead to automatic rejection. I expected rejection from everyone: my family, my closest friends, and certainly from Church acquaintances. I expected excommunication. I felt there was no one I could talk to, no one who would empathize with me. I became increasingly lonely and isolated. The mental pain was almost constant, and I thought,

"I'm going to be damned in any event, so I might as well just get it over with." I just wanted the pain to end.

He showed kindness

One of my roommates at the time used to talk about suicide. (Years later I would learn that he too was gay and going through a struggle similar to my own.) It worried me when he talked about it. I even called the counseling services at BYU to ask for help with my roommate. But I didn't dare talk to them about my own wish that I could just die somehow. By the time I went home for the summer of 1986, I had formulated a plan to end my life.

Fortunately, circumstances delayed my putting my plan into effect. Then one day I saw our neighbor, an Episcopal priest, walking down the street, and I felt drawn to him. I called him on the phone, and he invited me to his home to talk. He showed kindness and interest in me and hired me to work in his garden. This was very therapeutic and helped distract me from my problems.

Later that summer, I went on an internship to Finland. There I had a series of powerful spiritual experiences in which it became clear to me that my Heavenly Father wanted me to leave the Church for a time. I still do not entirely understand why my Heavenly Father would direct me to do such a thing. Maybe He knew that given my fragile state, it was more important for me to survive and begin to rebuild some of my self-worth than to stay in the Church under conditions that might leave me in such despair that I would rather take my own life.

We danced together

In August 1986, I asked to have my name removed from the records of the Church. Though I had not at that point committed any excommunicable offense, my bishop sent me a letter informing me that a Church court was to be held on my behalf, and I was formally excommunicated. I entered a time of prayer and fasting to decide how best to deal with my feelings of same-sex attraction. I continued to date women for a time but eventually realized that it would be wrong for me to get married. I joined the Evangelical Lutheran Church in America (ELCA) for a number of years, and I spent a summer in a

Roman Catholic monastery, to learn more about celibacy and what it might mean for me to live my life celibate.

I studied the problem out in my mind and then turned to my Heavenly Father. Gradually, I felt guided by the Spirit to explore the possibility of a same-sex relationship. I started going out dancing with friends. Often I noticed a particular slender, attractive African-American man. He was always stylishly dressed and was a graceful dancer. From the first time I saw him, I knew I wanted to get to know him better. One night as I was there sipping on my usual beverage (mineral water), someone tapped me on the shoulder. To my delight I turned around to see that it was this man. We danced together for the rest of the evening.

His name was Göran. He had chosen the name himself, partly as a way of making a new life for himself after leaving his hometown of Cedar Rapids, Iowa. Like many gay men of my generation, he had experienced rejection and conflict with his family over his sexual orientation. When I met him, he had had no contact with his family for several years. He chose a Swedish name because of his admiration for Swedish language and culture, one aspect of which was stoicism in the face of adversity.

Laughing and crying together

Göran says that he "always knew" we were meant to be together for the rest of our lives. It took me a bit longer to figure that out for myself. But after about a year and a half, Göran and I decided to move in together. We joined a community gospel choir, and in 1994 we joined a United Church of Christ congregation where gays and lesbians were welcomed into full participation. In 1995, we held a commitment ceremony, attended by both of our families, in which we promised to God, to our families, and to our communities that we would be faithful, true, and committed to one another.

Göran and I have been continuous companions, comforting and helping one another, laughing and crying together. In our relationship, I have found a sense of complementarity, wholeness, and near perfect joy. We passed through many tests of our commitment to each other. When I was unable to get work, he was there to support me. He was once physically assaulted by gay-bashers, leaving him with three broken teeth, and I had to lobby our state representative in order to get the police to bring his assailants to justice.

Once Göran slipped on some stairs and injured his tailbone. He was in extreme pain, and when I witnessed this, I passed out. We laughed about it later, when Göran pointed out that I wouldn't be much use to him if I did that every time he was in pain. But there was no pain that he felt that I did not also in some very real sense feel, and whatever made him happy filled me with joy. He literally became my alter-ego, the person without whom it is difficult for me to know who exactly I am.

I felt the Holy Spirit's presence

When I left the LDS Church in 1986, it had been clear to me that my Heavenly Father intended for me to leave the Church only for "a time". Later I grew to believe that I had outgrown the LDS Church, that I had no need for it, and that as a gay man I simply was not welcome there. I allowed much of my life to be controlled by anger and impatience with those who did not understand me.

In the fall and winter of 2002, I began a writing project related to Mormonism, and I read every book I could find about Joseph Smith and the history of the early Church. At the same time, a number of LDS former friends started to contact me. In the summer of 2005, a former BYU professor invited me to attend the Salt Lake Sunstone Symposium.

There I attended a session discussing the Church booklet, "True to the Faith". Without warning, I felt the Holy Spirit's presence in a most powerful, undeniable way. While I had had spiritual experiences in the nineteen years since leaving the Church, some very significant and powerful, none matched this one in intensity. Interestingly enough, though the session itself was somewhat critical of the booklet, the Spirit's clear, undeniable and distinct message to me was, "John, it's time to come back to the Church."

I was stunned. Though I was feeling quite critical of the Church, this prompting of the Spirit came so clearly, and with such an overpowering sense of unconditional love! I thought, "I can't do it. I'm gay and partnered. They don't want me. They would never have me back." And then I wondered, "The Spirit isn't possibly telling me I need to leave Göran, is it?" All these things were going through my mind, and I started crying, because of the beauty and power of the experience and my sense of the complete, overwhelming love of God. But I was also hurt and confused by it, because I simply didn't understand how it was possible to do what I felt the Spirit was asking me to do.

I wept tears of joy

Over the following months, the Spirit kept speaking to me, pushing me to consider coming back to the Church. Finally I had another spiritual experience in which the Spirit told me to just do what I could, one step at a time. By then I knew this was something I could not ignore, and I started to understand that there were steps I could take on the road back to the Church. I started by contacting Affirmation, an organization for gay and lesbian Mormons. But the step that I knew I really had to take was to actually start attending church. As I did, I found the Spirit frequently present, urging me to start praying and reading the scriptures daily again.

I wept tears of joy reading the Book of Mormon again, and found to my amazement that my renewed testimony of it was stronger than ever before, not in spite of but because I was aware of the criticisms of it. I had weighed them and found them not as convincing as the book itself. I had a religion professor at BYU who once advised me that the answer to my doubts about Joseph Smith and the early Church was not to read less, but to read more. I learned that this is true and discovered that the more deeply I studied the history of the Church, the more undeniably I saw the hand of God in it.

After attending church for a time, I met with my bishop and told him my story. The first words out of his mouth were, "Well, you have been on quite a journey, haven't you!" He made it clear to me that as long as I was in a relationship with my partner, I could not be re-baptized. But rather than pressuring me to leave my partner or trying to shame me or make me feel unworthy in any way, he encouraged me to incorporate as many gospel principles into my life as I possibly could. He told me, "No priesthood leader in this ward should have any problem with you attending church here, and if they give you any trouble, you let me know!" He encouraged me to attend meetings, to live the Word of Wisdom, to pray, to study the scriptures, and to do genealogical work. He assigned me home teachers, and permitted me to participate in the ward's music program. Every time I have applied a new principle of the gospel, I have found more and more blessings pouring into my life.

Tithing

A couple of years ago, I felt the Spirit prompting me to consider how I might apply the principle of tithing in my life. As an excommunicated member I knew I was not permitted to give tithes or offerings to the Church. I considered donating the money to some other church or charity. It also occurred to me to save my tithing in a bank account, in the hope that someday I might be restored to full membership and be able to give it to the Church. That is what felt best to me.

Over time, the sum in that bank account has grown quite large. Göran and I live within our means, but sometimes our finances are tight, and having my "tithing" money in a bank account in my name presents a constant temptation to dig into it and use it. Also, I feel conflicted about having the money just sitting there, doing nothing but collecting interest when there are so many good charities for the poor, and so many in need. So I continue to petition the Lord to give me some guidance about what to do in this situation. But so far, I have felt prompted simply to continue to put my tithing money into this special bank account and wait.

My "tithing fund" is, I guess, symbolic of the challenges I face as a gay man in a same-sex relationship who also happens to have a testimony of the gospel and a great love for the restored Church. I have felt incredibly blessed, ever since I followed the Spirit's prompting to incorporate the principle of tithing into my life. I have experienced a greater sense of closeness to my Heavenly Father and heightened sensitivity to the promptings of the Spirit. We have also never experienced financial want, and in fact have experienced great success in our financial goals. At the same time, it is a constant reminder to me of how awkward and strange my situation is.

A promise through the Spirit

As at every point throughout my life, as I have been faced with important decisions in this new leg of my journey, I have prayed and sought the guidance of my Heavenly Father. This has included praying about my relationship with my partner. It was extremely painful for me to lay this relationship before God and ask whether it was His will that I should end it. But I felt that I could not continue my journey with any integrity unless I did this.

It was made clear to me by the Holy Spirit that I should not leave my partner. Rather, I should apply the same principles of chastity to our relationship that I would apply to a heterosexual marriage. I received a promise through the Spirit that if I did this, and that if I in every other way possible applied as many of the teachings and principles of the gospel in my life as I could, that if I attended church, "standing in holy places", and remained loyal to the Church in every way I possibly could, that not only would I be blessed beyond my ability to receive, but that all would be well and that the Lord would take care of me both for this life and for the life to come. I have obeyed these promptings of the Spirit, and have made continuing obedience to the Spirit the highest priority in my life.

My bishop asked me how I could reconcile my commitment to my partner with the Church's teachings on homosexuality. I told him simply that I could not, but that I was doing the best I possibly could to live faithfully. My bishop and my ward embraced me and encouraged me to attend and participate to the extent allowed for those who are excommunicated from the Church. This is all I could possibly ask.

In 2008, when the California Supreme Court ruled that same-sex couples could not legally be denied the right to marry, Göran and I traveled to California to be married again — this time legally. My entire faithful LDS family attended the ceremony, performed by a minister of First Congregational United Church of Christ in Riverside. A framed copy of the marriage certificate hangs on our bedroom wall.

Each day is a gift

I have often wondered about the twists and turns of my personal history. What if, instead of speaking about homosexuality as abomination and perversion, my leaders had acknowledged as the Church does today that "Same-gender attractions include deep emotional, social, and physical feelings. All of Heavenly Father's children desire to love and be loved"? Instead of taking my temple recommend away and denying me a calling and the sacrament, what if my bishop had taken the time to get to know me better as a person, to let me know that I was loved and valued? Why was it that an Episcopal priest who knew nothing about me seemed more sensitive to my anguish than my own priesthood leaders?

I have often wondered if I would still be a member of the Church in good standing if the conditions that now exist in the Church had existed twenty years ago. And yet, when I consider everything that has happened in my life, in those same twists and turns I now see the hand of a loving God who is capable of causing all things to work for the good of His children. I will not waste time wondering about what might have been. I just accept each day as a gift, and continue to live my life in such a way as to be worthy of the guidance of the Spirit, to be sensitive and to listen, and to have courage.

There are many members of the Church who, unlike me, do not feel they can be open about their sexual orientation. They fear being misunderstood, and many of them struggle with feelings of isolation and loneliness. For their sake, I wish members of the Church could find appropriate ways to publicly indicate their support for those of us who are attracted to the same gender. When someone says something ignorant or unkind, it is an enormous encouragement when someone is willing to kindly correct such statements in the light of the Church's teachings of love and compassion.

I wish more members would understand what the Church is really asking us, to give up any prospect of finding the happiness in this life that comes from an intimate relationship. Many, perhaps the majority, of gay men and lesbians have left or will leave the Church because the thought of denying themselves the possibility of an intimate relationship is too lonely, too frightening, and too painful. Many, like me, have found loving relationships with same-sex partners and have nurtured lasting commitments to each other. My relationship with my partner has taught me important life lessons that I could not have learned any other way. It has helped me to become a more patient and hopeful person and has increased my capacity to love and serve others. I hope that married heterosexual Church members will consider the joy they find in their own marriage, and consider how readily they would cast that aside.

Although it is often painful and frustrating for me to be excluded from activities and service I would love to be a part of, I have also been blessed with an extra measure of the Spirit's presence, comforting me and encouraging me to honor the Sabbath, attend church regularly, to pray, to study the scriptures, to do genealogical work, to live the Word of Wisdom, to avoid pornography and impure thoughts, and to share my testimony whenever I am able. I would not offer myself as an example for anyone else, but I can say unequivocally that I am indeed blessed, and that my Heavenly Father has fulfilled all of his promises to me to overflowing.

I pray that my fellow Latter-day Saints will show love, kindness and compassion toward those in situations like my own, that they will not judge us unkindly, not make assumptions, and not lay burdens on us in addition to those we must already carry. Impatience and misunderstanding never can have as much transforming power as love.

Julia Hamilton

"A new commandment I give unto you, that ye love one another; as I have loved you, that ye also love one another."
– John 13:34

The summer before my fifth grade year, my dad sat me down and gave me some thoughtful advice about the importance of making female friends. I took his advice to heart. During the first week of class, at the beginning of recess, I found a ball and gave it to a group of girls as an offering of friendship. They tilted their heads in confusion as I gave up the ball and then quickly scurried away. Soon I was back to playing basketball and soccer with the boys.

During the second week of class, I had my eleventh birthday and moved up to a new class in Primary. One of the girls in my new class was "Sarah". One Sunday our teacher didn't show up, so Sarah taught the lesson. With eyes that brimmed with curiosity and a smile that lit up the room, Sarah taught us the simple truths found in the book of Matthew. As she taught, I sat quietly, watching her arm stretch up to create her perfect handwriting on the blackboard. She was so beautiful, so elegant, so happy and kind. Her smile made everything better, and she was always sharing one. She was brilliant and she had a testimony of the gospel — in short, this girl was basically perfect. She called on me, asking me a question about the lesson. Thankfully, just a few months earlier I had decided to sit down and read the gospel of Matthew, so I was able to reply mostly coherently. She praised me for my answer, and I felt my heart flutter.

It came time to decide what middle school I would attend. Sarah went to a public magnet school focusing on art; the only way to get into it was to pass a series of interviews, have solid recommendations, and write a superb essay. When I mentioned to Sarah that I was considering applying, her face lit up as she encouraged me, saying she knew I could make the cut. I wasn't sure, but I tried, and I got in!

Sarah and I became incredible friends. All I wanted was for her to be happy, and being around her made me happy. On the bus ride home, we would sit together and chat about our lives. When it snowed, she invited me over and we spent hours and hours playing together in the snow. We slid down the same hills over and over, squealing with innocent joy. It was the funnest winter I had ever had.

I found out that my English Literature teacher was gay. He was the first gay person I interacted with on a daily basis. He also worked as a theater teacher and was just a happy, flamboyant guy. The way he lived his life was a testimony to me. He wasn't some miserable person demonstrating how wickedness never was happiness. Rather, he loved his long-term partner and came to school smiling. This caused me to question — how could he be happy, be in love, when he was living at odds with Church teachings?

When I was in seventh grade, one evening my family gathered around to watch President Gordon B. Hinckley do an interview with Larry King on national television. I listened as he told us that he didn't know if gays were born that way or not: "I don't know. I'm not an expert on these things. I don't pretend to be an expert on these things." That resonated and stuck with me through the years.

Relieve me from this burden

One day, Sarah and I we were watching the middle school track team. Sarah watched as they walked by, commenting occasionally on cute guys. Suddenly, she said, "Eww," adding her musical giggle, "I feel bad, I'm looking at middle schoolers and finding them attractive." She twisted her face up. I laughed and, realizing that I was a middle schooler myself, wondered if she would consider me cute. This thought caught me off guard, and I violently cast it out of my mind. I convinced myself it must have come from nowhere, a random fluke in the universe.

I tried to get to sleep that night and I couldn't. When Sarah crossed my mind, all I could think was that I needed to leave, to get away from her, because I couldn't think of her the way I did. Should I go to a different school?

I separated myself from Sarah, avoiding her as much as possible. I struggled with feelings of worthlessness and apathy. I started wearing black and secluding myself. I stopped eating and started working out any time I had a minute. Before school I ran laps. During lunch I ran laps. After school I would do my homework, then go running. After that I would get on the family computer and try to chat with people I met online until I forgot my problems. I was spending more than thirty hours per week online, but I still wasn't happy.

I thought about death a lot. I wanted to die, but I also believed in a God who would be angry with me if I killed myself. I tried to pray, and when I did I would end up using phrases like "I'm thankful for the gospel," and then thinking to myself, "That's a lie, I can't even be honest in my prayers." I told myself that if nothing else, I would be honest with God. After that, my prayers turned to begging God to just kill me, to just take me home, to relieve me from this burden.

My grandparents came to my eighth grade graduation and told me how great I looked, exclaiming, "You've lost so much weight! You're growing into a beautiful young lady." I wanted to cry, or yell, or something, anything. I may have been growing into a beautiful young lady, but I was miserable, I hated myself, and I just wanted to be dead. I had no appetite, no friends, and didn't feel like anyone loved me or cared about me. I wrote a poem:

> It hurts.
> The sun still rises.
> The moon still shines.
> The world goes on.
> Without me.
> Expected to smile.
> Ignore the pain.
> "Why are you upset?"
> They inquire in vain.
> Not understanding.
> Even I don't fully.

I didn't know what to do or where to turn, but I knew that I wasn't going to see a psychologist. Needing professional help would mean that I wasn't good enough or strong enough. So I hid my feelings from my parents. I wanted to be the perfect child.

That summer, tragedy struck my family: my aunt killed herself. I didn't know how to handle the loss. I went over in my mind, time and time again, all the things I could have differently. Maybe if, instead of idly playing billiards the last time I was at her house, I had hugged her and told her I loved her. Maybe if I had told her that I thought her tattoo was cool instead of judging her for it. Maybe if I had told her how much I appreciated swimming in her pool and having her bring cookies out to us. The "maybes" went on and kept me from sleeping at night. Even though I hadn't been very close to her, I was anguished over her death. What about her children? Her husband? Her brothers? Just knowing that things didn't have to be this way, seeing the devastation that came from her choice — it shocked me and woke me up. After that, I could no longer consider suicide. I knew that I could not do that to my family.

This is normal

Later that summer, I went to Especially For Youth (EFY) at BYU. Before the program officially began, my EFY counselor sweetly made sure I was getting settled all right and that I had gotten something to eat. She was energetic, she had a strong testimony, she was fun, and she looked stunningly gorgeous, even in her pajama pants and baggy T-shirt with her hair put up. Seeing her put a grin on my face, and I couldn't deny it this time — I definitely found her attractive. But I thought, "Everyone finds girls cute on occasion, right?"

Over the following week, I just felt confused. I sat there, eating pizza with all the other girls and trying not to focus on the EFY counselor, repeating to myself, "This is normal. I'm normal."

At EFY there was a guy who really liked me. He was a kind gentleman. He put his arm around me, he escorted me everywhere. I didn't find him all that physically attractive, but knowing that I'd be able to go home and tell people about him, about us, made me happy. If only I could feel the same pull to him as I did to my EFY leader! But I figured that he just wasn't the right guy.

When I returned home, I wrote to my EFY leader. In the letter, I told her how amazing I thought she was and that she had had a positive influence on my life. I waited anxiously for a reply, but with each passing day my hope was dashed. I was disappointed to realize that I liked her and cared about her a lot more than she did about me.

That year I struggled to decide who I wanted to be; I read the entire Book of Mormon because I wanted to gain a testimony. I told myself that all people like girls — girls are beautiful. I figured that I just needed to pay more attention to guys.

At Church one Sunday, I heard about a new interview by the Church Public Affairs with Elder Oaks and Elder Wickman about homosexuality. I came straight home to read the entire thing. Once I finished, I felt like I needed to read it again, so I went through and thought about it more closely:

> The Church does not have a position on the causes of any of these susceptibilities or inclinations, including those related to same-gender attraction. Those are scientific questions — whether nature or nurture — those are things the Church doesn't have a position on ... Why somebody has a same-gender attraction, who can say? ...

> Find fulfillment in the many other facets of your character and your personality and your nature that extend beyond that. There's no denial that one's gender orientation is certainly a core characteristic of any person, but it's not the only one.

It was the trend at the time

Between my sophomore and junior year of high school, a friend introduced me to a girl "Jill". She was amazing, and I told her I thought so. Within about a week, she overheard me listening to a song, "I Kissed a Girl", by Katy Perry. She giggled as she heard the chorus; she had never heard it before and simply said, "That song is the story of my life." I raised an eyebrow but I don't remember commenting at all. I didn't know what to say. Later, I asked our friend what exactly she meant by that comment, and he gave a hearty laugh and said, "Oh, by the way ... Jill is bi."

I had known tons of girls in middle school who claimed they were bisexual, but the majority did it because it was the trend at the time. Once the popularity of it died down, they happily went back to identifying as straight. I never had a problem with it. I accepted that a person's sexual orientation was an inherent characteristic. So learning that Jill was bisexual didn't change anything about our friendship.

Dating guys

When I turned sixteen, I began dating. I liked spending the evening out with a nice guy. Honestly though, more than enjoying the actual date, I enjoyed telling my friends that I had gone on a date.

I threw myself head-first into dating. I would find a guy with common interests, start flirting with him and spending my spare time with him, and he would fall for me. I loved the excitement of getting his attention. Then I would feel like I had to analyze my feelings, and I would realize I wasn't attracted to him. This pattern was repeated time and time again.

"Paul" was the first boy of this string. I liked hanging out and playing video games with him, and even discussing football with him, but I wasn't attracted to him. On the other hand, I didn't want to reject him, and I didn't want to hurt him, so I stayed in there. I lasted about three months of seeing him almost every night and trying to make it work. He had fallen for me, but I couldn't reciprocate. So we broke things off. I felt bad, but there was nothing else I could do. Faking it wasn't working.

I told "Rob" about how I had broken things off with Paul, and he immediately told me how he had always had a crush on me and would love it if I gave him a chance to try dating me. I protested that I had just barely gotten out of a relationship. Plus I didn't want to get serious with Rob because he wasn't a member of the Church. I didn't completely reject him, but just said that it wasn't likely.

Later I began to grow closer to Rob emotionally. Most people considered Rob cute, but I just couldn't quite figure out how to fall for him. I tried, but it just didn't work. I was honest with him; I told him that I just wanted to maintain our friendship.

I dated boy after boy, and Jill started teasing me about my short attention span. Although I loudly protested her conclusion, I knew she was right. My "short attention span" was a direct consequence of the empty, hollow feeling that came with those relationships. There was a complete lack of chemistry with all of them. I didn't want to hurt the guys I dated, but without any attraction I felt trapped in the relationship. My solution was to break up and try again with someone else, sure that eventually I would find the "right guy".

Throughout this time, in between guys, I had been going on occasional dates with "Kyle". He was really good about not pressuring for a relationship or commitment or anything. I knew early on that I felt no attraction toward him, but I figured that maybe if I gave it time it would develop. It was fun to spend time with him as friends. After going on frequent dates for several months, we had our first kiss. Then, a few months later he asked me to be his girlfriend, which I agreed to.

I was worried about the lack of attraction I felt, and I talked to him about it in general terms. But he didn't seem worried; his response was basically, "We're 17, I don't plan to propose tomorrow." In the meantime, it was nice to have someone to go with to dances, someone to tell when something exciting had happened in my life, and most of all, an excuse not to date anyone else.

Opportunity of a lifetime

Soon afterwards, I found out that I had gotten a government grant to study at the University of Jordan in Amman over the summer. This was the opportunity of a lifetime, and I was extremely excited. I told Kyle that he should break up with me so he could be free for the summer, but he told me he would happily wait for me.

In Jordan, my roommate "Lindsey" was funny and amazingly brilliant. On my tough days, when I came home ready to cry of frustration, she was there and supported me. She helped me be spontaneous and adventurous and convinced me to try new things. When she told me that she was a lesbian, I supported her, and worked hard not to ask her out. Of course, nothing happened between us.

One time on an overnight trip, I shared a room with one of the other girls. That night, as she was changing from her jeans into her sweats, she said to me, "I'm glad you have a boyfriend — it is good to know that you're straight. I'm not so sure about some of those girls." Her tone made it clear that she considered gays to be disgusting. I felt hurt — I knew she was talking about Lindsey, who I adored. But it also led to a string of questions which hit me like a wall: "Am I really straight?" "Why do I have a boyfriend?" "Am I being unfair to him?" Ashamed that I hadn't stood up for Lindsey, and ashamed that I didn't know who I was, I crawled into bed and pretended to be asleep.

I might not be straight

When I arrived home, Kyle gushed about how much he had missed me. I felt guilty because I hadn't missed him. I combated this by throwing myself into my relationship with him, doing everything I could to make it work.

Kyle was one of my best friends in the world, but finally I had to tell him that although he was an amazing person, he was meant for some other girl. He took it well, but the night we broke up, I felt sad. Somehow I had defined a part of myself as "his girlfriend" and without this I suddenly felt lost.

My coping technique was to study physics. I picked up every book I could find on it and began watching videos about the subject. Jill introduced me to "Terry", a civil engineering major who adored physics and had never been on a date. After several dates, he asked if he could hug me. He was adorable. Unfortunately, he would some- times say little critical things about Jill. I felt a spark of indignation rise every time. He could easily have gotten away with saying them about anyone else, but not Jill. Jill was kind and giving and would do anything for a friend. She was beautiful and funny and I loved spending time with her.

It wasn't until I noticed how sensitive I was about his comments that I realized how much I liked Jill. It made my heart race. Running into her made me grin like crazy, and I couldn't get her out of my mind. I decided that I could never tell her.

Suddenly I was super-sensitive to her every action. "Jill stayed late to help me clean up ... I wonder what that means." "Jill told me that she likes my jacket. I wonder if she really does." "Jill went above and beyond to rescue me when I didn't have a way to get home." I had to know, or it was going to drive me insane. But I couldn't know. Knowing would mean admitting I liked her, which could never happen.

But one late night we were sitting together talking, and it just happened: I told her that I was not straight, that I had a long history of liking girls, and that I currently liked her. I looked at the ground as I asked, "So, I was wondering, do you like — like me?"

She struggled to find her words. First, she told me that she had a gut feeling and had suspected since the first week she had met me. More than that, she had actually asked our mutual friend if I was bi when she found me listening to that Katy Perry song, but he had told her that I couldn't be because I was Mormon. She also said that most straight girls don't spend ages ogling over Beyoncé's hips, dream of being with girls (she was my best friend and hence had been in charge of analyzing all of my weird dreams), or go to a foreign country only to come home gushing about how beautiful and amazing their roommate was.

I waited in suspense as she continued, but all she said was that she had never thought about me like that. I nodded and bit my lip. I tried to hide my hurt, but I knew that I hadn't done a great job.

That was a long night. This was the first time that I had seriously confronted the fact that I might not be straight. Up to this point, it had been easy enough to push it into the back of my mind. My first fear now was just, "What will I tell my future husband? Will I ever find a guy who will be willing to marry me?" The more I thought about it though, the more I realized that I didn't even particularly want a husband. I realized that I needed to figure out who I was before even considering something eternally binding, not to mention something that would affect the life of a good Mormon man.

Once I was willing to acknowledge that I wasn't straight, I became more aware of how many girls I was attracted to — not just the ones that took me off guard and made me catch my breath, but all the different girls in their beauty.

One foot in front of another

When I arrived at BYU campus, it was a fresh start, but I was scared. I felt like God had let me down: I had put faith and trust in him, I had served honorably in every calling, but he hadn't fixed me.

I decided I had to talk to someone. I didn't feel like God was answering me and I didn't know what to do. I was questioning whether I even wanted to be a member of the Church anymore. It was miserable, and I wanted to run as far away as possible.

I posted on an anonymous online forum asking for advice, and someone replied and told me about a group that meets on campus called Understanding Same-Gender Attraction. I felt like it was an answer to my prayers, finally a sign that not all people leave the Church who deal with same-sex attraction. It was also a support system filled with fabulous people that were okay with being themselves.

As I got to know myself better, I felt better about being more open with friends, family, and others. One day, four students, along with one of my BYU professors, stayed after a class discussing our thoughts on a talk relating to same-gender attraction. We talked about our feelings on gay marriage and gay rights. We were there for forty-five minutes, sitting on the tables as we talked. I mentioned the Oaks-Wickman interview and the Church pamphlet "God Loveth His Children". I knew that they might wonder how I knew so much, but I also knew that they were all supportive. In fact, the professor said that he considered sexuality to have wide variations and that he may be somewhere on the gay spectrum himself. So then I came out to him. Soon we had to leave. Over the following weeks, he took special care to ask me how my day was going and how I was doing.

I'm not sure what my path will be. I plan to keep the Honor Code while I'm a BYU student. Eventually I will have to make my decision, but for now I put one foot in front of another and hope for a day when the answers are clearer.

Keith Penrod

"This above all: to thine own self be true,
And it must follow, as the night the day,
Thou canst not then be false to any man."
– William Shakespeare

When I was a kid, one of my older brothers asked me, "Do you notice boys or girls more?" I replied, "Neither." He suggested that might indicate I am bisexual. At the time I didn't really have any clue what he meant. I went and told my mom, and she said I was too young to be thinking about that.

As a kid, I liked hanging out with the boys, playing, having sleepovers, and exploring the swampy empty lot in our neighborhood. I always had a tender heart:

> I like today espechaly because my mom ecpressed her
> fellings about me[.] she ecpressed her fellings about me
> in a speishal way that made me cry of joy ... (Oct 9,
> 1991)

I remember watching the kids play on the playground at elementary school. I would usually just sit by and watch them. Sometimes I thought that they were immature and silly. For example, a boy would steal a girl's jacket and then the girl would chase after him and try to get it back. It didn't make any sense to me. I just sat there thinking, "Why in the world would anyone do that?"

In fifth or sixth grade, there was a girl who had a crush on me. A rumor started that we liked each other. Well, I quite honestly refuted the story when it got around to me, but of course no one believed me. One time I was lying on the ground at recess, and she deliberately stood nearby so I could look up her skirt. I just thought, "Why in the world would I want to look up a girl's skirt?"

> My best friend lives in Washington Terrace, is friendly and has always been my friend since I met him ... I like him best ... I like [him] the best besides everyone in my family. The last time I went to his house, we talked about our futures. I want to be an electrical engineer when I grow up. (Mar 31, 1995)

One time when I was in junior high, some of my guy friends started talking about girls, and they asked me who in the whole school I would make out with. I answered quite honestly that there was no one in the whole school that I wanted to make out with. They wouldn't accept that as an answer, and they kept pushing me until I finally gave them a name. Luckily I named someone that the other guys thought was attractive, and they voiced their approval. It didn't occur to me that there was any difference between me and the other guys. I just thought that I did much better at controlling my thoughts and feelings than they did. At church we were taught not to lust after women, and I thought that I was doing an exceptional job.

High school

In high school, I started hanging out with more girls and after my 16th birthday, I started going on several dates. I would go on group dates with friends, and it was fun. At the same time, I started noticing, though, that I really really liked certain guys. I had a thing with sitting next to guys. At the time, I thought I was "feeling their spirit": I thought that if the guy I was sitting by was spiritual enough then I could feel his spirit and it was a good feeling. It never occurred to me to question why it was only guys that I did this with.

I remember one time there was this guy that I really liked. I can't remember what I had done or said to him, but for some reason I thought that he was mad at me. I felt like it was so bad that we might not ever be friends again. So, I decided to talk to my dad about it. I said "Dad, what do you do when you've really messed up a friendship and don't know if you can ever undo all the harm you've done?" or something to that effect. What surprised me is that he assumed I was talking about a girl. So I picked the first girl that came to mind and started talking about her instead. I felt that it would be easier than trying to explain to my dad why it was a guy not a girl that I was worried about. Afterward, I asked, "How did you know it was a girl?" partly because I wanted to keep him thinking that it was a girl, and partly because I wanted to see what was so bad about it being a guy in the first place. He replied that misunderstandings between guys are usually settled over a fistfight, and then each party forgives the other with the passing of time. I couldn't relate to this viewpoint since I had never punched a friend and was averse to the idea.

Although I noticed that I liked being around guys more than girls, I never really wanted to do anything sexual with anyone — male or female. And I never wanted to kiss any guys or even hold hands with them. I just wanted to be with them — maybe hug them, cuddle with them, and stuff like that. On the other hand, I also began looking at pornography off and on, and nearly all of what I looked at was men.

First year at BYU and mission

After finishing high school, I went to BYU. At the new student orientation, the freshmen were divided into "Y-groups" led by upper-classmen volunteers. Well, I remember I was attracted to my Y-group leaders. I thought they were really spiritual guys and I wanted to be like them.

At a stake conference, the stake president told us, "Young men, I want you to date regularly. That means at least once per week." I took the counsel to heart, and I did date almost every week my first year at BYU. It was a lot of fun. I don't think I ever took the same girl out twice. But I got to know lots of girls and I enjoyed all of the dates.

After a year at BYU, I went on my mission to Japan. I noticed that there were tons of Japanese guys that I really liked, and it was good to teach them the gospel. I honestly felt — and still do feel — that Heavenly Father made me attracted to them so I would want to help them accept the gospel and grow closer to Him. It was actually kind of funny because my second companion only wanted to teach females, and I got frustrated because we stopped seeing all the cute guys that I liked teaching.

In one area, there were several young men at church that I was attracted to. My missionary companion Elder "Smith" and I hung out with these guys as much as possible and had a lot of fun. I recently visited that ward again, after six years, and three of those young men told me what a lasting impression I had made on them. One told me that he might not have served a mission if I had not encouraged him to go. So I believe that God gave me those attractions for a reason.

In one area there was a gay young man who was taking lessons from another set of missionaries. I had a lot of compassion for him. I wasn't really attracted to him, but I found out that he was attracted to another guy at church who I found rather cute too. One night I got the chance to have a nice talk with one of the missionaries who was teaching him, and I explained about how I felt like I was gay. I hadn't completely decided, but I was relatively sure. He took it quite well. He asked how I had handled it, and I told him that since I had grown up with the gospel and knew all along that being gay was bad, that I had never acted on it.

A wonderful woman

When I got home from my mission, I immediately started to date Karen, a wonderful woman that I had known from high school. I had admired her very much for her intellect, her spirituality, her compassion, and her strength. She was diagnosed with Hodgkin's lymphoma just over two years before I started dating her. This kind of cancer has a high recovery rate, and though her cancer had continued to relapse even after she had been through many different kinds of treatment, we were hopeful that she would be rid of it soon.

She lived just a few minutes away from me, and we went together each week to Institute. After a while, whenever I went to visit her family, whoever saw me first would yell "Karen, Keith's here." But sometimes I was actually there just to see the family because I was friends with all of them. This was the first time I had ever pursued a relationship with a woman, so there were lots of things I was trying to figure out.

I took Karen to a few dances, and we had a lot of fun. One time, I took her to a Christmas carol sing-along, and that's when I had the strangest sensation ever: it was a feeling that I wanted to hold her hand. I had never wanted to hold anyone's hand like that. I didn't know what it meant. I knew it was good, though, because it meant that I was on the track to being attracted to her — which I hadn't been up to that point. I admired her. I knew that she was pretty, smart, and really fun to be with. But I wasn't attracted to her until this point in time. I almost reached down and grabbed her hand. But I was pretty sure that she wouldn't appreciate me taking her hand like that, so I didn't. Later on I talked to her brother about it, and he said that I made the right choice because he didn't think she would have appreciated it either.

Two months later, when we were at a dance together, at the end of the dance I asked her if I could hold her hand. She never really answered me, so I just made my hand extremely available while we were walking out to the car, and she grabbed it. It was like magic. I had never experienced anything like it before. I just lit up. I felt wonderful inside. It was so strange. Then, when we were in the car, I held her hand. I was content just holding it in the empty seat between us, but I don't think that was enough for her because she pulled my hand over to her lap and then proceeded to caress it with her other hand. It almost drove me crazy. It was like sensory overload. I had never held a girl's hand before (or a guy's) and all of a sudden she's stroking it. Before that night I had absolutely no idea that holding hands could be that wonderful.

Developments

The next time I saw Karen was during General Conference. I watched Conference with her at her house. We held hands and kind of cuddled on the couch together, and I'm afraid I really didn't get anything out of Conference. I was so excited by the physical affection that I couldn't think about anything else. On the other hand, I also felt uncomfortable because I felt like we were moving too fast, but it was so nice that I didn't dare say anything to her. Later on, one time when we were driving in the car, she placed her hand on my upper leg. I told her that was too exciting for me, so I asked her not to touch anywhere above my knee. Gradually, we developed lots of little rules like that.

I was sincerely growing attracted to her. I wasn't forcing anything and I wasn't being inauthentic. After a while I wanted to kiss her. It took me a long time to muster up the courage to do so, but finally I did, more than half a year after we first held hands. I have to admit the kiss wasn't as magical as the holding hands had been at first, but it was definitely a good experience. I refused, on principle, to kiss longer than a simple peck prior to marriage. She respected that and admired me for it.

We got engaged near the beginning of December. During Christmas vacation, when we were both home for the break, I apparently wasn't as affectionate as she expected me to be. She went to her sister and cried. She never said anything about it to me until after we got married.

Sometime while I was engaged to Karen, I was hanging out with my little brother. We were just chatting, when all of a sudden he started asking me about how excited I must be to do certain things with her body. Well, I was shocked. I didn't know what to think. In my mind Karen was a very virtuous woman and thinking about her like that just seemed to disgrace her character. I had never thought of anything like that, and I definitely wasn't excited about the prospect when he brought it up. In fact, the things he described were disgusting to me. So, when I say I was attracted to her, it still wasn't the same sexual attraction that most guys have for girls. But I wouldn't have married her if I hadn't been attracted to her.

I felt like the engagement was a good length of time — nearly seven months. I felt no great urge to make the time go faster. Our relationship developed mostly through email and phone conversations, since we were still attending different universities.

When we got married, we were both scared for the wedding night. But we were both okay with holding off the first night and waiting until we were both ready. Instead, what we did was make out, for the first time, and I had to admit that it was much more exciting than I had ever thought it would be.

Well, after a few months, I started looking at pornography again, so I went and talked to my bishop about it. This was the first bishop that actually asked specific questions, such as "What kind of images are you looking at?" I told him that I had been looking mostly at pictures of nude men, and then he asked, "Are you homosexual?" I replied, "I don't think so," which felt like an honest answer since I loved my wife and was genuinely attracted to her. And I had never wanted to have a sexual relationship with a man, so I figured that meant I probably wasn't gay. But even at the very moment I said that to the bishop, I thought of two or three guys in the ward that I was attracted to, and almost changed my statement to "maybe".

Eventually, I came out to Karen. Of course, I didn't understand it very well myself, so I didn't know how to explain it to her. At one point she said, "I don't think you're gay. I think you just have gay tendencies," which to me meant that she didn't understand it very well.

An old friend

In 2008, I was looking around on Facebook and found out that Elder Smith, my former mission companion, was gay and had married a man in California that summer. I was devastated. I didn't know what to think. I didn't know what to do. I wanted to say something to him, but I didn't know what. I just wanted him to know that I knew that he was gay and that I was okay with that. I wanted him to come back to the gospel and live it because it had brought so much happiness to my life.

At the same time, I felt kind of jealous, and in a way I started to live through him: I was excited that he was married to a man and it made me wish that I was too. But I loved my wife and was still just as attracted to her as I had ever been. Never at any point in time did I regret having married her nor did I truly wish that I had married a man. I was just starting to have feelings that maybe I would have been happy with a man.

Anyway, I told my wife of my discovery about Elder Smith. I didn't tell her about the feelings I was having, of being jealous of him, because I didn't think she would understand.

God's newest angel

During one of Karen's doctor visits, she was told that the cancer had spread to her brain and that she would need to start a new regime of chemotherapy. The first time the weight of this struck me was when she was in the hospital receiving a dosage of chemotherapy and her doctor said that she had two to four months to live. I hadn't realized that cancer in the brain was so often lethal.

My therapist encouraged us to discuss her impending death — what it would mean for each of us. We talked about things such as whether she would want me to remarry, which she did, and what I would do with my life. It was an intimidating and humbling experience.

After a few weeks of this new treatment, we decided that if she was going to die soon it would be better to be in Utah, with the bulk of our families around. We scheduled a trip for home — I was already out of school for the year and she was not able to work any longer, so we just left. We spent nearly two months out there, which gave her plenty of time to see everyone one last time. We didn't tell anyone out here in Tennessee what the nature of our vacation was, but those that were closest to us could tell. Neither of us articulated the fact, because Karen wanted to live the rest of her life as though she were going to live many more decades. We both had faith that God could heal her and that He would, if she were meant to live.

Shortly after we had celebrated our third anniversary, her condition rapidly declined. As I saw what was happening to her, I knew that I needed to give her a priesthood blessing and that I was to instruct her to go home to the Father who gave her life. It was the single most difficult thing I have done in my entire life, but I placed my hands on her head, together with my dad, her dad, and a few brothers. I stated precisely what the Holy Ghost had told me to say. Three days later she passed away.

Confusion

A few months after Karen's death, I began viewing pornography again. I had the idea that being gay is all about sex and people just wanting to satisfy their urges. Therefore, I had come to believe that if I was gay, then I had to be sexually attracted to men.

At one point, I went to a local used bookstore and purchased two gay romance novels. I was simultaneously ashamed and thrilled to make the purchase. I should point out that I really don't know much about gay culture or gay authors. So for these books, my method of selection was rather simple — I just picked two books that had really cute guys on the covers. Well, much to my surprise, as I began reading these books, I found that both of them contained the message that being gay is not about lust. Gay people long for love just like straight people do. Up until the point that I read these books, I would think things like, "Why would gay people want to get married? Why don't they just sleep with whomever they want?" because I didn't understand that there's still that desire to have a committed relationship.

So, in a sense, I have to admit that reading these books actually, if anything, calmed down all of the hormones that I had let rage over the prior few months. I started to realize that I can be gay and not want to have sex with every cute guy that crosses my path. In fact, as I was reading these stories I started to return to how I had felt in earlier years — such as high school — where I just wanted to be good friends with guys. And by good friends, I definitely mean something more deep and meaningful than friendship usually means among guys, but not sexual.

What's funny is that at the same time that I was resolving some of this confusion inside of me, I was also disappointed because I had purchased the books expecting that they contained lots of steamy gay sex scenes, which they did not. So, there was a sort of internal struggle with whether I actually enjoyed that kind of material or not.

Another old friend

It was nearly a year after my wife's passing before I started dating again, and even then my heart wasn't really in it. I went on a few dates with girls and it was fun, but then I just kind of stopped for a few months.

One day I read one of the notes that my friend Brent had posted on his Facebook Wall about homosexuality. I was quite intrigued; knowing that he likes to study a wide variety of topics — from Hebrew to operator theory — I just assumed it was another scholarly pursuit. I had known Brent off and on for about nine years. We were in the same ward my first year at BYU, and we both majored in mathematics. I thought he was a great guy, and I had been really excited to see him again after we both got home from our missions.

So I commented on the note and asked why he was interested in the topic. His reply didn't say that he was gay, but it alluded to the fact, so then I went back and read his other notes and realized he had been out for some time now, so I felt silly. Anyway, reading what he had written made my head spin for several weeks. It took some time to sort out all of this new information.

At first I just couldn't believe it. It seemed so impossible to me, the way he talked about wanting to stay in the Church but also live with a guy (in a committed, but celibate relationship). From my point of view, he might as well have said that God didn't exist. What did all of this mean? How could someone I respect as much as Brent say such terrible things? I called him on the phone, and as we talked, I learned more about his story. I wanted to better understand his position.

Making sense of things

Slowly, over the course of a few weeks, I started to assimilate the information that Brent had written, and the more I did so the more I understood. In fact, this was the first time that I truly felt like I understood my own sexual orientation. Up until that point I wasn't sure: I knew I liked guys more than girls, that I wouldn't mind holding a guy in my arms and maybe even cuddling with him, but I never wanted to be sexually intimate with a guy. All through my life even the thought of kissing another man disgusted me, which may sound strange considering the fact that I had looked at hundreds of pictures of guys kissing each other and those images excited me. But even when I'd look at pictures of men doing all sorts of things, I still wouldn't be able to picture myself doing those things. The thought, for some reason, was always disgusting to me. But finally I understood what the situation was: Brent is asexual, and I could relate to the feelings he expressed concerning that. To some degree, I would say that I am closer to being asexual than average.

Up until that time, I still had kind of believed that 1) being gay is a choice, 2) that pornography had caused me to become gay, or that during times when I looked at it I was "more gay" than at times when I refrained, and 3) that gay people were capable of changing and becoming attracted to people of the opposite sex. This of course was a natural conclusion for me to draw, since I had become attracted to a woman myself. But I mused then that "gay" might not be the best word to describe me, that perhaps "bi" would be a better word. But this could be misleading, because the only woman I have ever been attracted to was my wife, whereas I am naturally and routinely attracted to men. The word "asexual" could also be misleading, because although I don't naturally experience sexual attraction to either gender, I did enjoy sexual intimacy with my wife albeit probably not as strongly as most men do. I have since learned that there is another term, called "demi-sexual", for someone who does not experience sexual attraction based on physical appearance, but who can experience sexual attraction after having developed an emotional connection. To some extent this might apply to me too. Really, I think it's impossible to use one word to describe something as complex as a person's sexuality.

So, as I finally started making sense of my orientation, the things that Brent was talking about started making sense too. I saw that he didn't say anything that was against the doctrines of the Church. I had just misunderstood what the doctrine was. It restored my respect and faith in Brent.

While on a trip to Utah, I had a chance to visit with Brent and attend a meeting of an unofficial group at BYU called Understanding Same-Gender Attraction, which meets weekly on campus. I spoke up often during the meeting but did not indicate what my orientation was. It was a very positive experience for me, getting to meet other gay members of the Church and hearing their stories. Over the past year I have come to realize that there is strength in numbers — at church, in support groups, and social circles. It definitely helps to have other people alongside you who are facing what you are facing.

The future

Over the last month or two I have come to have much more compassion for homosexual people. I would never encourage anyone to leave the Church. But I now have more understanding for people who feel that their best choice for happiness is to live with a partner of the same gender. I can truly empathize with such persons, and I can understand how for someone with a strictly homosexual orientation, incapable of attraction to a member of the opposite sex, they might feel that marrying someone of the same sex is the best option for them. I will never judge another soul for that. I do not know the ground on which they stand, nor do I have room to criticize.

Before I read Brent's remarks I had never even considered the possibility that a faithful Mormon guy could consider finding a male partner to commit himself to and yet live in complete obedience to the law of chastity. At this point in time, I still felt that what I wanted to do is to start dating again, find another woman, and marry her in the temple.

I married my wife in the temple, and therefore I know that I am married to her for all eternity, even now while she is dead and I am still alive. I don't know how it would work out in the next life, but as far as I know, if I married in the temple again, that would mean I would have two wives for all the eternities. That thought is still a bit scary to me. All my life I grew up knowing that our church doesn't practice polygamy anymore, and that was always a comfort to me — especially after I got married and saw how close the two of us grew to each other. The thought of having to share my time with two women doesn't seem fair; I don't think it would be fair to them. I don't know; it just seems so complicated.

After considering my options for about two months, I was still relatively certain that I would not pursue any relation with a man. However, one of the guys that I met while I was visiting Utah seemed to relate very well to me. I expressed my thoughts and feelings to him, and he said that he had been in roughly the same place a couple years prior. We watched a movie at his apartment and he asked me if it would be okay to cuddle while we watched it. I was hesitant, but I agreed, knowing that I would enjoy it. I did enjoy it very much, and it really helped open my eyes to the true nature of the feelings I was having. It had nothing to do with lust at all. It wasn't because I needed to burn sexual energy with him, it was simply the desire to connect with him in a meaningful way. I felt a bond, stronger than any words could create. No, we didn't decide to become boyfriends, and I don't think there was that expectation on either party. But, there was definitely a connection.

And so, because I want to avoid the complication of having multiple wives, and probably more importantly because I feel like I may be happier with a man than with a woman, I am open to the idea of casually dating men and looking for one that I might consider entering a relationship with. Since homosexual relationships are not endorsed by the Church, at this time I do not feel like I would engage in any sexual behavior with such a partner, so it would need to be someone that was comfortable with being close but not sexual.

Well, that's where things stand now. What will the future bring? God alone knows, and I feel good about keeping it in His hands.

Jeromy Robison

"A real friend is someone who knows all your faults, but likes you anyway."
– Charles M. Schulz

I have an identical twin brother. People ask me what it's like to have a twin. It's a rare gig, and I feel special in that regard. I'm not alone in my existence. I am part of a team, a very special team with an identical genetic code. When he finds success I feel a sense of mutual accomplishment. People ask, do we speak a special language with each other? Did we ever switch places in school? Did we marry the same kind of girls? Valid questions indeed. A common misconception about twins is that we are basically the same person.

But aside from the usual novelty and jokes, there is a fact that seems to pose more questions than answers: Not only am I a twin, but I am gay — and my identical twin brother is not. The question is "Why?" If twins have identical genes, how does something as fundamental as sexuality deviate from one twin to another? Is it a biological anomaly? Is it environmental? What role does choice play in sexuality?

What was wrong with them?

Growing up, my brother and I shared the same bedroom, hung out with the same friends, went to Boy Scouts together, and gave talks in church together. It was like having a shadow, even at night. But by age eleven, I knew I was different. My twin brother, Jason, liked video games, while I was more interested in the piano. My brother hung out with the popular kids and got a new girlfriend every few months, while I was shy and had a secret crush on "Rob" in my fifth grade class.

Because we looked alike, Jason and I were often asked, "Which twin are you?" Friends would scrutinize our looks and mannerisms for the slightest deviations that would give us away. I felt a certain need to be just like Jason, but I didn't know how long I could pretend to be like him when I felt fundamentally different.

Dad had us watch the *Nova* program "The Miracle of Life". This was the first time I learned about sex. When I mentioned my disgust at the idea, my father promised I'd like it someday. I thought that perhaps every eleven-year-old boy was sickened by the idea of heterosexual intercourse. Isn't that why we run from girls on the playground? Something about cooties? Of course, the other boys had stopped running away years before.

Just at the point when Jason's hormones were raging in the normal "I like boobies" kind of way, mine went in the opposite direction. Suddenly men were becoming more and more attractive to me. I secretly eyed the tanned yard-workers at school while they dug and trimmed hedges with their shirts off. When sitting in our club house in the back yard, my brother and his friends would tell dirty jokes about girls. I felt out of sync but pretended to think it was funny. When I watched movies with Jason and Dad, sometimes they would cat call and coo at the ladies in the movies. Again I felt disgusted, and I wondered what was wrong with them. Then I wondered what was wrong with me.

I was a loner

As my curiosity about men grew stronger, so did my brother's watchful eye. When I drew pencil sketches of male nudes, Jason found them and confronted me. When I wrote same-sex romance stories and hid them under the club house in the backyard, he found those too. Muscle magazines, clippings from the men's sections in the Sears catalogue, and journal entries were all found by my brother. Every bit of evidence of my feelings was sniffed out — even my interest in music: when I got my first electric keyboard for Christmas, Jason made me set it up in our bedroom closet with headphones so he couldn't see or hear it. I played it with my back against the closet door and my head between the hanging clothes. I spent a lot of time in the closet with my keyboard. After a while, it became my hiding place. I could express myself in there comfortably.

They called me "gay" for the first time when I was in seventh grade. I had heard that word before in reference to other people. I knew it was a cruel word, meant to hurt. Now it was directed at me, and it did hurt. As Jason grew increasingly popular, I grew more introverted and awkward. His friends would make fun of me in front of him. Middle school was the worst period of my life. Not only was I a loner, but I was a loner in the shadow of my popular twin brother.

Dad and Jason played sports and video games together. When I joined them I only got smeared. Eventually I stopped playing video games and sports, if I could avoid it. I wished they would go to a play with me, or a museum or art gallery. I grew to both hate and envy the time my Dad and my brother spent together.

Every problem could be solved

Church played a big role in my life. At church, the pressures of the outside world didn't exist. I had the admiration of my Church leaders and fellow members. I played the piano often in church. One year I wrote the Christmas play while Jason helped direct it.

I learned to love a particular bishop who I believe knew about my attraction to men. He loved me and nurtured me regardless. He would smile at me, shake my hand, and hug me when he could. I loved those hugs. It was important to me to gain that trust in a Church leader.

I gained a testimony of Jesus Christ. I relied on it. I knew that Christ loved me in spite of my differences from other boys. I learned to pray hard. I tried to pray away my attractions. I believed that every problem could be solved by the scriptures. So I lived devoutly: I never missed church, I paid my tithing honestly, I confessed every single perceived sin, I learned to trust my priesthood leaders, and I looked forward to my mission.

The gospel provided a life-script. It was security. I knew where I fit in as long as I clung to its teachings. I loved the stability of the

Church. I liked the idea of covenants that promised prosperity if I lived up to my commitment. All I had to do was fulfill my part.

I learned to serve others

I was called to serve two years in the Florida, Fort Lauderdale mission. The areas in my mission were among the most sexually charged places on the east coast. While most missions have a so-called "single female" rule, my mission had an equal but opposite single male rule: When visiting single males we had to take a priesthood chaperone or conduct the meeting in plain sight.

Those two years were the most challenging, yet most formative years of my life. For the first time there was no shadow to compare me to. I learned to serve others, and I loved it. I was determined that God would bless me for my obedience, and I never once entertained the idea of exploring what was forbidden.

By the end of my mission I had felt the thrill of success and accomplishment. I had lost myself in the work and was ready to move forward on the road to my own future. The problem was, with the end of my mission came the end of my life-script.

I desired to reach out

On the day of my return home, my dad had flown all the way to my brother's mission and back with him on the same plane as a surprise. When I arrived at home they were already celebrating their return together. The familiar feeling of resentment awakened at the sight of them. I spent my first day at home crying. I swung from an extreme high to an extreme low.

I fit right back into the usual pattern. Jason and I shared a room together. I enrolled in college classes, and so did Jason. Jason found a girlfriend immediately, and I remained single and uninterested in dating. The feeling of angst turned into depression. I felt betrayed by the promise of a brilliant future. My life was worse than before my mission. Moreover, my interest in men escalated.

With the pressure of finding an eternal companion looming over me, I desired to reach out to others in my situation. I wanted to talk to other men who were experiencing the same attractions. I wanted to feel a part of something again.

I decided to move to Utah. I made arrangements to move in with an aunt in Provo, and I packed up my keyboard and left the world I knew in search of a new one. I now measure my life in two parts: before and after January 2, 2001. That's the day I admitted to myself that I was gay. It's the day I feel I breathed for the first time. I wanted the strength of the Church to remain a constant in my life while I waded through turbulent waters, and I knew there would be other men in Utah going through the same struggles.

A new perspective

This is where choice came into play. Being out of the closet would mean being accountable for the choices I would make. There was a lot to explore and also a lot at stake. I didn't choose to be gay, but I could choose my values. I knew that acting hastily in the beginning could have long-term consequences in the future, and that it was important to weigh the choices before committing to the outcome. For better or worse, I allowed myself the freedom to choose how I lived. Even if I chose to retain ideals and values from my former life, I wanted to do so of my own free will.

Immediately after moving in with my aunt, I told her I was gay. She was incredibly helpful. We talked a lot about it. She asked me, "Where do you stand with the Church now?" I was asking myself that question too. I knew the basic gospel principles were true. I had a testimony of Jesus Christ and the Atonement. As a gay man I relied upon it.

I went to church in my aunt's ward. When I took the sacrament, for the first time I actually questioned if I wanted to. But my answer was very plain: I did indeed. Everything I did within a religious context from that moment was strictly because I wanted to. It felt nice. It also felt nice knowing that my aunt, somebody besides me, knew I was gay and welcomed me anyway. That feeling of acceptance, in a place where I expected conflict, set a tone for the rest of my life.

My aunt helped me through a lot of personal issues. She listened and understood. She helped me find a therapist who could not only just listen, but offer real ways of dealing with the negative feelings I had for my twin brother and family. From a new perspective of acceptance and validation, I was able to deal with the feelings of insecurity that had plagued me from childhood. I was finally able to express the self-loathing I had felt for being so different. The result of expressing these long-suppressed emotions was magical. I was finally able to accept myself.

My confusion grew

After a few months, feeling lonely, I posted an ad on a website for gay men in Utah. A returned missionary living in Provo answered my ad. We decided to meet on BYU campus at an Institute class.

"David" was very nice and good looking. He was tall, with darker features. He had a charm all his own, and we instantly formed a bond. I hadn't felt this way before. Months went by, and I began spending more time with him. We watched late-night movies, went on long drives, and talked. I felt comfortable sharing the parts of my life that I had always been afraid of.

The first time David touched me was while watching a movie at his place. He only touched my shoulder, but it felt like electricity going through my body, and my heart began beating faster. When the movie ended, David held me. I lay in an ocean of ecstasy that I never knew was possible. Thoughts went through my mind, "Is this bad? Something so wonderful can't be bad. Then why do I feel like I should run away right now, run from this feeling of peace and safety?"

That was the first time I experienced the touch of a man. We remained semi-clothed, but we kissed and enjoyed it more than anything. I hadn't violated my temple covenants, but my confusion grew with regard to the gospel. I had been taught that a man who lies down with another man is next to a murderer. I didn't feel like a murderer. I felt better than I had ever felt. I concluded that my values no longer agreed with the reality I had come to know. It was an undeniable conflict. Something had to give.

I talked with my bishop and was surprised by the swift retribution I received: Immediate and indefinite probation. He took my temple recommend and sacrament privileges away. No more priesthood responsibility, period. I was given weekly reading assignments on the Atonement, including a full reading of *The Miracle of Forgiveness* (ouch). I was not to pray aloud in meetings. There was no love, no mention of mercy, no validation or acceptance. I think this particular bishop wanted to send a strong message, and he certainly did.

Over the next six months my bishop, elders quorum president, stake president, and home teachers treated me like a project. Feelings of depression grew. I stopped dating, and I quit my job. I felt I wasn't worthy of acceptance by anyone. It seemed a heavy price to pay for admitting my love for another man. I never saw David again.

Back into the closet

My brother Jason had broken up with his girlfriend in California and decided it was time to venture out in life, so he moved to Utah. I allowed myself to fall under Jason's shadow, thinking it would be safer and more stable than the torrents of life I had faced while out of the closet. He and I moved into an apartment together. We went to Institute together. He got a job in my office. We went to the same school. He made his friends out of my friends. Every part of our lives intermingled, especially our Church activity. While he lived with me, I successfully recovered my temple recommend.

Jason found success in many areas. He was well-liked by my friends and priesthood leaders. He excelled in school. He even found favor with one of my lady friends, whom he began dating. In a short time, it seemed that with my help Jason had made a fine life for himself. But while he rose to great heights, I grew increasingly depressed and withdrawn. Going back into the closet resulted in continually growing angst and resentment.

I knew that Jason and his girlfriend were getting serious. It would have been difficult not to notice them together in embrace, for what seemed like all the time, in our apartment. After one of my scheduled appointments with the bishop, Jason was waiting outside the bishop's office for an appointment of his own. I assumed there had been something in his relationship with his girlfriend which required priesthood guidance.

I was correct in my assumption as to the nature of Jason's meeting. However I was not prepared to learn that on top of that, he was called to be my elders quorum president. My testimony of priesthood leadership changed when Jason came out of the bishop's office. The bishop hugged him, patted him on the back, then jokingly said, "It's good to know you two have chemistry before popping the question. Now let's get you sustained." I noticed a significant difference in protocol with regard to confessions of love. When I confessed my love for David, it meant six months of drudgery. When Jason confessed to similar actions with a woman, he got a position of leadership. At that moment I felt the poisonous barb of bitterness twist in my side and lock firmly in place.

I still love you very much

Jason and I went our separate ways after that. Our relationship had grown too close for comfort, and we needed some distance. We let the lease on our apartment expire as he moved closer to BYU campus (and marriage) and I moved in with other Utah Valley University students. In all, Jason and I had lived together for about a year. It took me that long to realize how much happiness I was missing out on while living according to everyone else's expectations. I wanted to make my own choices again. I decided that life was not worth living unless I lived it happily. Being measured against my brother and being subjected to the inconsistencies of Church doctrine weren't on my life's menu anymore.

Over the next six months, I dated men, got involved in gay social clubs, and made friends. I excelled in school, found a really good job, and came out of the closet to several friends and coworkers. The Church was still firmly rooted in my life, but now I only went to church or Institute when I wanted to.

When I had grown accustomed to the idea that I was going to be gay for the rest of my life, I knew it was time to tell my family. Very late one night I called my mom and asked how she was doing. I was very nervous and it showed. I stuttered and couldn't breathe. She asked what was wrong and I told her that I was gay. I told her I had had a very hard time coming to grips with it, but had finally decided that I was going to live my life as a gay man or not live at all. My mother said, "I know Jeromy, and I still love you very much." Oh, the sweet words of acceptance again! She said she knew I was different since I was one year old. I was shocked. I asked her why she never said anything. She said that it wasn't something she could tell me, that I had to figure it out on my own. Honestly, she was right. She wondered why it took me so long to admit it to myself. I still don't know the answer to that.

Some of the sweetest words

I was too afraid to face my father in person. So my mom told him the news. He called me the next day to say he was concerned about me. He said, "Your mother told me about your 'condition'." He couldn't say the word. But my dad is a man of few words, and what he did was better than any words. He drove up to Utah to spend a week with me. We did the things I had always wanted to do with him, just the two of us. I finally took him to art museums and flower gardens. We played laser tag. We built a trellis together and planted flowers in the yard. We made music together, me on the piano with him on the guitar. We went on scenic drives up the canyon. We ate at nice restaurants. This time with my father said far more than any words over the phone could have conveyed.

Jason still lived in town, and he wanted to join all the fun with my dad. He kept calling my dad's cell phone to find out where we were and when he could join. I was so sure that I was going to end up sharing my "coming out" week with my twin brother that I had already resigned myself to making room for him. Without a cue from me, Dad called Jason and said, "Jason, I have spent so much time over the past many years with you, and I realize how little I really know about Jeromy. This week is for him." These were some of the sweetest words I had heard in my life.

The night before my father went home, after I had gone to sleep, I woke up and found he had been crying. He looked at me with such anguish. His heart was broken, not out of disappointment that I was gay, but because he blamed himself for my pain. We realized that there was nothing we could do about the past. All we could do was make amends and move forward. I hugged him, and we cried together.

"Which twin are you?"

My family went through a transformation after that. Love was spoken much more often. When I came out to my older sister, her response was, "Finally!" My younger sister said she always wanted a gay brother to go shopping with and talk about sex (as if gay men have that market cornered). It was nice to be so open and candid with my family. They mentioned a change in me after that too. They said I remained the same person, but somehow *more* of the same person than before.

Two weeks prior to Jason's wedding, I paid him a visit to finally explain that I was gay. When I told him, he denied it at first, but after about ten minutes, the acceptance and tears started. Now that it was finally safe to discuss, he told me that he had always known it. He not only had known I was gay, but had lived in anguish over it. When he used to confront me over the little evidences of my homosexuality, it wasn't to get me in trouble; it was to keep me safe. He told me he had always envied and admired my musical talents, my knack for art and creativity, and my sensitivity and honesty. Coming out of the closet to my brother was a defining moment in my life.

My life story is still being written. Did I ever discover what made my half of the genome-pair gay? No. It doesn't matter anymore. It is reality and is accepted by me and those who love me. Being honest with myself and others has led to an outpouring of blessings in my life. The greatest of all is the relationship I now have with my twin brother, Jason. The greatest compliment he ever paid me was his joking response to someone's question, "Which twin are you?" He replied with a smile, "I'm the gay twin!"

Adren Kimo Bird

"Always moving forward!
Failure is not an option!"

I am 41 years old and single. I was attracted to boys and male teenagers before I was eight years old, when my parents divorced. I remember when I saw men naked in the locker room for the first time, I was attracted because I thought it was beautiful to see. I wondered why I wasn't attracted to women.

No one in my family talked about sex or homosexuality. I had no idea about it until I came to junior high school. My classmates found out that I was gay and they were freaking out and started mocking me and calling me "faggot" or "queer". One of my best friends in junior high school found out from one of my classmates. He looked at me and asked me if it was true. I told him it was true. He left me and told me that he didn't want me to be his friend. My classmates started rumors at school and at church about me. I didn't understand why they were freaking out because I was gay. I thought being gay was nothing wrong. I thought it was natural.

I was converted to the Church when I was 13 years old. When I told my branch president I was gay, he reported to the stake president in Logan, Utah, to determine whether I should be disfellowshipped or excommunicated. I learned from him three things why I became gay: 1) lack of relationship between father and son, 2) puberty, and 3) attraction.

I broke down and cried

When I was 21 years old, I was a student at Utah State University, and I went to downtown Salt Lake City to visit for shopping. The Spirit of the Lord prompted me go to Temple Square; I felt drawn there so strongly like a magnet with the Spirit of the Lord. I enjoyed walking around Temple Square. When I left on my way home, the Spirit of the Lord sent me a message and said, "Go on a mission." I refused, because I had heard that the Church said that homosexual young men were not worthy to serve a mission, but the message kept repeating in my head, "Go on a mission." That's where I was confused and didn't understand why the Lord called me to go on a mission. I prayed and got strongly inspired from the Spirit of the Lord, and I obeyed and returned to church for six months before going on a mission. I kept all my secrets from my bishops, stake presidents, and mission presidents, because I was afraid that they would find out and would send me home in dishonor with disfellowshipment or excommunication.

I served my mission for a year and a half. On my mission, a companion asked me about my gay experiences, and he started to be curious about gay sexuality. We had sex, and he denied to the mission president and begged him to let him stay on his mission. I chose to give up my mission because I was gay and had not been completely honest to my bishop, stake president, and mission president. I asked the mission president to disfellowship me and send me home. I broke down and cried and cried. I was in pain and heartbroken when I got on the plane on my way home to Utah. That's how the members in my ward heard about it and rumors spread over the valley. I left the Church for ten years.

After I came home from my mission, I started dating and had relationships with a few ex-fiancées. They knew about my same-sex attraction (SSA) and supported me, but each was concerned if I married her then I would cheat on her for another man. They decided to break up with me because of my SSA, but we are good friends and they support me and accept me.

I came out to my mother right before I went to the university in Washington, D.C. She was upset with me. I tried to explain to her. She didn't want hear about it. I assumed that she might feel guilty and think that she hadn't taught me right or that I didn't understand everything in the real world because I couldn't hear (I am deaf). But she realized that I knew what gay meant. She told me that she would not tell my grandfather that I am gay because he is against homosexuality, so she kept silent for a long time. We agreed that I must not talk about gay issues at all.

"I love you"

One time I met my last companion in Cedar City, Utah. I had been angry at him for a while and had a difficult time forgiving him. He saw me and was so frightened that I was going to fight him, but instead I met him and gave him a big, sweet hug. He got confused but was happy to hug me. He took me upstairs and showed me a book he wrote about American Sign Language. He grabbed my arm, I turned, he put his hands on my shoulders and looked at me. With tears in his eyes he asked me to look at him. He begged me to forgive him and apologized for what he did to me. My heart was tender and with tears I told him I forgive him 100%, and we hugged each other a while and comforted each other. He felt peace and moved on with his life. We became good friends and he still supports me with my SSA feelings.

I met several deaf members who are struggling with SSA and they don't know what to do and are searching for the answers. I met them and explained to them and wanted to help them to understand why they are struggling with SSA. I told them about Evergreen International and North Star and other resources. Unfortunately, some of them decided they don't want to deal with the Church because they feel that they judge them and say bad things about them. They are not interested in the resources I referred them to. I remember one guy who I have a lot of respect for, and he set a good example. I am so impressed what he said to my friend who shared with me. He told my friend, "I have SSA feelings, and I have been struggling for a long time, but I do honor my priesthood."

Years later, I saw my father; I hadn't seen him for ten years. We caught up with everything, and he asked me, "Are you gay?" I could not lie to him, because he's my father, so I came out and told him, "Yes I am gay." He was surprised but said, "It doesn't bother me. It is your life, you have to live it." He asked, "When did you know you were gay?" I said, "When I was eight years old." He said to me, "I love you and you are my son. No matter who you are, you are my son." He accepted me and supported me. He asked me and I told him I knew gay is wrong. My dad said, "I'm sorry I wasn't a better father to you. I know it must have been really hard for you. I'm sorry it took so long for us to get together." That's where I decided to forgive him; I know he was trying to be a better father to me.

It helps me to understand better

I have seen a therapist for a while. I learned from him, and he explained that I have sexual addiction and pornography addiction. I have been studying and researching to help me to understand why I have both addictions. I was manic depressive, confused, and had attempted to kill myself when I was a teenager.

Now I am fully accepting of who I am. I have SSA, sexual addiction, and pornography addiction for purposes that God sent me here to learn — to understand others that I may be able to help them, to teach them, to love them without being judgmental, and to be fully supportive.

I know that homosexuality is wrong, and I know that the Church is true. The gospel of Jesus Christ is the true word of God. My hope is that I will be able to change and will no longer feel SSA and will be able to overcome and be free from sexual addiction and pornography addiction. I was excommunicated in June 2010 because of gay issues.

I want to share my testimony that I know Heavenly Father loves me and Jesus Christ, our Savior of the world, loves me. I know that the Church is true and Joseph Smith was a true prophet of God. I witnessed and saw the gold plates in a dream during my mission. I touched and I felt the engravings on the gold plates. I will never deny what I saw in my dream. I would seal my testimony for the rest of my life and for all eternity. I know someday I will return to be re-baptized at the right time and at the right place. I am very grateful that God gave me great tribulations, affections, and trials and experiences; it helps me to understand better.

I remember that day I was complaining to God why I became gay, and how I wanted to be rid of my SSA feelings. The Spirit of the Lord prompted me to read my patriarchal blessing, "It has the answers for you." I read my patriarchal blessing and it said, "Adversity comes to all, and you will be blessed to meet this adversity and make it a learning experience in your life." I realized that the answer was from the Lord, and He knew that I had to go through a time of adversity. I stopped complaining, and I have to learn to be humble and to accept that fact.

I have hope and try to be patient

Because of what I have been through, I have greater love for all my brethren and sisters who are struggling with SSA. I will always support them and I will pray for their strength with full hope and love. I am very grateful for awesome friends and members in the Church who give me their support with much love and understanding for what I have been through. If I hadn't joined the Lord's true church, my life would have been miserable, bitter, angry, and loveless. I was grateful that I joined Lord's true church and the gospel of Jesus Christ saved my life and has changed me through family's and friends' examples and their love for me. Those who are SSA have helped me to understand why I became SSA. I am very grateful for North Star and Evergreen International for the resources they provide, for the answers I was looking for.

My hope is to establish a new program for deaf and hard-of-hearing people who struggle with their SSA, sexual addiction, and pornography addiction. I want to be an advocate to help them understand why they become SSA and struggle with their addictions. My therapist advises me to wait until I give up pornography and sexual activity and recover completely before I can establish the program.

I have fears about marriage. I want to be a husband. I want to be a father. I want to be sealed to my eternal companion for all eternity. There are beautiful and rich blessings in marriage. I met a lot of men who have feelings with SSA, and most of them got divorced. It makes me feel afraid of marriage because I don't want to hurt my wife if I cheated on her for another man. I don't know if I will remain celibate the rest of my life while having SSA feelings? My patriarchal blessing said:

> At an appropriate time you will find a fine young lady, who along with you, will qualify to go to the Temple of the Lord and there be married and sealed to each other for time and eternity. You will take upon yourselves vows and covenants, which if you live up to them, will bring you many blessings.

That's where I got confused and questioned: my patriarchal blessing said I will marry a young fine lady, but why wasn't I attracted to women? The Church taught me that it was required for me to be married in the temple of the Lord to be sealed for time and eternity. I had to obey the commandments of the Lord, and I wanted to find a young fine lady somewhere out there. Will I in the near future meet a young fine lady? I don't know, but God knows that my heart desired to marry in the temple of the Lord and be sealed for time and eternity. Was I a failure for not obeying my patriarchal blessing? Was it all my fault? Did I choose SSA over God? I love my God, Heavenly Father, and Jesus Christ, and I have always loved them, and I will always love them for all eternity, but I still have confused feelings and unanswered questions about this.

I don't know if I was born that way, to be SSA. I don't know how I became SSA. I have no idea how. I am no longer dating women for now but maybe in the near future I will be ready? I have hope and try to be patient and positive and happy and accept myself as who I am.

Eric-Preston Hamren

"Respect all life around you, whether it be a plant or a person, because all life is sacred no matter what form it takes. Plus I would rather stay on the good side of Karma."

I was born in the covenant and raised in the Church. I went to preschool with other kids in the ward. When I was in kindergarten, about five years old, there was a boy, "Daniel", that I was best friends with. I didn't put a label on it, but I knew I just liked him. As I got closer to puberty, I became more aware that I *really* liked him. At the same time, I started tuning in to the things that were being said about homosexuality by my parents and by Church members. If the topic ever came up, it was never spoken kindly of. It was just understood that this is something bad, like drinking alcohol. No one really went into detail about it, but I learned pretty quickly: people shouldn't be gay.

And so I kept my feelings quiet. I kind of separated myself from most kids at school. I was afraid that if they learned too much about me they might figure it out. I always tried to keep my distance in the locker room; I would change in a stall. In Scouts, I had a major crush on a boy in my ward. It was kind of hard, because when we went on camping trips together, we'd sleep in the same tent, and I was worried that I would be aroused by him. In church I was the deacons quorum president, and later the teachers quorum president. I knew I had to set a good example for the other boys.

I can't be gay

When I was in seventh grade, Daniel would sometimes bring bits of pornography to school and try to sell it to other kids. Sometimes we were in class together, and he would give it to me to pass along to someone who was buying it. I remember the first time I saw porn that had a guy and a girl in it, and the whole time I was just looking at the guy, and I couldn't figure out why at first, but my mind was just thinking, "This is just hot!"

So when I got home, I started looking it up on the Internet and started realizing that yes, I am gay. My dad, being the computer wiz he is, found everything I did, even if I had deleted it. So yeah, I was busted! And then he asked, why was I looking at this kind of porn? I said I was just curious, because I had seen all the other kinds of porn and was wondering what this was like. I was hoping he would buy that explanation. He didn't press me any further, but he sat down and gave me a lecture about how sex works and about the importance of keeping the Church standards. After this, I decided, "I can't be gay; I need to get rid of this."

Years later, my dad told me that on the day I was born, the first time he held me in his arms he had the impression, "This is odd, this one is a little different." He never knew why, just that the spark or connection he felt the first time he held my siblings didn't happen with me. So he always kept an extra eye on me. And then as I grew older, he suspected I might be gay. And now, when he caught me looking at this porn, it was the first real confirmation that I might be gay, although he still hoped and tried his hardest to influence me otherwise.

After that, I really held strong to the Church. I was afraid that if I strayed away from it then I would end up having sex with strangers, and I would get AIDS. This is the stereotype that I had gotten from others. I didn't want to be that. I wanted to have a family. I wanted to have kids. And even though I didn't really have a testimony and was unsure about the truthfulness of the Church, it was all I had ever known, and I couldn't imagine leaving it behind. So I held onto it for dear life, hoping that by staying close to the Church, I would be able to not be gay, that it would go away, that things would get better.

Sometimes I think because of this internal struggle with my orientation, I was never fully able to feel the Spirit. It was always kind of disappointing, because you grow up hearing about these amazing spiritual experiences when you enter the temple, but I never felt anything close to what I expected. It was kind of a letdown. I felt like somehow I didn't qualify for it. And it made me worry more about my testimony and about this fact that I'm attracted to guys. I turned even more to the Church, hoping that if I could gain a testimony, then my feelings would go away and I would be able to deal with this.

People in my family would sometimes ask, "So are you interested in any girls?" And I wasn't. On the other hand my sister would always ask, "So do you have a boyfriend yet?" I would get upset and say, "No! Why would I ever have a boyfriend?" And she would just laugh. We hadn't talked about it, but she just always seemed to know.

Holding onto the Church

When I was about 17, my grandmother died. She was probably the most spiritual person that I knew. She was absolutely kind to everyone. When she died, it shook up my family pretty hard. At her funeral, I don't remember what was said, but I remember something clicked with me and I made the decision that I would live a celibate life. I would never have a relationship. I would never experience a family or any of those things. With my orientation, this seemed to be the only way I could keep in tune with the Church.

For about the next six months, I would wake up, go to seminary, go to school, come home, do my homework, read the scriptures for the rest of the day, have dinner, and go to bed. I wouldn't watch TV. I would stay away from music except Church music. I tried to detach myself from anything worldly.

When I felt most in tune with the Spirit, after my prayers I had the feeling that I was being prompted to move to Utah. I had an aunt and uncle who lived there. I also researched correctional facilities, hoping there was someplace I could go where they could help me not be gay.

I was at a crossroads. I wanted to keep going to church, but I wanted to accept myself. It was probably the most conflicting and trying time for me. It was when I contemplated suicide the most. In my spare time, I would cry, not knowing what to do. I wanted to stay at my school in California because I was involved in so many things there. I talked to my mom about moving to Utah, and she told me to pray about it and listen to what the Spirit says. I was frustrated that this always seemed to be her answer for everything. I wanted to tell her, "I *have* been praying about it!"

Near the end of my junior year, while I was in choir, a boy came out of the closet. He was a friend of mine and sat next to me in choir. He told everyone in choir that he was gay, and he was really worried about what everyone would think. In order to make him feel comfortable and let him know that it wasn't a big deal, a lot of the guys in choir became cozy with him: they would sit closer to him and put their hand on his knee like close friends. One time I saw one of the guys sitting right next to him, leaning on him in an affectionate way, like a couple. As I was watching, I was thinking, "Oh my goodness, I want to do that too." This was my first time seeing people who were okay with someone being gay. I saw things in a different light for the first time.

I kind of gravitated toward him. When he would need help with a solo, I would be the one to offer to play the piano for him while he learned the song. Sometimes I would talk with him about his orientation and how he felt about that. A few times we ended up experimenting sexually, never doing too much, but just exploring each other. And he started asking me if I was gay, and I would always say, "Nope, I'm Mormon, I can't be gay."

When it came to my senior year and I was 18, I kind of pushed him away. In my mind, I was thinking, "I need to get ready to go on my mission, and I can't be doing this." I told my bishop about it. Going on a mission was what was always expected. But even though I wanted to, deep down I knew I wasn't going to go, partly because I was gay and didn't feel comfortable hiding that part of me, and partly because I didn't feel right going and teaching people about a plan of happiness which I knew that I myself would not be able to follow. It just felt like another thing that I didn't qualify for. But I was still holding onto the Church for dear life because I was afraid of what would happen if I ever strayed away.

Other ways of living

My senior year I started becoming more comfortable with myself. I became more outgoing and made some real friends, people I became close to. After I graduated, I got a job at Recreational Equipment Incorporated. I loved the outdoors, and this was a place where everything was outdoors. There was a lot of diversity, and a few of the women were lesbians. Most people there were spiritual but didn't tie themselves to any one religion. As I worked with them and got to know them, I realized that you don't necessarily have to be Mormon to be a good person, that there were other ways of living.

Since I was becoming an adult, the expectation between me and my dad was that I would move out in four or five months. While I was still living at home, my dad gave me the responsibility to pay the water bill; it was an incentive for me to move out sooner.

That November, after Thanksgiving, my little brother encouraged me to create a MySpace account. I did, and after a month I started browsing for other gay Mormons, or just gay people in general. Although it didn't say my orientation on my profile, I was now able to meet other people like me and talk with them.

Some of them were more inclined to do other things than just talk. So I kind of got into this world of "internet sex" — not really doing anything, but just talking dirty. I did that for a couple months, finally exploring the sexual side of myself and my attraction to men that had been locked away for so long. I was able to explore what I liked and what I definitely didn't like. That was a weird time of my life. Looking back, I kind of felt like a pervert, but at the time it was my only resource to other gay people, and I wanted to have that resource, even though I knew it wasn't necessarily the best resource.

My dad found out about it. He caught me sending a nude picture of myself to someone else. He was really concerned about me exchanging pictures; he said if I got a picture from a guy who turned out to be under 18, then it could be considered child pornography, and since it was his computer, my dad could be arrested, which would make things difficult for the whole family if he couldn't work. He said this was something he would not tolerate. He told me to be out of the house within a week. My mom was sitting right there when my dad was yelling at me. She thought I shouldn't leave, that I still needed more parental guidance. She knew the kind of stuff I had been looking at, that it had been guys and not girls, but for some reason she didn't seem to view it as, "My son is gay," but more as, "He's going astray and is confused." It was Sunday afternoon, Jan 27, 2008, the same day that President Hinckley died.

I can have a family

I felt kicked out of the house, although I really wasn't. It was more of a mutual agreement that it was the best thing for the time. When my dad told me to leave, I went to my room and immediately started packing. I still had to find a place to go. When I was about to start crying, I realized, "This is probably the happiest moment of my life!" I had a new freedom, and at that moment I decided, "I am gay, I accept that, and I will no longer hide it."

I changed my orientation on MySpace to "gay". I felt so proud of myself. At the same time, I was terrified. But along with being terrified, I was happy, and I realized that if any of my friends were not okay with this, then I was okay with that. I could find new friends. It was like the birth to a new life.

I got on the computer and sent a message to my sister. I said, "I'm gay, and Dad is kicking me out of the house." Immediately she replied, "Finally. I've been telling you to get a boyfriend since you were twelve. Come live with me."

I also sent a message to a friend online: he and his boyfriend had been raised in my area and did a lot of the same things that my family did. When I told them what happened, they were like, "That's great! Let's take you to the club and celebrate." Since I was still living at home, I told my mom I was going to stay the night with someone from work. They picked me up, so I met them for the first time in person, and they took me to "Tiger Heat", a gay club in Hollywood. The whole time in the car I was shaking. I was so nervous, so scared, not of them but of going to a gay club for the first time.

We got inside, and they immediately took off their shirts and started dancing. I was kind of a wallflower, so they helped pull me in and sent people over to dance with me. It was fun. I had always had kind of a low self-esteem of myself, of my body. I knew I was always a little more feminine than other guys, so I was conscious of how I carried myself. But now to have people coming up to me and saying things like, "You're attractive! You're cute! You're hot!" — It was very new to me and confidence-boosting.

I ended up sleeping in the same bed with the other two guys. Of course we didn't do anything, but it was kind of nice. We were all cuddled together, and I just thought, "This is what I want." For the first time it occurred to me, "I can have a relationship. I can have a family. This is what I want. I don't want to live a lie. I don't want to not have these things." It didn't matter that I was gay. I wanted to have a partner, to have a family and have kids. So I stayed awake a little longer that night thinking about things. That was Thursday.

This is nothing to kid around with

I spent all day Friday looking at houses. One of the guys that took me to the club helped me look at places. He had a truck and helped me move on Saturday.

I found out where my new ward was, but I wasn't ready to go back to church yet. I didn't tell my mom where I lived, because I didn't want her to change my address in Church records. I didn't come out to my new roommates yet, but I told everyone at work and my friends from school. They were all supportive. Most of them said, "We know. We were just waiting for you to tell us."

About two months after moving out, I got a call from my mother. She wanted to visit, so I gave her directions to my place, without giving her the address. Of course she figured it out and transferred my Church records; within a day, missionaries were at my door. Between my roommates and me, it became a house rule to check the door before answering, to make sure it wasn't the missionaries.

One day, my mom called, and I could hear she was holding back some emotion. "So, some people have told me what it says on your MySpace." I said, "What's that?" pretending not to know what she was implying. She said, "Well, I don't need to say, but just so you know, people from church can see it, and I don't think they're comfortable with that. This is nothing to kid around with. You should change it back to 'straight' because you're not 'gay'." She thought I was playing some kind of joke.

How can you choose this?

In April, I met a guy "Sam" and we started dating; he wasn't LDS but he had similar standards. He had been out since he was thirteen. He took me home one day to meet his parents, and it was such a new experience for me! They were on the couch holding hands, and we were on the couch holding hands. It seemed weird for them to be okay with that, to be so open. A few weeks later they took us to see "Wicked" in Hollywood. So there I was, holding hands with a boy in public. It was completely new, but I was becoming comfortable with the fact that I was gay, and it was okay. This was just another part of it that I was eager to discover.

I knew that I needed to actually say to my mother, "I'm gay." My sisters invited me to go with them to the Rainbow Gathering for a week in Wyoming. After I got back, my mom wanted to see all the pictures. I got my laptop and planned it all out: I dressed as gay as I could: I did my hair and wore capris and a V-neck shirt; I wanted to throw it in her face as much as possible so that there could be no denial. I started showing her pictures of Rainbow, and then mixed in there would be pictures of me and Sam, which I would quickly skip over. One of them was us kissing. After I got past that one, I asked, "So how was your week?" She was still staring at the computer even though I had closed the image. She said, "Who was that?" I said, "Sam." She asked, "Who's that?" And I said, "He's my boyfriend. Cute, huh?"

I closed the computer, and she was still staring at it. She started crying and asked me, "Are you gay?" I said confidently, "Yes." She said, "How can you choose this? You're turning your back on everything you've been taught." She saw it as something I chose, that I was never going to be happy, that I would never make it to the celestial kingdom this way. I replied, "Mom, I don't think the terrestrial kingdom is that bad. I'm okay with being there if it means I get to live forever with the person I want to be with." She said, "You won't live forever with a partner." I said, "— not with a woman. But I'm okay with that, if it means the person that I want to spend forever and all eternity with is in the terrestrial kingdom with me." She just kept crying and saying, "This is stupid." She wasn't saying it to be mean; it was just something she would say when she was frustrated with something.

I was still very fond of the Church

I had started going back to church. During this time, Proposition 8 was going on. I talked to my bishop and explained that I had come out of the closet, moved out, and was still struggling with whether to be involved in the Church. I said I understood where the Church was coming from with Proposition 8, and I offered to help. I was still struggling with my stance on Proposition 8, but I thought I would be in a good position to talk to people, since I was gay and Mormon. He said he would put me down on the list and connect me with the coalition leader from our stake, and that I would get a list of houses to go door-to-door to, to talk about the issue.

I didn't get a phone call, so I tried calling the church to check with the bishop, but they said he was busy. When I would see him at church, I would try to talk to him, but he always hurried off to his office after the meeting was over before I could reach him. I had been consistently getting visits from missionaries at least once a week, and I had let them come into the house a few times. But after I told the bishop I was gay, the missionaries never came to my house anymore.

That's when I started to feel that this campaign wasn't really about marriage, that it was about the fact that they weren't okay with people being gay. Every temple in California was being protested at, and I stayed away from all that. I still had a real strong attachment to the Church.

I moved up with my sister in northern California not long after New Year's in 2009, and she sent me to Burning Man several months later, which was an amazing experience. I became comfortable with myself, my true self. It made me recognize all the false personas I had put on my whole life to try to hide the fact that I was gay. It helped me find a deeper spirituality and recognize that I didn't necessarily have to be attached to an organized religion. But I still was very fond of the Church and the standards of the Church; I didn't like drinking, smoking, or porn.

The last straw

In September 2009, I came to Utah to visit some friends, and especially to visit Jake, the guy I had been dating long-distance. I ended up calling my sister and telling her, "The universe has decided for me to stay in Utah," and I just stayed. I went to church a few times and told members, "I'm gay. I just moved here to Salt Lake City." Members were nice and invited me to come to the single adult activities.

In October 2010, I heard on the news about Boyd K. Packer's talk. I had to hear it for myself, because I knew that people can misconstrue things. So I went on the Church website and watched all of General Conference. It was a long day. When I came to Boyd K. Packer's speech, and heard him say what he said, that we are not born with these tendencies, that God would never do that to a person, it hurt. It still makes me choke up. And I know that not everyone interpreted it that way, but I read it again and again to make sure I wasn't misreading it. Before, I had never been told by my church, point blank, that *I* was a sin. How do you tell a five-year-old child that they were not born this way, that there is something wrong with them? And how can you tell that to a deacon or a Beehive?

The bottom line is that the Heavenly Father I was raised with would never say something like that to His children. He wants us to be good, happy people, kind to everyone. I think that one of Heavenly Father's highest standards is to love thy neighbor as thyself. All through seminary that was my favorite scripture. That was the one value that through everything I always upheld and tried to live by, that regardless of whether or not you were raised in the Church, that Heavenly Father really just wants you to be a good person.

But the things that were said over that pulpit went against the Heavenly Father that I was raised with, that I had a testimony of. From that point, in my mind the Church was no longer associated with God, with Jesus, or with anything spiritual in any shape or form. It was the last straw for me. It was the end of my relationship with the Church.

Other ways to happiness

I've been with Jake now for almost two years. I love him to death. I would like to continue my life with him and one day have a family.

The Church does a lot of good. There is no denying that. Their welfare program is amazing. Many of the standards of the Church I still agree with. I have seen the value of avoiding alcohol and coffee. My body is a temple. Even though I can no longer associate the Church with the word of Heavenly Father, it is what I was raised with. My favorite song to this day is "The Spirit of God"! I still sing that song all the time when I'm in the shower.

I'm an intern now at the Utah Pride Center helping with gay-straight alliances (GSAs) at schools across the state. That prompting I had so many years before, about why I needed to move to Utah, is clear now. I feel like the reason is because I was needed here. I don't want any kid to go through what I experienced growing up: the bullying, the feeling of self-loathing, that there's something wrong with you. That's why I do what I do with the GSAs. I hope to continue to make a difference here and help people's lives not to go in the direction that I was almost headed in, of suicide, or denying yourself all happiness.

If you're someone who's struggling to deal with this, know that you're not the only one. That is the one thing I wish I had known growing up; I felt like I was the only gay Mormon. But there is an entire world out there. The Church's plan of happiness is great for a lot of people. But there are other ways to happiness. It is possible to live your life, have a family, and be successful and happy! You just have to find what makes you happy!

Marcela Brimhall

*"The future belongs to those who believe
in the beauty of their dreams."*
– Eleanor Roosevelt

I was born in Provo, Utah and am blessed with a loving family. I loved going to church and was a proud member. From Sunbeams to Achievement Days, I learned and loved it all. In our family we always had family prayer, scripture study, family home evenings, and weekly planning meetings. Righteous people surrounded me. Life revolved around the Church. Friends, family, neighbors, classmates, teachers, etc. were primarily LDS.

In my family, I am the youngest of nine kids. I have two adopted Native American brothers, and I always knew that I was adopted as well. Unfortunately I'm not ethnically Native American, but I felt especially connected with these brothers growing up (even though they teased me like crazy). I am the baby of the family, and I was sealed in the temple to my family when I was young.

When I was about six years old, I found out that my sister Alicia was my birth mom, which meant my parents were actually my grand-parents. My parents and Alicia had an agreement not to tell me until I was 18. Good thing I was a smart kid, as I would see pictures of her when she was young and always thought it was weird she looked so much like me. Alicia told me when I was way younger than the agreed age, which caused conflict. The truth came out, and my parents took me to dinner and we had a nice, emotional chat about the situation. I was so young, trying to make sense of such a strange concept. Birth mother? Real mother? Who knows.

I will never know exactly what everything was like before I was in this world, but as time went on and I got older, more of the story was unraveled — and I share this with Alicia's permission. Before I was born, Alicia was attending BYU, and she was date raped. She wanted to heal and come to a healthier conclusion of what sex was really like, so she threw down some moves on her friend she had known since high school. Here's where I feel something lucky happened for me: after just one time, I was created. This threw my family a curve ball and they dealt with the situation accordingly. She went to live in Arizona with our grandma before I was born, and a year later she served in Chile as a sister missionary for the Church.

She had an agreement with my parents that if she married a man in the temple when she got home, then she would be able to raise me. After her mission, she came back to BYU and was proposed to by a wonderful man. I was only about four years old at the time, but I remember him; he was really nice to me. My parents adored him as well. This was a huge turning point in her life, as she realized she liked women and couldn't consent to his proposal. She only thought of him as a friend.

Time passed, and my parents — Alicia's parents — raised me as their child. I traveled with them, and I learned to value the wisdom of the elderly! I went to school and had so much fun with all my friends in the neighborhood, always staying active with games, bikes, forts, climbing trees, imagination, sports, pretty rocks, etc. Everything had significance growing up.

When I was about twelve years old, Alicia came out to me as lesbian. It felt like a collision between two worlds, but I learned to accept her for the person she is and to love her regardless. Unconditional love is something I believe in and have known all my life.

"Just hold my hand"

I started going to Young Women's, and it was really great! I had the most wonderful leaders, and there was a great energy there. I held callings and loved to serve. There were no young women in my age group (only young men), so I either had to hang out with the older and younger girls, or settle with the "immature" boys at group activities.

In school, I was always social and athletic. I loved playing basketball, but I enjoyed soccer as well. When I was a Mia Maid, there was an organized basketball game at the stake center, and the guys my age invited me to play. I was really stoked that they considered me on the same skill level! To make the long story short, the leaders asked me not to play. They were worried that the boys might inadvertently touch me inappropriately; somehow I was deemed to be a temptation in the situation. Yet I was *the* most modest girl around. I made sure I was always covered well and did not dress immodestly around boys ever. Phrases like "modest is hottest" were mottos I clung to. It didn't make any sense to me. I was frustrated to tears they wouldn't let me play because I was a girl! It shifted my thinking as I reflected on the inequality of the experience.

When I was 16, I began dating a friend. Somehow we ended up being boyfriend and girlfriend. It was a strange, cute, lovely relationship and I had some precious moments with him. He was and is a fascinating human being. We never kissed, but we would hold hands and seemed to be quite emotionally involved. One time at a girls basketball game at our school, he saw a friend "Becky" sitting all the way across the gym. She came over, and he introduced us. In that moment, I saw something and felt something that changed me. From the first time she came near me, I just adored her. She seemed so lost that night. I could tell there was more to her. Slowly I began to find out who she was, and what she was all about. As with many others in Provo she was also actively LDS. She was fun, smart, beautiful, adventurous, and passionate.

One night I was hanging out at a friend's house with my boyfriend. Coincidentally my friend lived right next to Becky. Becky and all the girls hopped into my car and we drove to Wendy's (I was the oldest and had my license!). We played cards till they closed, and we had a great time. Later that night, we all went back to the house and as everyone went inside, Becky lingered outside with me. We just lay on the hood of my car, looking at the stars and talking late into the night. She was really sad because a boy didn't like her, among other things. Without even taking time to process it, I said, "Just hold my hand. It will be okay." I don't know what I actually meant by that, but my intention was to comfort her and just be there for her, to be a kind, open friend, to listen and feel what she was experiencing. As time went on, we got more and more cuddly, as we intertwined. I felt so blessed and grateful just to know her and to have her in my life.

Everything happens for a reason. A few months later my boyfriend and I broke up.

It was so incredible

That summer, my brother came with me and a bunch of friends to the Fourth of July parade on University Avenue. Becky and I were sitting on a blanket near the library, and we were just being cute, having a great time with all our friends. There were lots of people walking around and sitting, prepared with their camping gear. That night, Becky and I went on a walk around the block, and we almost kissed, but didn't. The intensity was overwhelming. We were so emotionally connected, which was what I loved most about the relationship.

Later that night I was talking with my best friend, and she said, "By the way, your brother asked if you and Becky were 'together'?" I just shrugged it off and said, "No, I wonder why he said that." At the time it was absolutely true, as whatever was happening between us was completely innocent. I didn't know what was going on, because I was pretty much in denial about the whole situation. But I kept smiling. I was infatuated and didn't know what the meaning of it was. So I decided to feel it out with my head held high.

The next day, I went to girls camp at Mia Shalom. It was such a beautiful, spiritual place to me. This was my third year at camp, and I was so excited about the experience. Every day after dinner there was time set aside for us to write in our journals. Instead of doing that, I wrote Becky a long letter, addressing the intensity of all my feelings for her. It was a record of thoughts within myself, deciding whether or not I was going to let myself feel what I was feeling.

When I got home, I gave it to her, and she read it while I took a shower. I was nervous to see her reaction. After I was done, I came in and lay on my bed with her, and we just talked about it and looked deeply into each other's eyes. A week apart had seemed like an eternity for some reason. After many intense moments passed, I kissed her. She went for it too. It was so incredible, and words are too simple to describe such a moment.

Such love and connection

When I tried to sleep that night, I started thinking, "What's going on? Do I like girls? Or do I just like Becky?" I didn't regret it; I didn't feel guilty. I was just processing what my actions really meant. After that, Becky and I started seeing each other a lot, and our friends started to find out we were getting closer. My brother was always really nice to Becky, which I always appreciated and thought was really cute. I was in denial for so long about him knowing. It's funny to think he knew from the beginning.

Becky introduced me to a boy we went to school with, and he was the first homosexual man I became friends with. One night I was in the car with him and some other friends, and they called me out, "Hey, we know you and Becky are together." I denied it for a second, but they were like, "Come on. Come on, we already know!" So I confessed, "Yes. Becky and I have been seeing each other." Then they tried to get me to go further into detail, but being the wholesome young lady that I was, I did not go there.

Years melted by, and Becky and I had so many incredible times together. We played in the mountains, the canyons, in the water, in each other's houses — always playing and growing together, having the best adventures and learning from all our experiences. It was great to have the support system of our friend group. We all grew together in Provo and experienced such love and connection with each other as we made sense of the world around us.

There were times when I would talk with Becky, posing questions: If we were meant to be together, does that mean we weren't going to marry men in the temple? Would we spend the rest of our lives together? What happens with all eternity? All we knew is we were doing what we were doing and just decided to stick with that — kind of.

"Don't you feel guilty?"

After I graduated from high school, I went on a trip with my family to Nauvoo. My mom was really excited about everyone going to the new temple, but I knew I couldn't go inside. I didn't even try; I thought I wasn't worthy. I thought, "You can't kiss girls and go in the temple." My recommend hadn't been renewed anyway, so I just blamed it on that. I was kind of stressed out and sick that day anyway so I stayed in the hotel. The rest of the trip was delightful.

I loved traveling, and we went to lots of historical sites. Our family was spread across the country, so it was great to be reunited in such a special place.

When we got home, I went to Especially For Youth (EFY) in Provo. It was at BYU, but the whole time I kept sneaking away with my friends who met me on campus. My mom even caught me away from EFY once, which was funny.

Things got rocky and chaotic as my life took a strange turn. I went to Hawaii to live with Alicia and brought some friends. During those months I made some bad decisions, but we all had some learning experiences that I wouldn't trade for anything. The way I see it, you can learn from every opportunity life has to offer you. The way we process experience is crucial to our personal development and progression.

I started attending Utah Valley State College, and after about a year, my mom asked me, "Is there something more going on between you and your friend Becky?" At first I played dumb, "Well, what do you mean?" But eventually I gave in and said, "Yeah, I'm more than friends with her." She kept asking me, "Don't you feel guilty?" And I kept saying, "No, I've never felt guilty for this." It was an intense conversation, and I got slightly frustrated because it felt like she was trying to put words into my mouth about my situation. The bottom line she communicated was that she loved me and just wanted me to be making good choices.

My dad was out of town at the time, but when he came back, he sat me down and interviewed and counseled me, "You can't be doing that. You shouldn't see her anymore." He encouraged me to talk to my bishop. After that, I felt like I needed a place away from my family. I needed to become a more independent individual and live my life. So I made the big decision and moved to Taylorsville. I started attending Salt Lake Community College, and I also transferred my job to a store in Salt Lake City.

This opportunity to live

Becky would come up to Salt Lake City a couple times a week to see me. It was rough not living in the same city anymore, not being able to see each other whenever we pleased as before. There were holes in the relationship and eventually they grew too big to fix. It hurt a lot, as I felt I had given the relationship all I had. But I understood, because the reason she gave was that she was going to marry a man in the temple someday. She knew that regardless of what she was doing now, that was her goal. As always, I love her unconditionally and understand that people do the best they can, and for her and myself, it wasn't meant to be.

I've done well to be open and hold the values I've been raised with. I realize I am the same person I've always been, but different at the same time. I believe in working hard. I believe in the undeniable infinite worth of souls. Human desire is strong and motivates action, which causes a reaction. Gratitude, Humility, Respect, Honor, Loyalty, and Truth are all values I hold. I believe there is a reason why I am given the opportunity to be here, and a reason for every single occurrence that happens in my life.

I could choose to look at my life and feel, "I'm a mistake. I don't know why I was born into these circumstances. Why has this happened?" I choose to be positive and understand the place I have in this incredible reality we call life. The point is that I am here, and I am given this opportunity to live. I strive to live the wonderful life that I always looked forward to when I was young. I choose to do that in my own way, whatever it means.

A life of balance

After the break-up, I began to recover and tried to mend my broken heart. I met my second girlfriend just a few weeks later. We moved into the relationship way too quickly, without knowing one another's boundaries, personalities, and goals. Although the relationship was intense and developed at an accelerated speed, I was still trying to get over my emotional attachment to Becky. I am so grateful that the universe brought this new girl into my reality. From all the things I put her through, and which she put me through, we learned together fundamental lessons of life that will never be forgotten. She is the smartest person I know. We grew and connected together in ways I thought impossible to be real. As time passes, it's funny how your brain and heart cling to deep feelings and connections. Unfortunately, the relationship took a turn for the worse, and I guess we both decided to drop it and move on. Now I'm single, pretty much for the first time since I was 16, shifting to being independent.

Thus far, I've been in good relationships and bad relationships in my young adult life, and I'm trying to figure out where the beauty of love lies. I haven't really ever been interested in boys. I get along with boys just fine and have been close a few times. I never really felt like I could connect with a boy on the same frequency that I know I can share with a girl. Then again, who am I to judge a person based on their gender. Instead of "labeling" myself as someone with restrictions to only one gender, I realize that I have a tendency to fall in love with women. I am in awe of how much passion and beauty women possess.

Last summer, at my family reunion I truly came out to my parents. It was a rough conversation as I came out to them as "gay". I was nervous. I had thought about this conversation a million times and how I would have liked it to go down, but life never happens the way you plan it. My dad gave the definition of "gay" as meaning carefree or happy. This was the beginning of a complicated conversation. I realized that the bottom line was that they loved me and wanted me to be happy. I understood they felt they knew the correct path for me. But nobody can choose the path for another.

I told them that I was making changes in my life. Even though I wasn't sure they were the changes they wanted to see, I just wanted them to know that I'm taking care of myself, body, mind, and spirit, while traveling on my quest searching for a life of balance.

I love to experience life

At this point, I couldn't go back to church and feel comfortable there the same as in my childhood. I don't feel like I would be accepted in that community. Maybe it's just me assuming, because every LDS person I've "come out to" has responded well. In our generation, young LDS people are so loving and open; it is literally changing the world. It seems like they are really taking the doctrine to heart, treating everyone equal, like we're all children of God. But I just don't know what it would be like at church.

For myself, I've found peace in the spirituality that I practice. My mind has opened itself to a different way of thinking. But I will always be LDS, because it is in me, rooted deep in me since I was a little seed. It is in my culture. I love the doctrine. I love the things that I've learned at church, as I've loved the things I learned at school and in life as well.

I just love to feel, and I love to experience life. Emotions are crucial to understanding where I am in my life. I want to keep moving forward towards making a difference in this world, to have a family someday, to create beauty and abundance. I want to do my part to care for nature. I love the earth, and strive to preserve what is left of her remarkable beauty. Everyone has the ability to make their own decisions. I know it is important for me to experience what is in the present, to process the thought or emotion, deal with it, and then let it go. I can be happy if I choose to find happiness and live well.

Blake Yuen

"Love is the irresistible desire to be irresistibly desired."
– Robert Frost

My earliest memory of being attracted to members of the same sex was at about the age of five. I was with my family camping in the California Redwoods, and the campsite had shower facilities. When my father took us to the shower to get clean, I remember being fascinated by the bodies of the naked men there. At that point it wasn't a sexual attraction, but I just found their whole bodies wonderful and interesting.

After I hit puberty, I was always checking out other men and I had a lot of crushes. I had a seminary teacher my freshman year who I thought was the most handsome man I had ever met! He was young, tall, and well-built. In school there were several handsome boys in my classes, and they always brought a smile to my face.

I assumed that it was just a phase or something that I would outgrow. I figured that God wouldn't make me gay. I prayed, read my scriptures, went to church and did everything else that God had asked me to do, but I still carried around this curse, this millstone around my neck!

Just after high school I started attending my stake singles ward and quickly made friends. Although there were a lot of pretty young women in the ward, I was more interested in becoming friends with them than I was in dating any of them. Of course, I had to pretend that I was interested in some of them to keep up the appearance that I was "straight". I did date one girl for about six months. I tried really hard to be the heterosexual young man that everyone expected; I just couldn't force myself to be that.

The time eventually came for me to start preparing for a mission, but I feared that my secret would be found out if I had to shower with the other missionaries at the Missionary Training Center. So I kept putting it off. People at church kept nagging me about when I was going to go, but I never did end up serving a mission.

Years passed and I continued to stay active in church, hoping my desires would change. After a while I began to feel great confusion. I knew God loved me — I felt it in my heart and in my soul. I just didn't understand why He would curse me like this. Why would He make me gay when I wanted to follow His gospel and be good? Why did He hate me? What could I possibly have done, in this life or the previous one, to deserve such a punishment?

When I was 30 I moved away from California to Utah with a friend who was leaving to go to BYU. When I was about 33, I was asked to leave the young single adult ward, which I did. I tried to attend the older single adult ward, but it seemed like everyone in the ward had lost hope. They seemed somewhat dead inside, like they had lost all vigor for life! It was a weird experience. I eventually stopped going.

I hated this curse that prevented me from being what I thought God wanted me to be! Although I always knew that I was attracted to men, I could not accept the fact that I was gay. I mean, I knew that I wasn't attracted to women, but I felt like accepting my homosexuality would be a death sentence. I wanted to be with men, but I believed that this was wrong. And so, accepting my homosexuality would have meant consigning myself to a life of loneliness, devoid of love.

Eventually I came to know that God loves me just the way I am, the way He made me. I am now the happiest I have ever been in my life. I finally found love after having given up hope of ever finding someone to love! Many people consider Utah Valley to be the heart of "Mormonism", so it's ironic that it was there that I found the love of my life. We have been dating for about a year and a half. I proposed to him a few months ago and, if all goes according to plans, we will get married on July 28, 2012.

Randal Graham

"True religion is about what we love, not about what we think. True religion is about what you and I hold sacred. The practice of true religion is faithfulness to what we love."
– Peter Morales, President of the Unitarian Universalist Association

I can't say for sure when exactly I began to recognize my interest in others of my same sex. In my early years, I looked at pornography and had experiences with other boys, but I didn't recognize it as an attraction to them. All I really knew was that I liked to look at men and that I did not like to look at women in the same way.

During my teens, I never felt a strong need to be with a man; any longing that I felt was strictly sexual, and I never saw that as being "gay". Meanwhile, I was attracted to girls, but never sexually. I remember having a crush on a female classmate in third, sixth and ninth grade. In ninth grade I met a girl who for years held my heart. She was first a best friend and then a love interest; nonetheless, I never had any real desire to be intimate with her, merely to be with her. What I felt for her was a strong platonic love, not romantic love, much less sexual attraction. That flame has long since died, but we have remained good friends.

Men had always been able to inspire something in me that women didn't. Plainly put, guys got me hot; girls didn't. I tried to take some of the thoughts I had of men and replace them with women, but my mind always reverted back to the same gender.

I was often ashamed, and I began to make attempts to change. As I prepared for a mission, I was disappointed in myself, knowing that I had failed to make myself totally "clean". I had not had sexual contact with anyone since my childhood, but I still struggled with private habits which I hadn't told my bishop about, and which were considered sinful. I do not regret serving a mission, but I do regret that I continued to perpetuate the façade of a "good Mormon boy".

I had hoped my mission would set me on track and that I would be able to get married soon afterwards. This was not the case, and as I faced my emotions, I began to feel that I was not meant to remain within the Church, but I decided I still had to strive to overcome and remain faithful to my covenants. When I came out to my parents, they supported me in these efforts.

After I came out to myself and my parents, I began to really understand what I was experiencing. I had a continued strong desire to be with a man, and this desire was becoming an increasingly emotional one: wanting to be held, wanting to be loved, wanting to be understood by a man. The thought of ever being with a woman, which I had entertained for so long, was now almost entirely out of my mind.

I did not yet realize that, the day before I came out to my parents, I had met the man who three weeks later would give me my first kiss. When I later informed my parents of my disillusionment with the Church and of my new relationship, they expressed intense dismay and disapproval and encouraged me to think carefully about my decision.

I am happy now. There are very few things now that I wish to change. My parents have asked that my relationship with my boyfriend be kept from the knowledge of my siblings; I dislike this secrecy and the fact that at times it requires me to bend the truth. I hope that this will soon end. I hope that I can soon be honest with my family, and open about the fact that I am different. I love my partner and want my family to understand that I am happy — even without being active in the Mormon faith. I love my family and want them to understand that they know and love someone gay.

There is so much more in my life that makes me happy. I have a wonderful job; I live happily alongside my partner, getting to hold him close each day and wake up next to him every morning; I have friends who love and accept us; I have not yet lost any friends, and, rather, have seen many of these relationships strengthened. I am striving to make a difference in the world and am satisfied with those efforts; I am no longer guilt-ridden. Life has treated me so well, and I am grateful.

In my pursuit of happiness I have learned valuable lessons. Friendship, or any relationship, is strengthened through honesty and sincerity. I can make a difference, even through small means, simply by being myself. There are others like me. I am not alone, and neither are you. God loves me just as he loves my neighbor. Respect, patience, and inner peace help lift the pain of disapproval expressed by those most dear. If I allow fear to hold me back, it hurts me and those around me.

With these lessons in happiness, I have also experienced a new sense of liberation and illumination. I believe that there is good in every religion. I don't believe that the Church of Jesus Christ of Latter-day Saints, or any other church, has all we need. Each has that which it does best. I believe God wants *harmony*, not homogeny; I believe God wants us to be ourselves. I believe Jesus' greatest commandment was to love God and love our neighbor. This love between beings, romantic or platonic, is sacred; love is a gift, and I think that's why we're here: to learn to love.

I still have much to do. Fear has not yet lost all power over me, but I'm not going to be held back. Life is hard, but every challenge that we face makes us stronger and better. Happiness lies behind every obstacle, but we must overcome and embrace our joy once we find it.

Joshua Johanson

"Our deepest fear is not that we are inadequate. Our deepest fear is that we are powerful beyond measure. It is our light, not our darkness, that most frightens us. We ask ourselves, who am I to be brilliant, gorgeous, talented, and fabulous? Actually, who are you not to be? You are a child of God."
- Marianne Williamson

I was blessed to be born into a wonderful LDS family. I was raised by wonderful parents who taught me the gospel throughout my life. Through them I was blessed with an inquisitive mind and a thirst for knowledge. As I learned more, I became skeptical that of all the world's religions, I would just happen to be born in the correct one. This led to a serious study of my faith.

By the time I was 15, I was reading the Book of Mormon for the third time. I was in Alma where he addressed those who had a desire to believe. It caught my attention because I thought that described my situation. He then said to experiment on the word. If it were true, it would give good fruits. I began to think about all the experiences I had in the Church, and the Spirit bore witness that what I had been feeling was the Spirit. A powerful feeling came over me, and I knew that God had answered my prayers. I knew the Church was true, and I decided I would do anything to feel the peace of the Spirit. Since then I have had many other experiences that have confirmed my testimony.

My testimony helped set the foundation for my life as I started learning more about myself. I always felt different from everyone else, especially other boys. They seemed crude, lazy, and insensitive and were always getting into trouble. It was the complete opposite of what I wanted to be. I was very sensitive and always tried to do what was right. I understood girls a lot better, and I spent most of my time playing with them. Yet there was still a strong draw to guys. While I despised many of their traits, there were still others that I coveted. They seemed so confident and strong, features that I lacked.

All the other guys talked about girls, but I was never interested in them as anything more than friends. Men were so much more interesting. I began fantasizing about guys. It was nonsexual at first, but as I matured it took on a more sexual tone. I would spend hours looking at Greek statues of naked men in the encyclopedia. I assumed that it would change when I hit puberty, but it never did.

I was always taught that being gay was a choice. It didn't occur to me that I might be gay, because I knew I had never made that choice. When I asked about gay people, I was told they wore earrings and crossed their legs funny. I became super self-conscious about the way I crossed my legs and uncomfortable around guys wearing earrings. Whatever gay was, I didn't want to choose it.

When I was 17, I went to BYU. That was also about the time that the Internet started being widespread, and all students had an account. The Internet provided greater access to more of the type of pictures I had seen as a kid. Slowly, they got more extreme. I was always taught that pornography was looking at inappropriate pictures of women, so I was able to justify my addiction. I really didn't understand what was going on. I didn't want to tell anyone. I was ashamed. I was too ashamed to even admit it to myself.

I wasn't quite ready to admit it

Since I didn't realize my viewing pornography was really an issue, I went on my mission without addressing it. There were some problems on my mission, and although it wasn't anything too serious, I realized that what I had done was wrong, and I went to talk to my mission president. He said I could stay on my mission, but warned me that they are usually pretty strict about gay things on the mission. It wasn't until he said that, that I finally realized that what I was doing was gay.

When I came back, my problems with pornography increased. It wasn't until I was actually caught at BYU having looked at pornography, that I was willing to address it. I got put on probation, and I had to go to counseling. In a group session, there was a guy who came out as gay. He was married and had had problems with pornography while he was married, but for the most part he had been faithful to his wife and had a good marriage.

I started talking with him, asking some questions about what he went through. Eventually he asked if I was going through some of the same things as him. At that point, I wasn't quite ready to admit it. I said I was bisexual. I lied and said I looked at both kinds of pornography. He didn't believe me; he said there was no such thing as bisexual. We talked, and he really helped me out a lot, but we lost contact shortly afterwards when I finished at BYU.

During this process, I would talk with my bishops about my problems with pornography. I didn't tell them what type of pornography I was viewing, so they didn't really understand the full scope of the problem. I wasn't addressing the underlying issues, because more than pornography, it was that I was isolated; it was the fact that I was hiding. A lot of problems multiply when you're hiding.

Talking with parents and counselors

After I graduated from BYU, I finally told my parents. I had been really scared to talk to them about my attractions. I knew they would always love me, but that they would be disappointed. After I told my mom, she gave me an article about how same-sex attractions were a choice. Over time I tried to convince her that although I was responsible for looking at pornography, I hadn't chosen my attractions. We had several family home evenings where I shared some of the Church's teaching that same-sex attractions are not a choice. At first she was reluctant to change her viewpoint, despite reading quotes from the prophets, but she eventually listened and changed her view.

She wanted me to go to counseling, so I went and met with Dr. Jeffrey Robinson for about nine months. I really liked his approach. He focused a lot on taking control of your life and not being a victim, which I think is sound advice for anyone. I wished I had been able to learn more from him. I was struggling with depression at the time, and wasn't ready to really address my attractions.

After that, I went to the University of Washington for graduate school. I started seeing an LDS counselor there. He didn't specialize in same-sex attraction, but he pointed me to some videos on the website www.ldsresources.info. He had me meet with someone who called himself a gay Mormon. He talked about the decisions he had made to follow all of the teachings of the Church, except to be with a man instead of a woman. I tried to listen with an open mind, but it didn't feel right. I wanted to be squarely in line with the gospel of Jesus Christ.

"I'm here for you, man"

I then moved to California, and things started to look better. I had a good roommate and I met a girl who I was really excited about dating. After an amazing week of dating, she suddenly broke the relationship off. I asked her why, and she said that she didn't know. She said from her perspective everything seemed to be going great, but that she had prayed about it and didn't feel comfortable and thought she should break up with me. It was very disappointing, because here I was, trying to do what I was supposed to do, and God stopped it when it was going well. Wasn't dating women what He wanted me to do?

My roommate could tell I was upset. He kept saying, "It's cool. You can tell me. I'm here for you, man." When he insisted, I finally told him that I was attracted to men, that I was trying to date women, that it wasn't working out and I was frustrated. He said he understood it must be tough, that it didn't change anything, and that if I ever needed anything I could let him know.

The next day, when I got home from work, all of his stuff was gone. He left a note for me that said he would pay his portion of the rent even though he didn't feel comfortable living there anymore, and that I shouldn't contact him. I couldn't believe it. I was so frustrated I didn't know what to do. I just dropped everything and ran out the door. I didn't know where I was going; I just wanted to get away.

I ended up at a girl's house who I barely knew. I told both her and her roommate everything about what I was going through. I didn't care anymore. I told them things I had never told anyone. They were very understanding and it was so liberating to finally talk openly.

Having a friend simply leave like that was really devastating, but in a way, it was also very empowering. Before this experience I had always been held back by the fear of what might happen if someone found out about me. Now the worst had already happened. There wasn't anything else to fear.

The opportunity to be real

Meanwhile my parents had found out about Journey into Manhood, a weekend retreat for men dealing with same-sex attraction. They were excited for me to attend and offered to pay for it, so I decided to go. I purposely went to a retreat in Utah, hoping that there would be more members of the Church there. My bet paid off. It was weird being with so many other guys who knew of my attractions. I didn't feel so alone anymore. One of the things that impressed me was that some of them were really confident in who they were, something that I severely lacked. For me, there was a lot of shame in my attractions. I felt that in order to have self-esteem I would need to be straight. Yet here I saw all these people who were fine with themselves and were living the gospel. It really helped me look at things in a different light.

That's when I really started getting connected to people. I realized that one of the things I enjoyed most was the opportunity to be real, to be authentic, to not have to be fake, and to not have to lie. I also started reading everything that the Church put out about same-sex attraction or about homosexuality. I got involved in Exodus International and also went to an Evergreen conference. It was good to be able to process my feelings with other people. Within these organizations I always encountered some people who had an attitude of "You have to become straight," which I didn't agree with, but overall I had many great experiences.

As I was becoming more comfortable with myself, I found it easier to make friends. I began developing closer friendships with a couple of my roommates. They started putting the pieces together and asked if I was attracted to men. I opened up to them, and they became my confidants whenever I needed to talk. They always listened and never judged. It felt really good to be accepted, especially by straight men.

I got to the point where I realized there was no point in being ashamed of my attractions. Since Church leaders said there was no sin in having same-sex attraction, I shouldn't act as though there were. Some people were saying, "Well you shouldn't talk about it, because you shouldn't talk about past transgressions," but I knew that my attractions weren't transgressions. I determined that the only way to get around the shame was to stop acting as if it were shameful.

God's love for us

At church, I was asked to speak in sacrament meeting about God's love for us. I decided to talk about how I had found God's love through dealing with same-sex attraction. I talked to the bishop about my intended angle, and he was cool with it, so I went ahead. People were surprised that I would be so open, but they also supported me. One of my roommates cried through my entire talk, and he came up and gave me a big hug afterwards. I had friends before, but now I felt like I was making friends all over again. This time, they knew the real me. It was a huge boost to my confidence to know people would still want to be friends with me even when they knew about my attractions.

I was surprised how little changed after coming out. My friends were still my friends. People still treated me the same. I thought people would have tons of questions, but no one talked about it much. Some even forgot. One thing that did surprise me was that it was easier to date girls after I came out. There was a lot less anxiety. There was one girl who I started dating shortly after coming out. It was a good experience. I had a lot of fun hanging out with her, but there was nothing beyond that. She was very understanding and didn't want to pressure me to kiss her. After a couple months we broke up amicably, and we remained good friends.

The next year, I took my parents to the Evergreen conference. A family spoke about how important it is to love your children no matter what, and it really touched my mom. She saw a lot of people there, normal people who were dealing with these attractions and still had strong testimonies. Many were even married. I think it helped ease her concerns about the issue and instilled hope in the possibility of my ability to marry a woman.

I showed my parents the Church pamphlet "God Loveth His Children", and my dad started giving copies of it out to different people. When someone spoke about homosexuality or gay people in a disparaging way, he would speak up and correct them. One time a same-sex couple attended their ward to hear a friend who was speaking, and my mom went up to them, welcomed them, and said they were always welcome at church. These actions made me really proud of my parents.

"Falling in love"

I first met my wife at a salsa dance. (Although I didn't get the fashion genes of being gay, I did get the dancing genes.) She was a good dancer, and things seemed to click between us. I got her phone number and started asking her out. Our second date was Valentine's Day, and we went dancing again. Things were going well, and I wanted to be close to her. She took that as a sign that I wanted to hold her hand (which hadn't even crossed my mind) and so she grabbed my hand. I was surprised but impressed with how forward she was. I thought I had better make the next move. Things just seemed so right. We lingered after I dropped her off at her car. We didn't want to leave each other. I took her to a point where we could look over the city. I started singing "I'm a Believer", and she looked at me with eyes full of joy. I decided to go for it. I leant over and kissed her. It was really nice, but kind of weird. I only gave her a peck. I enjoyed that but definitely did not want to do anything more. Still, that peck was magical.

This was followed by many more dates. I loved being with her, but my anxiety started to build. I hadn't told her about my attractions yet. I didn't want to hide or act shameful, but at the same time I didn't want it to be the only thing she knew about me. I wanted her to know me for who I was first. Since I had already kissed her, I felt she expected me to continue to kiss her, and give her more than just a peck. I tried to kiss her a bit deeper, but that was really awkward, which didn't help my anxiety at all. The whole situation was starting to become unbearable.

She could tell something was up. One day she asked me what was going on. I knew she would find out soon. I had run through this scenario a million times in my head, but I still found myself at a loss for words. I liked her, and was so scared that I might lose her, but I couldn't live with the anxiety anymore. I started by saying: "You know I like you, right?" Then I told her about my attractions to men. Just telling her lifted a huge weight off my shoulders. It felt so good, I almost didn't care how she reacted. Meanwhile, my introduction made her think I was going to break up with her. When it didn't happen, she finally asked, "So, you're not breaking up with me?" I was so relieved she even wanted to be with me, and assured her that I wanted to continue dating. I was surprised at how understanding she was of everything. It had taken me so long to come to terms with how same-sex attractions fit in with the gospel, but everything made perfect sense to her. I took her to the Love Won Out conference and the Evergreen conference, but it seemed she already understood many of the principles.

One thing that she appreciated about my attractions is that she knew I loved her for who she was. She had seen a lot of relationships where hormones would accelerate things too early in the relationship, and people would fall in love with being in love, rather than with the person. For us, our relationship developed before anything physical. With the anxiety gone, I became more and more comfortable with her physically. While most of the process was gradual, there was a definite threshold that I crossed where I started to thoroughly enjoy being intimate with her and wanted more than I would permit myself before marriage. She noticed it and brought it up; I had noticed too.

As time progressed, I received a strong impression that I was to marry her. I was still hesitant because of all of the bad things I had heard about mixed-orientation marriages, but every time I prayed the answer was the same. About a year after we started dating, we were married in the temple for time and all eternity. I have been really surprised about how easy everything came once we were married. I think both of us were expecting a harder transition.

Making it work for me

I've been married for about two years now. While I am still head over heels for my wife, I am still very much attracted to other guys. The severity comes and goes with time. My wife is very patient, and understands that people still have attractions. Whether I am attracted to men or women makes little difference to her. As long as I keep my attractions under control, she is okay with it. What is more important to her is that I am faithful to her and live in a manner consistent with the gospel.

When I had been intimate with other men before my marriage, I felt alive and real, more so than I ever had before. While homosexual intimacy was intoxicating, I felt a loss of peace. I came to understand that I value the peace of living the gospel to the extent that I was willing to give up the thrill of intimacy for that peace. One of the biggest surprises about being intimate with my wife is that I was able to feel that thrill and excitement of intimacy, but also an overwhelming peace at the same time. I had thought that I would have to choose between intimacy and peace, but God, in His infinite grace, has blessed me with both at the same time.

One key for me was focusing on meeting my needs and finding

fulfillment in ways that were consistent with my values. I found one of the best things about being intimate with guys was the authenticity that it brought. By coming out and having people love me for who I was, I was able to find that authenticity in living the gospel. Desires for other men were reinterpreted as a need for male bonding. When I feel a romantic or emotional attraction for a guy, I try to spend time hanging out with my male friends. My wife understands a great deal of my challenges and has been very supportive of my need to spend time with other guys, probably more than I do. She will sometimes say things like, "You need some guy time. Why don't you call up 'so-and-so' and have him come over? I can get out of your way so you can have some good bonding." I have heard controversy about whether a lack of positive male interaction causes same-sex attraction, so I don't want to preach that as if it is gospel truth. However, feeling like I'm one of the guys is what works best for me. I think everyone needs to find something that works with their value system.

Another thing that helps is weekly companionship inventory. It is an opportunity for us to talk about different things in our marriage. I feel free to talk about my attractions to other guys, any difficulties I have had that week, and what I am doing to improve. She also gets a chance to discuss her issues and how she is making changes. Our inventory isn't always perfect. It was especially challenging at the beginning, because there was a lot of confusion and hurt feelings when we tried to talk about difficult subjects. It has been hard to let go of expectations and focus on what our spouse needs. It is always tough to accept weaknesses, both our personal weaknesses as well as our spouse's shortcomings, but we've made a lot of progress.

When I started my marriage, I was aware that some people thought marriage wasn't a possibility for gay guys, and that it was unfair for the wives. I think one of the things that held me back from dating was being worried about hurting the woman I was dating. When I was dating my wife, she told me how happy I made her, and it helped me realize that it wouldn't be fair to her for me not to date her. I think there are some women out there that just need a gay guy, and my wife is one of them. I understand the concern in these types of marriages, and I have tried to be proactive to making sure our marriage is strong. I feel pretty good with where we are at now. I have made a covenant and am dedicated to make our relationship work no matter the cost.

You can't let negativity drag you down. Growing up, I saw a lot of my friends whose parents got divorced. They became convinced that marriage would never work, and I think that really held them back.

Regardless of what others have been through, you need to make your own road, and your own life. If you let fears get to you, you're never going to be successful. I truly believe that any two people can make things work out if they put their faith in God. It might be hard, but I've never been one to shy away from a challenge.

I feel that my marriage was very much a blessing from God. At one point, I fully expected I would have to be celibate for the rest of my life. It is a very daunting prospect to think you might live the rest of your life alone, but that is the prospect many people who are attracted to the same sex find themselves in. Living a chaste life isn't easy, but sometimes it is through the greatest challenges that we receive the greatest blessings. Be willing to submit to the Lord's will, whatever it is.

Trust in God

I have come to the point where I am truly grateful for my attractions. My experiences have helped me understand the Atonement. I used to view God as more of a disciplinarian — "If you mess up, you're going to pay or suffer." Now I view Him as a loving God. He wants us to be happy. He wants us to be okay with who we are, and He wants us to feel His love. My attractions brought me to Him. I needed my attractions to bring me to Him. I don't think I could have done it without them. He knew that all along. He gives us commandments that He knows will challenge us, but it is through those challenges that we grow. If we but put our faith in Him, He will make all things work for the good of those that love Him.

My journey has also taught me compassion for others. I made mistakes along the way. I did things that were against my values. I regretted them. We all do things against our values. People might not have a name and an identity for what they are struggling with, like I have for being gay, but that doesn't mean it isn't a struggle for them. It makes sense that others would make mistakes, so I try to be more forgiving.

I hope that the culture around this issue will change, and that it will become easier for people to be open and feel comfortable with who they are — not just with same-sex attraction, but with anything they find to be a struggle. As members of the Church we are commanded to mourn with those that mourn, but too often we are forced to mourn alone and put on a happy face around others. In order to mourn with those that mourn, we need to be able accept their weaknesses. If members of the Church start seeing gay people as sons and daughters of God, the way God sees us, I think more gay people will feel of God's love and seek to live their lives in accordance with the great plan of happiness.

For someone trying to sort out their feelings and goals, I would say this: Seek out the Lord's will for you. All too often people end up trying to please others rather than God, due to all of the societal and religious pressures we face. For a long time, I thought God wanted me to pretend to be straight, and to walk or talk a certain way. But that wasn't me. God made me like this for a reason. The true Joshua is a son of God, who walks and talks a little effeminate, but is in charge of himself. We are made to act, not to be acted upon. That is the true me. If we trust in God, He will lead us in the ways of truth and righteousness.

Mark Packer

"Life is about not knowing, taking the moment and making the best of it without knowing what's going to happen next. Delicious ambiguity."
– Gilda Radner

I was born in Ogden, Utah in 1952, into a very strong Mormon family. A few months later we moved to Smithfield where I grew up. The Church was the centerpiece of my life. I knew I wanted to follow the path I had been taught: to be a good boy, to go on a mission when I was 19, then come home and not wait too long before getting married in the temple and having kids.

When I was deacon, twelve or thirteen years old, I remember sitting on the front row of the chapel, and my leg was touching another deacon's leg. It was like electricity, or like a fire was in me! I didn't know what it was, but it was so strong. I didn't put any meaning to it because I hadn't heard the words *homosexual* or *gay*, or if I had heard the words before, I didn't understand what it all meant.

I remember guys standing around talking about girls and their experiences with them, and the thing that always jumped into my mind was, "Wow, I'm sure glad I don't have temptation like that!" And, "I'm really blessed because I've never been tempted to do anything sexual with girls!" And it's true, I was never tempted to do anything sexual with girls.

While in my second year of high school, I went on a band competition trip to San Diego with the school marching band. As we were returning home on the bus, late at night, I ended up having sexual experiences with two of my buddies, two separate incidents within about an hour or so. That was the first time anything like that had happened. Afterward I felt really guilty, but eventually I forgot about it.

Mission and marriage

When I was nineteen I went on a mission to Japan. I remember a particular Japanese guy that we were teaching; he was about my age, and I felt really good about being friends with him. I liked teaching him the gospel and being in the same room with him. I didn't put any meaning to it, but I was very attracted to him.

A few years after returning home from my mission, people started asking questions like, "Are you dating?" or "Do you have a girlfriend?" I just knew I wasn't interested in getting married yet. While attending Brigham Young University I met my future wife "Angela" through a student family home evening group. Angela and I shared many interests: musicals, ballet, theater, etc. I grew to like her a lot, and we hung out together as friends, dating off and on for three years.

I knew Angela was very interested in moving our relationship forward. But although I enjoyed hanging out with her, I didn't feel any strong feelings, and I didn't want to lead her on. We actually "broke up" twice. But eventually, I caved in to the pressure, not just from her, but from all around me, and finally asked her to marry me. In 1977 we were married in the Salt Lake Temple. Looking back, I realize that when I married her I didn't love her, but I liked her a lot. She was a really good friend.

Wow, that's weird

Later, while living in Washington, D.C., we met a new guy in my ward. The first time I saw him I just thought, "Oh, I'd like to meet this guy, and I'd like to be friends with him." So that is what happened; and for a number of months my wife and I hung out with him. We would go to movies, or out to eat, which I really loved doing because I really liked him. He was a great friend! I had no idea that I was really attracted to him!

This kind of thing continued to happen through the years. In the Fall of 1988 while singing in a rehearsal with the Southern California Mormon Choir, I remember looking across the way at the organist and realizing I wanted to be his friend! After the rehearsal, I walked up to him, shook his hand, and introduced myself. His name was Weston.

The following spring I saw Weston again, as the choir was doing a recording at the St. James Catholic Church, immediately behind the Los Angeles Temple. I could see his face as he played the organ while we sang. I remember that I kept looking at him, and he at me; and then he winked at me. The first thought that came into my mind was, "Guys don't wink at other guys!" But I didn't feel any negative feelings; I just thought, "Wow, that's weird, he keeps winking at me!"

I was hiding

At some point I gave Weston my phone number. Soon afterward, he called me and we talked for about two hours. We talked about our backgrounds, our lives, and everything. A few weeks later I received a letter in the mail from Weston. It was handwritten, about twelve pages, on regular stationary. About five or six pages into it he said something like, "You're the type of person I would like to spend eternity with." I read through the whole letter, and then I took it to Angela and said, "What do you think this means?" She read all the way up to that point, then stopped. She couldn't read any more.

I said to her, "Do you think he might be gay?" She just looked at me like I had been dropped on my head. It didn't make any sense to me because from what I knew about homosexuals, about gays, he was not like them at all. I was just thinking, "Wow that's weird!" As far as I knew I had never actually met a gay person before that. I didn't answer the letter. I wanted to answer because he was highly complimentary to me, but I just didn't know what to say.

Shortly thereafter, the Southern California Mormon Choir had its annual party celebrating its founding. We met in a stake center in the Los Angeles area, and Angela was with me. Well, Weston and I kept looking at each other across the hall during the dinner, and I remember Angela saying a couple times, "Mark! Stop! Stop that! Stop looking at him!"

After dinner and a short program, we all went into the chapel. A month earlier we had joined the Mormon Tabernacle Choir in their weekly program, "Music and the Spoken Word", broadcast worldwide via radio and television, and now they were playing the recording of that broadcast. We sat on a row that was packed with people, my wife on my left and Weston on my right. While we were watching the broadcast they turned off the lights, and I ended up holding hands with my wife and with Weston at the same time. I don't remember how that happened. It was a strange experience.

Through the years I grew to love Angela. You can't live fifteen years with somebody being relatively okay with the marriage and not have feelings for them. But I remember when I was holding Weston's hand, there was this amazing feeling, and I had never had feelings like that for Angela. So there I was, holding hands with my wife and with Weston at the same time. I know she didn't see it. I was hiding; I didn't want her to see. None of this was planned, but I did realize I needed to sit down and talk with Weston face to face.

A weight lifted from my shoulders

Weston and I set up a time to meet for lunch just a few days later. At the lunch we set up another meeting — at his place in Manhattan Beach. I shared all this information with Angela. I left work early that Friday afternoon and headed to Weston's. We spent the entire afternoon together, eating at a restaurant and walking and talking along the beach. When we got back to his apartment, we hugged. At that precise moment, all of it finally hit me. The best comparison I can make to this is when I received my testimony of the Book of Mormon. It was like a revelation! There were no words for it; I just remember feeling absolutely incredible. I realized, "I'm gay," and I felt fantastic. I knew from that point forward that my life was going to be completely different. I was thirty-seven years old.

I had this unbelievable feeling of euphoria as I was driving home. It was absolutely incredible, wonderfully incredible! A weight that I had carried my entire life was lifted from my shoulders. I was so happy, so joyous!

I knew that I needed to come out to Angela as soon as possible. I planned to sit down with her on the first night that we got the kids to bed at a decent time. That opportunity came the following Thursday. I told Angela that I needed to talk to her about something, and we sat down on the couch in our living room. I began talking, and after several minutes said, "... And I'm gay." Her response to that was a simple, "Oh." I sat stunned for a few seconds because all she said was, "Oh." I said, "Uhhh, did you hear what I said?" And she said, "Yes." I responded, "I said I'm a homosexual." And she said simply, "I know." I paused again, then I said, "I don't understand. I expected more of a reaction." And she said "Well, I've thought you were gay for a while." And I just said, "What? How long?" She said, "Probably several years." She explained that she hadn't been sure, but pretty well thought I was gay.

Angela is a very observant and very sensitive person. She told me later that during the summers, years before I met Weston, she had observed when we were driving down the street, my head would always turn as we were passing guys with their shirts off. I didn't even realize I was doing this, or that it was anything unusual! But she noticed, and apparently she started to figure things out. So, I asked her, "Well, if you knew I was gay, or figured I was gay, why didn't you say something to me?" I'll never forget her response. She just looked at me, gave me a little smile, reached over and grabbed one of my hands between both of hers and said, "Now Mark, if I had approached you several years ago and said that I think you're gay, how would you have responded?" I said, "Oh. Okay." I didn't have to answer her, and she didn't need to have me answer, because we both knew how I would have responded: even a year and a half earlier I would have denied it, and I would have honestly denied it. That's how naive I was.

We can make it work

My wife was very supportive, and for the next two months, our relationship was better than it had ever been during our entire marriage. The only way I've been able to explain this is that I was finally able to be me. And, on the Kinsey Scale, obviously I'm not a six (exclusively homosexual); I'm probably about a four-and-a-half (predominantly homosexual, but a little more than incidentally heterosexual). And so for the next several months I was as happy as I've ever been in my entire life.

Looking back I realize that what I experienced in my marriage up to that point was an okay life, but I was not really happy. It wasn't that I was horribly unhappy or anything, but I was never really happy. I was always troubled. It was not right, and I didn't know why. But now, every day, it was great to get up and live the day. It was like my life had begun anew. It was a very, very happy time.

Not too long after I came out to Angela, we started talking about our marriage. We decided that we were going to make our marriage work, even though I was gay.

I was meeting with Weston regularly at this point. Once or twice a week after work, I would drive down to the Episcopal church where Weston was rebuilding the organ, and I would talk with him, sometimes for twenty minutes, sometimes for three hours. What Weston did was make me look inside and start learning about myself, because I had completely suppressed myself for 37 years. So we would talk for hours at a time, and every time I went to leave, we would hug. I remember he always walked me to my car, and I didn't want to go! But I knew I had to go home; I had a wife and kids.

I was so confused

In the meantime Angela and I were getting along well. I was still joyful and happy, and we were going to make our marriage work. As time went on, I kept wanting to visit Weston more, and talk with him longer. Finally, after one of our talks, as I was preparing to leave, we kissed. The first thought that jumped into my head was, "Wow! His lips are so soft!" It felt so good to kiss him. I told Angela about it, and I didn't feel guilty, because it wasn't sexual — it was just a kiss.

Eventually Weston invited me to come down to his place after work and stay overnight. I really wanted to do that. When I told Angela about it, she immediately became frightened. I knew what it could possibly mean, but I kept that out of my mind. All I was doing was going down to stay overnight with Weston. Period! But Weston, as the date got closer, kept pressing me as to what I wanted. He was asking, did I want more physical contact, did I want sexual contact? I couldn't deal with it, and I wouldn't answer him. Weston was always very patient with me, but this was the closest I'd ever seen him to running out of patience. He thought I was playing games with him. I said, "I'm not playing games, but I can't answer your question, because I don't know!"

Eventually the day arrived, the last Friday in January of 1990. After work I drove down, and boy was I excited! We had something to eat and then walked along the beach. The moon was out. It was really beautiful on the water. We went back to his place and watched "Maurice", the first gay-themed movie I'd ever seen. And then Weston started to become romantic with me, and I resisted. I liked it, but I just couldn't deal with it emotionally. He finally said,

"Listen, you sleep out here and I'll sleep in the bed," and I said, "No, I want to sleep with you." I didn't know what to do.

Finally, we went into his bedroom and went to sleep. We cuddled together as we slept. Early in the morning I woke up, and that's when things started to happen. I remember feeling a euphoria that I had never felt with my wife. And there were two things happening in my head simultaneously. The first was, "Oh wow! I've never felt like this ever before in my life." And the second was, "Oh my gosh Mark, you were married in the temple. You have four children. You have a position in the ward. What in the blazes are you doing?" We finally got up around noon and went out and got some milk for cereal, had breakfast, talked for a while, and then I went home.

We need help

When I walked in the door that evening my wife was at the kitchen sink. She turned her head, took one look at my face, and knew immediately. There were no words exchanged, but she knew. When the kids were in bed that night, I told her what had happened. The next day, I met with the bishop and confessed to him. When I told him what had happened, he had no idea what to do; he looked like a deer in headlights. He asked, "Can I tell the stake president?" I said, "Sure."

Later that day, I called my sister and said, "We need help." She flew down and spent about three days with us. She was amazing! She held us together. While I was at work she would spend the day with Angela, talking with her while helping with the housework.

Over the next few weeks the bishop and I met several times, and at one point he wanted to know who it was that I had the sexual contact with. I wouldn't tell him. I went home and talked to Angela; she couldn't believe that the bishop wanted his name. She thought it was wrong that he would ask, and she was very supportive of me. When I went back to talk with the bishop again he said, "If you give me his name, we'll just put you on probation." But I would not give him Weston's name.

In March of 1990 a bishop's court convened and I was disfellowshipped. They gave me a list of things to do in order to be refellowshipped. I met periodically with the bishop throughout the year. That fall I went with Weston to my first Affirmation meeting, an organization for gay and lesbian Mormons. There were about thirty people in attendance. I was scared to go, but I also thought it was really cool!

What are you doing?

Angela and I were still going to make our marriage work. I hadn't had any further sexual contact with guys, not with Weston, not with anybody. As time went on, I actually took Angela with me to a couple of Affirmation meetings. But after about a year, I started having experiences with other guys, here and there. Every couple of months or so something would happen. This went on for about a year, and I told Angela every single time. And it just killed me to tell her, because it hurt her. But I couldn't lie to her, I couldn't hold back from her. Eventually some of my friends said, "What are you doing? All you're doing is hurting your wife. Why are you telling her these things?" So I stopped telling her.

In January of 1992, I went to the first Gamofite retreat, a new organization for gay Mormon fathers. There I met Ernie. We began to spend a lot of time together. I would visit him once or twice a week after work. Angela knew that Ernie and I hung out a lot together. Eventually, I began to fall in love with him. Our friendship turned sexual around April of 1992. That summer I took Angela and the kids down to Ernie's place and met his three kids. We all swam together in the pool at his apartment complex. At the time, Angela didn't know about the sexual encounters, but eventually she asked me and I told her. Once that happened I stopped seeing Ernie completely.

Gradually, I came to realize that our marriage wasn't going to survive. We did a lot of talking, and Angela realized what was happening. We used to drive out to a beach by Santa Barbara and would walk and talk for hours. The last time, in September of 1992, as we were walking along the beach, she turned to me and said, "We're not going to make it, are we?" I looked at her and said, "No, we're not." And that was the beginning of the end. I found out later that she had thought that I was going to say, "Oh no, we can make it, we can make this work." She was actually surprised when I agreed with her.

In November, Angela and I separated. I moved her and the kids up to Utah, to an apartment we had found. At the time I had a job assignment in Kansas City, so I flew from Salt Lake City to Kansas City, which marked the beginning of our official separation.

Shortly thereafter, I contacted Ernie. Eventually, we decided to settle down. Our relationship started off rocky for a number of reasons; the main one was that politically he was very liberal, while I was very conservative. And we saw the Church differently: he had stopped going to church entirely, while I was still active. But we really loved each other, and as time went on, we grew much closer. It was especially great being with Ernie in public and social situations; we enjoyed being physically close while mixing with friends and other people. We just liked being together! In 2005, I quit my job (after 27 years with the same employer), and we decided to move to Utah. Our relationship ended within weeks following the move, after 13 years. But we had spent many wonderful years together.

What a life it has been!

Five years have passed and I now know that if Ernie and I had stayed together, I would not have progressed to the point where I am spiritually. I have a strong testimony of the gospel of Jesus Christ. At that time I was very comfortable in my relationship with Ernie, and I didn't really feel the need to have a strong spiritual connection with my Father in Heaven, or with the Savior.

I had an amazing dream in August of 2008 that completely changed my life and my relationship with the Savior. I learned of His infinite and unconditional love for me. I continue to have my ups and downs with the Church, because of disagreements with Church policy in especially one area, but I have no issues with the gospel of Jesus Christ or my Savior. Although excommunicated in 1999, I have faithfully attended church through the years. I would like to continue to attend church regularly, but since I "came out" in testimony meeting on November 7, 2010, the reaction of my local leaders has made attending church very difficult for me.

I really worry about the youth of the Church, boys and girls who go into the bishop's office and say, "I think I'm gay." Many bishops are telling them that they can suppress it to the point where they can get married to someone of the opposite gender. Well, it doesn't necessarily work that way, and it does a lot of damage to promise kids these things. This must change. It is something that deeply concerns me.

In the future, I would like to find a man that will love me and that I can love, and I'd like to be married. That may not happen in Utah, but I don't know what the future holds. I do know that my desire is to be in a long-term, loving relationship.

During the three years between the time I came out to Angela and when we separated, I used to drive to work, and I would pray and cry nearly the entire drive because I didn't know what to do. As awful as some of those times were, which I'm very happy are behind me, I'm not sure I would change anything. Now this may sound strange, because if I had figured out I was gay before I got married, then I wouldn't have had to worry about a separation or any of the horrible feelings that went along with it. But here's the kicker: I wouldn't have four children that I love with all of my heart, and four grandchildren as well. I don't know why my life went this way, but the Lord allowed me to get married and have children. Although the separation and divorce was the worst experience of my life, I wouldn't change anything, especially because of my kids and grandkids! What a life it has been! I don't know what will come next, but I'm sure it will be wonderful and good!

Amy Booth

"Look around you ... the people to your left and to your right — everyone has a story. We all have value. We all have something important to share. And you never know who you're sitting next to."
– Major Nicole Malachowski,
  United States Air Force

In 1983, I was born in Murray, Utah, a suburb of Salt Lake City. I am the oldest of three girls. Growing up, the Church was everything; it was a part of every aspect of our lives. I held callings in the Beehive, Mia Maid, and Laurel presidencies, and I earned my Young Woman Medallion. I attended the temple and did baptisms and confirmations for the dead. I was enrolled in seminary and graduated with a four-year seminary certificate. I received my patriarchal blessing when I was a senior in high school.

At church, I listened to lesson after lesson about the Spirit and what it should feel like, and I felt like a failure because I didn't feel it. I would look at the girls my age, and I knew that I was different from them. I didn't like the same things. I wasn't interested in shopping. I didn't want to wear the styles that were in. And most obviously, I wasn't interested in boys. My sister covered her walls with posters of Jonathan Taylor Thomas and Andrew Keegan. Mine had posters of John Stockton and the BYU football team. I remember thinking sometimes that it would have been so much easier if I was a boy. I liked basketball, football, climbing trees, and wearing hats, T-shirts, jeans, and sneakers.

As I became an adolescent, the feeling of being different created walls around me. I couldn't articulate it, but I felt like there was something wrong with me which no one in my life could relate to. I began cutting myself at the age of fourteen; it was a way of releasing the emotions I was dealing with.

Right about the same time, there was suddenly a rumor going around my junior high about me. I was horrified. I still have no idea how it got started or why. The rumor was that I was a lesbian.

I had to hear it from my sister, who was even more horrified than I was. As my sister, she was embarrassed because of what the other kids were saying. And though it deeply hurt me, I didn't know what to do about the situation. I knew that lesbians were girls who liked other girls the way you are supposed to like boys. I also knew that it was very bad to be one. I wasn't trying to be a bad person. I didn't consider myself to be sinful, like I was told lesbians were. I didn't want to be called by that name. But having no idea why anyone would say it also meant that I had no idea how to change it.

For a few weeks, people gave me awkward stares or avoided me. I spent a lot of time alone or with my CD player. Like most rumors, it fizzled out after a few weeks, and eventually junior high was over.

It couldn't be true

In the years I attended high school, I hung out with the boys, because we shared similar interests. I didn't worry about who was cuter and which one should be my boyfriend. It wasn't on my mind. I didn't consciously experience an attraction to girls, but I knew that I wasn't attracted to guys. Guys were my friends and I didn't see them as more than that. But I did have a boyfriend during my senior year of high school. He was a year younger than me. When he asked me to be his girlfriend, I didn't want to tell him no. We got along really well and became closer. I didn't mind cuddling with him, or even kissing him.

After high school, I enrolled in Westminster College in Salt Lake City. It was a small campus with more diversity than I had ever known. In my second semester, I took a philosophy class. I remember a discussion we had one day about gay marriage. There were differing opinions on the subject. I remember sitting in my car in the parking garage after class that day. I couldn't believe that I had just sat through that discussion. I had never listened to a conversation like that *ever*. That was the first time I thought I might be gay and wondered if that might be what was wrong with me. But I immediately shut down the thought. It couldn't be possible. It was a terrifying thought, and I put it out of my mind. I remembered how I was treated in junior high when that rumor was circulating. It couldn't be true. I wouldn't let it be.

This wasn't how it was supposed to be

I still vividly remember the moment when I met "Derek". For his job he had been going door-to-door, and my dad had been talking with him at the front of our house. The sun was beating down, I saw him, and I had the impression that he would be my husband. I knew hardly anything about him, but I knew that I would marry him. It was a strange feeling, but in a way it comforted me. Marriage is what I had been taught to aim for. It was wonderful and here it was, on my doorstep, like it came to find me. Derek and I dated for six months before we got engaged, and were engaged for five months before getting married in the Salt Lake Temple in February 2004. I was twenty-one years old.

Marriage was a huge eye-opener for me as far as the intimate details go. My whole life, I had been taught how important it was to avoid sex until marriage, because it was sacred and special and not to be taken lightly. Then I got married and magically all the restraints were lifted. It's supposed to be the greatest thing in the world. Or at least, that's what I had been told. Not for me. My mind didn't shift that easily. I assumed that my way of thinking was the problem and that it would get better with time. It would take time to adjust, of course. This was a new experience. Understandable.

But it didn't get better. Instead, it became worse. I honestly can't remember a time where it wouldn't make me cry. It felt very wrong and I dreaded it with every fiber of my being. This wasn't how it was supposed to be. Derek seemed to enjoy it as best he could, though I knew he was disappointed when my reaction was not the same as his. What was wrong with me then? Why didn't I enjoy it? I didn't have the answer, and time was not helping. I felt trapped. I would volunteer to stay late at work in the hopes that my husband would be asleep when I got home.

I just wanted to be near her

When we moved into our first apartment, Derek was eager to meet the people in our new ward. Shortly after we moved in, we were given a calling in the nursery. But I struggled with being at church. I didn't feel warm fuzzy feelings. It was a weekly reminder to me that I was a failure. Somehow, that thought had gotten twisted into believing that God didn't love or care about me. I was hurting myself on purpose, and for that, I believed that God hated me.

Although we were both students when we met, we now couldn't afford for both of us to continue in school. So I took it upon myself to find a job. I was hired at a restaurant and worked there during the evening. I was also working as a dental assistant during the day. The long hours made for a good excuse some nights when I just wanted to go to bed and not worry about fending off the unwanted advances of poor Derek.

At work I met "Miranda". We became friends rather quickly. I suspect it's because we had a similar sense of humor. She was a Jehovah's Witness. For some reason, the more we got to know each other, the more she decided that she was going to save me. This worked out for us, because I wanted to be saved. She knew that I wasn't happy, she knew that I was hurting myself, and she knew that I doubted that God could love me. She set out to change that. We met once a week with another member of her congregation to study the Bible. She invited me to worship with her on the occasional Sunday. And we grew closer.

Emotionally, I was more connected with her than I was with my husband. I would miss her terribly when we weren't together. I ached to be with her. There were nights when I was at home, watching Derek play video games or watching a movie with him, and I couldn't keep my mind from wondering what Miranda was doing, where she was, who she was with. I wished we were together. When I was thinking of her, I just wanted to be near her. I never thought about our relationship in a physical way. We were just really good friends and when I was with her, something in me changed. I could see happiness in life. I could feel happiness. We laughed a lot. She helped me try to quit cutting. She held me when I would cry. I genuinely felt like she wanted to help my life be more enjoyable. And it was, when I was with her.

Nothing ever happened between us, but I was so attached to her, and I couldn't imagine what my life would be like if she wasn't a part of it.

I needed to do something drastic

At some point, Derek and I decided that we should move closer to work and school. We looked for cheaper living arrangements and found a basement apartment in Kaysville. At this point, I had decided that it would be better for me not to attend church. I gladly volunteered to work on Sundays. Derek didn't like going to church alone, but he faithfully went every week.

My mental health was also rapidly deteriorating. The cutting was accelerating, despite my attempts to stop. Derek didn't know what to do. Neither did I. One night, unhappy and in despair, I took a large handful of migraine medication. It was a long night and I was very sick. Once the effects wore off, I knew that I needed to do something drastic. So in August of 2006, with Miranda by my side and without my husband's knowledge, I checked myself into the psychiatric ward of a nearby hospital.

I called Derek the next morning to let him know where I was. I tried to explain why I was there, why I needed to be there. He wasn't very happy. But I knew that neither of us had been happy for some time.

That was probably the last straw. When I was released and back at home, I was hopeful. I told Derek that there were things we could do to manage my diagnosis and that it might take time, but things could get better. He didn't share my outlook. He thought it would be better to talk to the bishop about what was going on. So we did.

The bishop recommended that we see a marriage counselor. He gave us the name of someone who was a member of the Church and would work with us. Derek called the next morning to schedule an appointment. At the very first session, when the therapist asked us if we thought we could make it work, Derek said he didn't think so. I knew that my marriage was basically over.

We separated shortly after that. I came home one day to find a note from Derek on the stairs, saying that he had talked it over with the bishop, family, and friends and decided it was best if we divorced.

I tormented myself with questions

I felt as if I had failed yet again. Miranda helped me through a lot of the really difficult moments. I threw myself into work. I moved back home and tried to move on. But I placed the blame squarely on my shoulders. I vowed that I would never get married again. My mom cringed when I would say it, but it was a very easy decision to make. I honestly did not want to get married for a second time. What if I failed again? What if I had the same reaction when it came to intimate moments? What if it was worse than before? There were too many uncertainties, and I refused to take that risk. It was a decision that brought me a lot of peace though, knowing that I wouldn't have to go through it again. I knew I could be happy by myself. I knew that I could find the life I wanted to live.

And I did. I got an apartment with one of my friends from high school. I continued to work at the restaurant and received promotions. I still struggled in some areas, but I made it work. I said goodbye to Derek. He was remarried six months after our divorce was finalized.

For a long time, I tormented myself with questions. I wondered why I was supposed to marry him if it wasn't going to work. I kept remembering the way his eyes looked as we knelt across the altar from each other. But I also recognized that this chapter of my life was over. I knew that it wasn't doing any good to dwell on it.

Miranda worked at the restaurant for about another year. Then she got a different job. It was very difficult for me to accept that I wasn't going to be seeing her as much. I was very attached to her. She had been such a constant support in my life and I wasn't sure how to make it work without that.

I tried to find answers

After several years, I finally found a therapist and a program that worked. I worked diligently to incorporate the program known as Dialectical Behavior Therapy into my life. I learned essential emotional skills that helped me cope better with my daily life. It was a difficult process but also a fantastic experience. I was even able to end my worst habit. After eleven years, I gave up cutting for good.

But there was still something nagging at me. I could feel it bubbling up from the depths of where I buried it so long ago. I knew that it was moving. I knew that it was rising. Gradually, the thought from years ago began resurfacing, "Am I gay?" If that was the conclusion, then there were so many things in my life that would finally make sense. But more than anything, I didn't want it to be true. I knew that being gay would cost me everything. I thought there was no way my family would ever accept me or love me again if they thought I was gay.

In November of 2008, I went on a cruise with my family. I remember being up on the top deck one sunny afternoon early in the seven-day trip. There weren't a lot of people around, but there was a woman in a bikini, all stretched out on a deck chair for a good dose of sunbathing. I remember consciously thinking that she was beautiful. For a few moments, I just stared, awestruck and fascinated. And then I realized what I was doing. Shame overpowered me and I left the area for another deck. But for the rest of the cruise, that experience haunted me. I couldn't get it out of my head and I couldn't understand why.

There were a lot of sleepless nights on that cruise. I tossed and turned, worried, wrestled with my thoughts, prayed for forgiveness and a miracle. "Please God, don't let me be gay ... but what if I'm gay?" Over and over and over.

I tortured myself in agonizing silence for the next couple months. I felt like such a terrible person. I was LDS, so I couldn't be gay. But I was realizing that I was gay, so I couldn't be LDS anymore. It was a circular argument replaying in my head. I tried to find answers. I prayed harder and more often than I had ever prayed in my life. But I couldn't feel peace and I wasn't comforted.

A breath of fresh air

In February, after much reassurance and encouragement that whatever was eating at me couldn't possibly be as bad as it seemed in my head, I tearfully confessed to my therapist that I thought I was gay. I apologized over and over for what I was feeling. I had tried to be good. I had tried to live the life I was supposed to, tried to be a wife, but I couldn't do it. I couldn't change what I was feeling and I couldn't run from it anymore.

I didn't know what would happen, but her reaction was and continues to be an absolute beacon of hope to me. She didn't think I was terrible, and she didn't judge me at all. She was amazing in helping me come out and be myself. She taught me how to stop hating myself for being gay.

I was terrified to tell anyone else, but it ate at me. I was quickly realizing that being gay was a part of who I was. It was stifling to keep it secret. As much as I didn't want anyone to know, I didn't want to hide it either. I felt incredibly torn. So I took a very cautious approach and told only a few people. They were accepting and were not surprised. It's still funny to me how other people knew before I even consciously knew. These friends helped me through those rocky first months of coming out, and I will be forever grateful to them for that.

With the encouragement of my therapist, I also looked online for some sort of support. Through the Affirmation website, I stumbled upon the blogging world of MoHos ("Mormon Homosexuals"). I read blog after blog and wept with joy that I wasn't the only gay Mormon out there. I started my own blog and slowly became a part of the MoHo blogger community. I reached out to a few bloggers on Facebook. I was able to find people who were in my shoes. I was able to meet some of them and make some really amazing friends. It was such a breath of fresh air to be surrounded by people who knew of the struggle to reconcile personal feelings with deeply held spiritual beliefs, and to be able to let my guard down and be myself with them.

We are best friends

One day, I sat down and had a heart-to-heart conversation with a girl at work. She had started only a few months before, but she was openly gay, and it was still difficult for me to believe that it was really okay to be openly gay. There were still only about four people who knew my secret. But we were able to have a nice talk, and she invited me to come hang out with her and her older brother and his partner, as he was also gay. She wanted me to see that life goes on, whether you're gay or straight. We exchanged numbers and made plans and were able to get together about a week or so later.

The original plan was to be friends. Neither of us had the intention or the expectation to be anything more than that. But the first time we hung out, watching a movie at her brother's place, there was something between us that just clicked. There was a spark there that I had never felt before. We went to a baseball game the next day, and the rest is history. We've been dating since August 2009 and loving every second of it. Once word got out, it was a very easy way to come out without having to actually tell everyone, "Guess what, I'm gay." The people at work have been very accepting. Many of them have known me for years. Some of them have mentioned how nice it is to finally see me happy.

Sometimes it still surprises me how easy it is to be with her. Our relationship is undoubtedly the best thing that has ever happened to me. We are best friends. We laugh all the time. We have so much fun together. It's just how I always imagined being in love would be. We might have fallen in love by accident, but I wouldn't change a thing. And while she's the first girl I've dated, I hope she'll also be the last. We plan on spending the rest of our lives together.

This is only the beginning

For some of my family, my coming out has been difficult. But with time, things are getting better. My mom has been amazing, and I'm so grateful for that. My youngest sister and her husband have been very welcoming to my girlfriend, and that means so much to me. For others, I know that it's difficult for them to accept, but I also know that they're working on it. I am so appreciative of their efforts, because my biggest fear in coming out was the possibility that I would lose my family.

Since coming out, my perspective about the Church has changed, but not drastically. My feelings about being spiritual haven't changed. I know that the gospel of Jesus Christ, as I was taught it, is the basis for my faith. I still consider myself to be LDS, because that is the foundation of my beliefs. But I am no longer an active member. I haven't been to Church since 2007, with the exception of baby blessings for nieces and nephews. I have found that it really is better for me to focus on my spirituality in both an individual and personal manner. What I believe is what I believe. I know that God exists and that His Son, Jesus Christ, is our Savior. I believe they know and love me just as I am. I believe they know where I struggle and where I do well, and I believe that they can see I'm doing the best I can. Someday, I will stand face to face with them. We'll talk about my life and the choices I've made and the consequences, both good and bad, that must follow. But I know they will know the entire story.

My family continues to be very active in the Church, and because of that, I know that the Church will always be a part of my life. I try to be patient and forgiving. I try to hold on to the simple faith that I have, and to the knowledge that God loves all His children, regardless of who they love.

For now, what I know is this: it hasn't been an easy path to walk, but the difficulties have helped me be strong. I have known pain. I have known doubt. I have known fear. But I have found courage. I have found hope. I have found love. We are taught that we have the bitter so we can appreciate the sweet. I know that is true.

My life is moving forward in a direction that I am very happy with. I have gone back to school and am working towards a career with aviation, one of my first loves. My girlfriend and I have plans to one day have a home, and a dog, and a wonderful life together. I have gained the confidence to be proud of who I am. I'm not loud about it, but it is such an extraordinary feeling to be who you are in spite of what other people choose to say. I have already gained so much by untying the knots I bound myself with, and giving myself permission to be me. I don't think I could have done it without the struggles. There were times where I wanted to give up. There were times when I tried to end my life. And I am so glad that I didn't. I would have missed so many beautiful experiences with amazing people. In many ways, this is only the beginning of my story.

Jim Wilt

"And see that ye have faith, hope, and charity, and then ye will always abound in good works."
– Alma 7:24

I was born in 1962 in Altoona, Pennsylvania. I was raised Catholic and went to Catholic schools until I was 14. I thought maybe I wanted to grow up and be a priest. I was aware of being attracted to those of the same gender at a very early age. It was a very natural feeling, and I was not conflicted about it. It was just a part of who I was. In grade school, I was very close to other boys emotionally, and I knew there was an attraction beyond friendship.

In high school I became involved with a male friend, and this lasted from age 14 to 19. It was a very intense relationship. Around others, we acted like we were just close friends, but in private it was very sexual. However, it was not romantic, and it was incomplete to me in that respect.

We weren't going to forget each other

One night in January 1982, I went to a party at a friend's house, and I met a young man named Michael Oleg Gorboff. He was of

Russian descent and had lived most of his life in Bordeaux, France. We talked for several hours; it was effortless, engaging, and euphoric. I made a bold move and invited him to my place for strawberries and champagne. He responded, "Why would I want strawberries and champagne?" Without hesitation, I responded confidently, "My invitation for strawberries and champagne is a pretext for sex with you." He said, "We can just stay here and have sex." It was said in a reassuring way, and I knew that we weren't going to forget about each other, that it wasn't just going to be a one-night stand.

We did spend the night together. It was a confirmation of a yet unspoken commitment. A few months later, I was buying food and wine at an Epicurean shop where his sisters worked; by coincidence he was there, and he helped me home with my purchases. I offered him a glass of wine. He objected in a very polite way that I should not open the bottle on his account, but I wasted no time in uncorking it, explaining that it was for guests. We relaxed and talked for about 45 minutes. As he was leaving we shared a kiss, the intensity of which was felt from head to toe; it was the most beautiful kiss I can remember with anyone.

At this time, I lived in Dallas, Texas and worked for Texas Instruments. Later that year I moved to Austin. During this period Michael and I would talk on the phone but only occasionally get together.

It did not make me love him less

In 1988 I returned to Dallas. I called Michael, and he invited me to come over. We spent the evening together, and he told me that he had HIV. I knew that his time might be limited, but it did not make me love him less. I didn't really want to think about how much time we might have together. I just wanted to live in the moment.

I moved in with Michael, and we grew very comfortable together sharing a home. We appreciated life's beauty and lived well; we were surrounded by period French and English furniture, ate very well, and really felt at ease with each other in a well-rounded way.

HIV was pretty rampant in the gay community (as it still is), and it was a common idea that it was just a hindrance to get tested; people figured that as soon as someone was diagnosed they wouldn't live much longer anyway. There was little or no treatment available. There was a lot of fear but also a lot of denial — because if we're in denial, then we don't have to acknowledge the fear.

Michael accepted and understood my insistence on using protection (which greatly reduces but does not entirely eliminate the risk of infection). However, there was one time when he slipped off his condom, and I knew it but still continued. After that, I just decided not to use protection from then on. We practiced "coitus interruptus", which we ignorantly thought would keep us safe. They say, "Ignorance is bliss," but it really isn't.

We were still much in love

There were hard parts of our relationship. Michael had a drinking problem, and he would often accuse me of being unfaithful to him. It may have had to do with a fear of abandonment that he developed as a teenager. As a young man, he had a lover who had told him that he wanted to "share an open relationship with another man." Michael understood this to mean being able to be completely honest with each other, unconditionally. But what he meant by "open relationship" was that they could sleep around whenever they wanted; and that was troublesome to Michael when he found out.

In spite of these issues, it was so wonderful being with Michael. When there were family get-togethers, my mother would always hug him and say, "I love you. You're my son too." That was really nice.

But at the beginning of 1990, after a particularly heated argument fueled by alcohol, I walked away from our home with only the shirt on my back. Within two weeks I was working at a hotel and living independently. Michael then moved in with his sister. Although we were not far from each other and were still much in love, it was essential that we live separately.

"It doesn't hurt anymore"

At the beginning of 1992, Michael's health began to deteriorate rapidly. He was hospitalized with serosis of the liver, and I visited him almost daily. He had IVs in his arms, and when I would reach out and put my hand on his arm, this could cause him discomfort. We really began to feel unconditional love, knowing that HIV and alcoholism could not deprive us of appreciating the precious time we had together. I saw him the week of Thanksgiving, and it was wonderful to be in each other's presence. On Wednesday, I arrived at work an hour earlier than scheduled. Upon walking into the office the phone rang. It was Michael; he said he called to tell me that he loved me. I told him that I loved him. That was the last time we spoke.

The next day, Thanksgiving day, I tried to call him, but he was napping, and his sister and I decided not to disturb him. That night I went to sleep, and the next morning before daylight I had a dream which was more like a vision. I was being led into a room that was darkened, but beyond that was a room that was very bright. Upon entering, I saw Michael, and he was being cleansed in a way that was visible to me. I reached out to touch his arm, but I pulled back. I didn't want to hurt him. He said to me, "It's okay now. It doesn't hurt anymore." Within a split second, I woke up and called his sister. She said to me, "Jim, we have been trying to get a hold of you. Michael just died." I dropped the phone in a moment of shock, but also a moment of clarity.

Shortly after his death, his sister welcomed me into her home, and I stayed there for about a week. I did Michael's laundry, folded it, put it away in his room, and thought, "Why am I doing this? He's dead. He doesn't need his laundry put away."

I let the family know that wherever they decided to have the funeral service, whether it was in Texas or in Alabama where his parents lived, I would be there. There were a few options being discussed, but everyone was still grieving and didn't know what to do, and eventually his parents made the final decision to have him cremated and have his ashes sent to them in Alabama. There wasn't a funeral, and of course Michael and I were not legally married, so I felt like I didn't really have a right to say what should happen. It was difficult to find closure, but the thing that made it easier was that he had come to me in a vision and told me he was okay, and I believed him. It was a pivotal experience; it was where I first really believed there is something after this life.

I asked a lot of questions

The summer before Michael's death, he strongly urged me to be tested for HIV. I agreed and was not surprised to find out the results were positive. At that point, I didn't plan for any future, because I thought there wouldn't be much time left.

A few months later, I was out at a gay club, and a really good-looking guy "Brian" came up to me. He told me that he was LDS and had just returned home from serving his mission. His family had disowned him and wouldn't have anything to do with him; he hadn't talked with them since he told them he was gay. I asked him a lot of questions about the Church, and he got really quiet.

Our relationship lasted several months and was pretty intense. I was upfront with Brian about my HIV status, and we were careful to use protection. We would stay at each other's house, and I would cook for him. I would spend the night and then leave in the morning for work. It was a normal relationship. But I wanted to know more about his church. Thinking back on it now, I didn't realize how much pain it was causing when I would ask him those questions.

It was very easy for me to believe

I started HIV treatment at a public clinic in 1992, but over the years, I began experiencing serious bouts of chronic fatigue. By 1997 I had deteriorated to the point where I couldn't work. I went and applied for Social Security disability. I didn't really have much hope that there would be much of a future for me.

In 1998, I started looking around to find better treatment options. During that time, I was taking as many as twelve different medications per day at different times of day. In 2006, after qualifying for Medicare I started treatment at a private practice. I started growing stronger, and it was encouraging; that's when I realized that there was a possibility of a future.

In the spring of 2007, I came in contact with a pair of missionaries. They asked if it would be okay to have them in my home to read the scriptures, and I readily agreed. The appointments and lessons were fascinating. They showed me the 20-minute film "The Restoration", and it was very easy for me to believe in Joseph Smith's visions. A lot of that had to do with my Catholic upbringing, because in Catholicism, visions and miracles are very much a part of the faith. But I wasn't ready to be baptized.

Shortly after that, I moved to Denton, Texas. On a beautiful day, January 26, 2008, while out biking I passed the missionaries and asked them, "How's it going?" When I got back to my apartment, I realized it was foolish of me not to have stopped and talked with them. So I went out to try to find them. I saw them across the street, called out, and we approached each other and set up an appointment for two days later.

When I went to church, everything made sense. But it was more than just a Sunday thing. It was a lifestyle that was all-encompassing! I liked the fact that when it came to spiritual matters, there was an answer to everything. I prayed about if the Book of Mormon is true, and there was a very high level of clarity as I realized that it was. It's interesting, because my conversion came at a point where I had a positive outlook on the future, rather than coming years earlier when I thought the end of my life was near. On March 16, 2008, I was baptized.

I felt an extremely empty feeling

Just after being confirmed a member, I was called as ward single adult representative. It wasn't a secret that I was gay, but unless it was pertinent, I never really talked about it. The bishop knew, but we had never addressed it.

A few weeks after the October 2010 General Conference, I was in elders quorum, and the meeting started by the instructor reading a hypothetical letter by a young man telling his parents, "If you loved me, you would respect me and my partner as you do your married children." He said, "You know what they mean by 'partner'." That's when my ears perked up, and I said, "Well let's say, for example, that the young man and his 'partner' are living together, obeying the law of chastity, and are there for each other to provide emotional support." Members of the quorum said that it wouldn't matter, that they shouldn't be together under the same roof. It seemed completely un-Christlike to me; it basically left a gay man in the Church zero options of ever having a roommate of any kind.

I got up and calmly walked out of the meeting. I live only three blocks from the stake center, so I rode my bike home. When I walked in, I felt an extremely empty feeling. My ward family was the only reliable support I had had in the last few years, and I had just walked away from them. So I sent the executive secretary a text message and an email, saying I needed to sit down and talk with the bishop ASAP. Within half an hour, I heard back from him, and he said, "Can you be back at the stake center in 15 minutes?" I said, "Absolutely." I brought some articles from the Ensign as well as Carol Lynn Pearson's book *No More Goodbyes* and some materials from the Affirmation website. It was as if I was getting ready for some sort of fight (which didn't need to happen).

The bishop asked me what had happened, and I told him about the elders quorum meeting. He said — and this is directly out the bishop's mouth, "So, it sounds like they were gay-bashing?" And I'm thinking, "What?" I said, "Yes, bishop, the Spirit was not there." He said that I had done the right thing.

We had a comfortable discussion, and he told me he was counseling a couple other people in the ward who had come out to him as being gay. He was really happy that I came forward. He has come up to me in sacrament meeting and put his arm around my shoulder and thanked me for things I've provided him. Recently at a fireside at his house, as he went around the room introducing people, when he came to me, he said, "That's Jim. He has taught me a lot."

"I have a heterosexual boyfriend"

When I first moved to Denton, I didn't know anyone, but when I would go out and walk the dog, I would often see a guy tossing a ball around with friends; he would greet me, and I would give him a friendly nod. His name was Matthew. It wasn't until after I got baptized that he asked, "How is it that you've been walking by all the time, and we haven't sat down and talked?" After that, we became close. It's basically like having a really great boyfriend, except sex is not an issue. We have different sexual orientations. So I have a boyfriend *and* obey the law of chastity. It seems like a fortuitous loophole.

A lot of people see us together; if we go out to dinner or a movie, we interact like a gay couple. Sometimes he spends the night, and I know a lot of people's minds go straight to what they want to think is going on. Fortunately Matt is really comfortable with himself, and it's easy for us, even if it's hard for other people to understand because it can't be labeled and put in a box. We're still growing into it. Even at first, it was really nice, but over the years it has only grown more comfortable. Sometimes he sends me texts like, "I love you." He's okay with letting his softer side show.

My bishop once expressed concern about my emotional support, knowing that I'm gay. I was pleased to tell him, "That's fine, because funny you should ask — I have a heterosexual boyfriend." My bishop didn't even seem to bat an eye at that, and most people at church who know me best are comfortable with it. They know I have a temple recommend. I think it's what our Church leaders want, for us to be able to find that emotional support. Matt is not LDS, but he was there, and he's still here.

A couple months ago, I was toying with the idea of moving out of state. Matt looked really sad and said, "What? You're going to leave me?" He wasn't joking. So the emotions are not just one-sided, and I realize that my personal decisions are going to have an effect on him too.

I can't predict the future

I have thought a lot about the law of consecration, where we devote everything we have to the Church. One time when I was in the temple, I had a revelation that one of my talents is being gay, and that I should devote that to the Church. I hope that my being open and active in the Church may help it be a safer place for our youth to be open. I want people to know that it is possible for someone to be gay and maintain Church standards and not hide. I'm almost 50 years old now, and I can control my desires and obey the law of chastity, although I do not envy teenage boys and their raging hormones.

I'm still learning to trust my friends, to be more honest about myself and give them a chance to support me. Right now my best friends are other MoHos ("Mormon Homosexuals"). But the thing is, it's not really about me. It's about these teenagers who are coming out to their families and bishops right now, who really need support.

I know people who I respect, who are gay, who have temple recommends but say they would give that up for a committed relationship. I think that is a quandary. If it really came down to it, if I found myself having to choose between being in a committed relationship and holding the priesthood, I might choose the relationship. I'm not setting out to do that; it's just a possibility that I can't deny, being gay. It's like asking someone who's heterosexual, "If you found someone to marry, and you had to choose between that or your Church membership, which would you pick?" Of course, they wouldn't have to choose.

A lot of people seem to think that since treatments have improved, getting HIV is not a big deal: "I can take a pill and I'll be okay." The truth is it's going to be more like 10 pills every day for the rest of your life, they're expensive, there can be serious side effects, and they don't always work; there are drug-resistant strains of HIV. Millions of people still die from AIDS every year. Once you're infected, it creates a lot to worry about for the rest of your life. It's a lot easier to prevent than get treatment, by obeying the law of chastity and waiting until you're absolutely sure that it's the one person you want to be with.

I don't think I'm ever going to be married to a woman. I can't predict the future, but I just can't see that happening. So as far as Church callings, that's going to be pretty limiting, but I would just hope that I can remain strong in my faith and remain an active member.

Alex Wells

"The real voyage of discovery consists not in seeking new landscapes but in having new eyes."
– Marcel Proust

"Mom, I'm tired." I said, sobbing.

"What are you tired of?" my mother questioned.

"I'm tired of lying about every single part of my life."

My mother, being extremely intuitive to everything within the family, replied, "You're gay, aren't you?"

It was from this conversation that my whole world was turned upside down, and I began on a journey for which I will always be grateful. I was always and still am a very obedient member of my family. I always have helped my parents out with anything, have followed their guidance, and have trusted in their leadership. I was raised in the Church of Jesus Christ of Latter-day Saints but was always taught to think for myself and to find my own path. My family encouraged me to make my own decisions and set lofty goals for myself. I believe that my successes are greatly related to their phenomenal parenting and their undying love for me.

Growing up

When I was in the first grade, I remember looking up to the older boys in my Sunday School classes. They were so cool the way they carried themselves, and as I watched them hang out with each other, I longed for the companionship that they shared as friends. The same was true in grade school. Boys hanging out with each other, playing sports together, laughing and sharing some sort of fraternal bond was always so intriguing and attractive to me.

Girls never had cooties, or if they did, I wanted them. I was that boy who would chase girls around the playground, teasing them at any chance I had. Girls were fun, so easy to get along with and so easy to befriend. I did not understand why it was so difficult for me to befriend boys my own age when the girls my age liked me so much.

I began to really figure out what was going on when I turned twelve years old. One of my few boy friends told me how he had a crush on a girl in our Church group. I was her friend but did not have any interest in her, or any girl for that matter. I thought it strange that the feelings he was having for her, I was having toward him. I got a little frustrated when he would bring this girl up, because I thought he would begin wanting to hang out with her instead of me. Was this normal? Should I have a crush on a girl too? I had no clue what was going on in my head except that something was a little off.

Spirituality and self-acceptance

From twelve to fifteen years old I began to realize that I was in fact gay, that I did long for a deeper relationship with other boys and that if I were to continue being comfortable with my family and my friends, I would have to hide it. If anyone were ever to find out, my reputation as being an obedient, faithful, straight boy would be ruined. I had hoped that I was going through some sort of phase and that as time went on, I would have similar feelings to that of my friends.

When I was sixteen years old, I began to focus on my church and God. I would pray often and became very strong in my religion. I thought that maybe this would make my attractions go away. My feelings never changed.

While focusing on God and my religion, however, I never felt remorse or guilt for the attractions I had. I was taught that the attractions were wrong, but never once did I feel like I was a bad person or that God loved me any less. I knew that my church as an organization would never accept my homosexuality, but I was finding myself reconciling my attractions with my relationship with God. I knew I was not alone, was a good person, and as long as I stayed a respectable good person, I wasn't at fault for the attractions I had.

Finding a place

I began meeting with other young gay boys at the University of Utah Union building on Wednesday nights in lieu of young men's mutual group. Here I met boys just like me who were struggling with coming out, staying close with their families, and making friends. It was here that I found refuge and my first real gay friends. While I met with this group, my relationship with my parents began to suffer. I had built up in my mind that once I told my parents about my feelings, they would stop loving me, kick me out of the house, and take everything away from me, as this is what had happened to many of my new-found friends.

I began to be more closed off. I would lie about whom I was going to hang out with, where I was going, and what I was doing. It hurt me to sneak around because this was not like me, but it was the only way I knew how to keep my "gay life" a secret. I was taking control of the time when I thought my parents would stop loving me. I had planned to tell my parents about my sexuality when I moved out of the house. I knew that there would be a right time and a right place to do it.

Coming out

Coming out was the most spiritual time in my life and has brought me closer to God and my family than I ever thought it would. As I sat in my room contemplating the many possible outcomes of coming out to my parents, I was overcome with a feeling that I will never forget. I knew then that that moment was set aside by God for my parents and me to open up and for me to finally begin to accept myself for who I truly was. I knew that I would not be telling my parents that I was gay when I moved out of the house after all. I would be telling my parents that night, that moment.

I was seventeen years old on December 30, 2005. It was nighttime and my parents had just sat down to watch TV. I was in my bedroom and my mom was sitting by the fire when that overwhelming warmth came over me. Some force got me out of bed, up into the family room, and right by my mother. I began to cry. As a desperate attempt to get away from the situation, I told my mom that I needed to clean my room. I rushed down to my room still crying while my mom followed closely behind. I sat on my bed, she sat there next to me, and the conversation unfolded.

After a long conversation with my mom, my dad was next. My mom went upstairs to tell him what I had just told her. It seemed like forever that I was down in my room. I moved to my comfortable chair in the corner under my blanket, sat, and waited until my father would come down and punish me for who I said I was. Finally, my parents both entered my room, and my dad advanced towards me with the sternest look I have ever seen him give. He got right up in my face and at that moment gave me the biggest hug he had ever given me. It was then that I knew that my parents were not going to stop loving me, were not going to take my home and family away, and would in fact be the biggest support system I would ever have in my life.

I began to truly be myself

After a month of non-denominational counseling, I began to open up to my parents, and they began to become my best friends. My mom and I began talking on a regular basis, and my dad and I started doing more activities together. My gay friends that I knew from the University of Utah were able to come over, and on the weekends I was allowed to go out with them until the late hours of the night. The trust that my parents gave me was just what I needed to feel fully accepted in my family circle. My friends were all very accepting, and I seemed to instantly gain respect from my peers toward the end of high school.

Coming out was truly liberating and I began to lose myself within the gay community of Salt Lake City. I began to play into a gay stereotype rather than to truly be myself. I was really cheating myself out of being the best person I could be. Although I seemed to be having fun, I was never really happy or content with what I was doing.

With the help of my amazing parents, I moved out of their house at nineteen years old and continued my education at the University of Utah. I strived from the moment I moved out to make my parents proud and to hold close to the beliefs and teachings they had instilled in me. I realized that being gay was not something that ran my life, but was a miniscule part of my true person. I began to truly be myself, not hiding my sexuality, but incorporating it into my everyday life.

I joined my dad's fraternity at the University of Utah and gained the respect of over 50 boys, both gay and straight. I advanced in the fraternity quickly and earned the respect of my brothers to become treasurer of the chapter. I learned here that my sexuality really had no correlation with what I could accomplish. The acceptance here was unlike anything I had ever experienced, and I realized that I had finally fully accepted myself. Shortly after, I graduated with a bachelor's degree in Urban Planning.

Stay true to yourself

I have a high respect for the religious institution I grew up in, but ultimately I feel at peace with who I am through my personal relationship with God. I have never personally been treated poorly by my church and have never felt a need to retaliate against it. Its doctrine has brought me such peace in my life and for that I am grateful. Self-acceptance is such a difficult journey and requires a lot of patience and selflessness. I feel that it took me a few years to accept myself and it may take others a while to accept me as well. I try to carry myself in a polite and respectable manner every day. I work hard, strive to be kind, and bring a positive light to the people around me. I am so fortunate to be surrounded by such accepting and supportive people.

My adolescence has been such a crazy experience, and I would never trade my experiences for anything. These times can be so hard, and if I can offer any advice to those going through what I have gone through, it would be this: Stay true to who you are and who you were taught to be. It is important to always try to understand and be sensitive to the people around you if you care to be treated the same way. It may actually be harder on them than it is on you. Never put your sexuality in the forefront of your life. Who you are sexually does not define you as a person. It is so important to stay positive and be as happy as you can be. Life is good, and can be so great if you just let it be. Nobody is ever alone; you just have to let people in!

I am here to help and would never turn down the chance to give any friendship or advice. Feel free to email me anytime: adwells314@gmail.com.

Joseph Scoma

"A dreamer is one who can only find his way by moonlight, and his punishment is that he sees the dawn before the rest of the world."
– Oscar Wilde

I've been aware of my orientation since age seven. I was raised by loving parents and was never abused physically, sexually, or emotionally by anyone in or out of the home.

With every ecclesiastic advancement, baptism, Aaronic Priesthood ordination, patriarchal blessing, Melchizedek Priesthood ordination, and my mission, I anticipated attractions for women would emerge. I prayed and fasted for this to happen. Eventually, although I recognized I had no romantic interest in women generally, I hoped to be guided to just one "special woman" with whom I would find happiness.

While attending BYU, for several months I dated a young woman "Kelly" from church. I forced myself to show her affection and physical intimacy but I never felt the slightest twinge of attraction for her despite the fact she was a lovely, accomplished, spiritual young woman. I was in constant emotional distress during this time. Feeling very desperate, I sought help from BYU counselors.

After an initial interview with a supervising therapist I was referred to a graduate student. With great effort I finally verbalized my situation: I was a faithful, worthy priesthood holder who has never been attracted to women and has had strong attractions for men since early childhood. By attraction, I meant the compelling physical and sexual draw that most people feel toward members of the opposite gender. In addition to this desire I also felt a deep emotional, romantic attraction to other men. In every way that a straight man is drawn to the beauty and personality of a woman, I was honestly attracted to other men (and obviously I found some men more attractive than others).

The counselor let me vent for an hour, and then he tentatively offered a suggestion for eliminating these attractions: He asked me whether my orientation might change if I had sex with a woman. I supposed he meant within the bonds of marriage. The idea of marrying someone without feeling any romantic or sexual desire for her in the hope that intercourse might fix me was absurd. I turned the question on him and asked whether sex with a man would alter his orientation in any way. He admitted it wouldn't. I thanked him for his time and left. Professional counseling for "my thorn in the flesh" was futile. This was my mortal cross to bear.

That very evening, after a date with Kelly, I told her about my orientation and assured her that I wanted to remain a faithful member of the Church, raise a righteous family, and be sealed in the temple. We were optimistic at first, but this soon gave way to a torrent of doubt and frustration as my ability to show honest affection for Kelly remained feeble. Though we both tried our best the relationship ended bitterly a few months later.

During all of this, I became friends with Kelly's best friend Gwen. I was open with her about my orientation and over time she admitted to having the same struggle. It was a "struggle" because each day was a battle to reconcile what we naturally felt with what we believed to be Truth, namely the restored gospel. We wanted to conform to the gender roles and guidelines contained in "The Family: A Proclamation to the World".

In January 2010, Gwen and I decided to get married after she graduated from college. It would be an unconventional marriage, without sex or romance, but we would have companionship. For several months we moved forward with our plan, but in May we both realized simultaneously that God didn't want us to get married. God didn't want us to live our lives inside a totally unnatural union. Our love as best friends could never be the love between spouses. But God didn't want us to be alone either. We are the way God made us, and we are just as capable of forming loving committed relationships as any straight person. Just because I fall in love with a man and Gwen falls in love with another woman doesn't make that love any less real or sacred.

Confident that God was okay with me being gay, I set a goal of coming out to all my friends and family. Now that my orientation wasn't a struggle anymore, I was ready to be honest with everyone. I've received a huge outpouring of love and support, and a tremendous weight of secrecy has been lifted from me. Gwen has received similar support and relief too.

We both consider ourselves survivors. Countless gay people have killed themselves because they felt they had failed themselves, their families, and God by not becoming straight. Gwen and I have both experienced years of despair and suicidal thoughts, believing it would be better to die than to live gay.

Thankfully we are now both walking a bright, hope-filled path of self-acceptance and growing inner peace.

Sarah Nicholson

"I speak for romantic love. I speak, too, for trusting the mystery, for forgiveness, and for believing that love in all its forms once created can never be undone. And that not only in eternity, but here, hidden under the grey, all is well, and all manner of things shall be well."
– Carol Lynn Pearson

I first met Scott in high school. He and I ended up in assigned seats next to each other in madrigal choir our senior year. I was drawn not only to his gorgeous bass voice, but also to his funny, yet quiet personality.

When I had the opportunity, I decided to ask him to the Sadie Hawkins girl's choice dance, which was coming up in November. I asked him by writing a message on a puzzle and putting it in a pumpkin. He answered by baking me a pumpkin pie and putting a paper that said "yes" underneath the crust. Wow, he could cook, too! We hit it off at that first dance. Soon he asked me out to a movie, and then to the Christmas dance.

We spent a lot of time together. When I accomplished something great or was having a bad day, he would bring me flowers. We became known as the cute choir couple of the year. Our friends would tell us how cute our kids would be, and that someday they expected Scott to be the bishop and me to be the Relief Society president. We went on hikes together. We watched movies together. We sang together. We baked chocolate chip cookies together and spent long hours talking and kissing. At his request, I taught him how to knit and crochet. We did baptisms at the temple together. I became quite attached to his little brother and sister, and his dad seemed to really like me. It was like a dream come true.

My heart would ache for him

I had never really dated anyone else or felt desirable at all. And all of a sudden I had a boyfriend: a talented, intelligent, sweet, handsome boyfriend that treated me like a princess.

Before too long, I was moving away to attend Snow College, and he was preparing for a mission. We spent long hours on the phone. Sending him across the country to Philadelphia on his mission was one of the hardest things I have ever done. Every day my heart would ache for him. I longed to hold his hand and cuddle with him. I missed the sweet sound of his singing voice. And I missed having him around to cheer me up or calm my stress the way no one else could.

I wrote to him the whole two years at least once and sometimes twice a week. I tried to keep my letters upbeat and spiritual. I heard from him much less often than that, but I knew he was busy, and when I did get a letter from him, I devoured it joyously. His mission experiences and faith uplifted me and I loved him more and more with each letter.

He seemed to write better during the second half of his mission, after I wrote to him about someone I was dating. He wrote back panicked, told me that he could not imagine marrying anyone else, and that he hoped I would still be available when he got home. I had an incredible spiritual experience while reading that letter, and I felt like I really should wait for him. Within two weeks of him getting home, we were engaged, and within three months we were married.

The routine of our lives

Scott's mission president had encouraged all of the missionaries to trust in God when they had their families, and to let the babies come. So two months before our first anniversary we had a beautiful baby girl, and sixteen months later (a bit sooner than we would have liked or could afford) we were blessed with a baby boy.

That year was a particularly difficult time in our marriage. Scott had quit school the year before to take a full-time job, but they ended up letting him go. He attempted to start his own business, but that was not working out either. We had no money and lived on our credit cards for several months. By the end of the summer, I decided I should apply for a job. A few days after applying, I received a call from a local high school. They just had a math teacher quit and desperately needed a replacement to start out the school year the following week.

I had always wanted to be a stay-at-home mom, and I was not sure that I wanted to commit to a teaching contract, but based on our lack of income, it seemed foolish not to take it. We attended the temple a few days later, and while we were there, words came distinctly to my mind, that my children would be okay while I taught school but that someone else's children needed me.

So began the routine of our lives: I worked full time while Scott stayed home with the kids and worked on computer projects to supplement our income. I had been going a bit crazy with two young children at home, and working helped me have a much-needed break so that I could be a better mom when I was at home. Our marriage improved drastically with some of the financial problems behind us. We soon bought a house closer to my job, and together we enjoyed remodeling and decorating our home.

There was no way

When we spoke in church for the first time in our new ward, I introduced our little family. I said that Scott and I were kind of backwards when it came to gender roles in our family: I worked while he was home with the kids; and he did most of the cooking and shopping, while I did most of the yard work.

Scott would make homemade chocolates, and I would take them around to my friends at work. One time as I was handing them out, one of the ladies said, "Oh, what a pretty necklace!"

I thanked her and mentioned that Scott had made it for me for our anniversary, that it had become somewhat of a tradition of his to make jewelry for me every year. Then another lady said, "Did you get a haircut?"

"No," I replied, "but Scott did color it for me last night."

By this time, one of the men was raising his eyebrows and giving me a funny look. "He makes chocolates and jewelry, colors your hair, and stays home with the kids. Are you sure he's not ...?"

I laughed. "No, he's not. We are just kind of backwards. I work and mow the lawn; he cooks and stays home with the kids."

It was around that time that he was elders quorum president. We had been married several years and had three or four children. With whatever I knew or understood about homosexuality at that time (which I now know was very little), that could not be him. There was no way.

Please tell me that you aren't gay

Early in the year 2008, one night we were lying in bed and I was desirous of some intimate time with him, but he was not interested. This was not uncommon, and sometimes I dealt with it just fine, but at other times I did not. This particular night I was quite frustrated, and spouted off questions to him: "Is there something wrong with me? Is there something wrong with you? Have you ever asked the doctor about getting your testosterone levels checked or if it could be something else?"

Scott assured me that it wasn't me, that it was him, that any time a picture of a naked or nearly naked woman popped up on the internet accidentally, that it did nothing for him.

"Then are you gay or something?" I asked with exasperation. He was silent. I started to freak out. "Please say something. I've heard horror stories of women who find out after they're married that their husband is gay."

Still silent.

"Please tell me that you aren't gay. Answer me!" By this time I was sobbing through my desperate plea for an answer.

"I'm not gay," he said softly.

Ok. I rolled over, my body still convulsing with the sobs that consumed me a few moments before, and slowly relaxed and fell asleep.

Is everything okay?

Around the beginning of July, I noticed that Scott started getting up at about 5:30 or 6:00 in the morning. This behavior was kind of strange, since he has never been a morning person. Then when he came home from work, he would help make dinner and then sit quietly and read a book. He loves to read, so the reading was not unusual, but he seemed distant somehow. I asked him a couple times if everything was okay, and he sincerely answered yes but did not want to talk much. He only wanted to read his book.

Okay, whatever. We've been through this before. It's not worth getting upset about.

One day he said, "We should go to the temple sometime soon." It had been a while, so it was not strange to suggest that we should go, but it was usually me that presented the idea, not him. That seemed a little weird to me. I asked him if there was any reason in particular, and he said no, just that it had been a long time and he thought we should go.

On July 11th, my daughter and I hosted a mother-daughter Mary Kay party while Scott and the three boys went to a barbecue. They returned home when the party was winding down. After getting the kids to bed, Scott helped me clean up and helped me decide what Mary Kay products to order with the credit from my party. He started turning off the lights to get the house ready for bed. Then he went out to the garage and brought in a plastic bag with something in it.

He had kind of a strange look on his face, so I asked him what was in the bag. He said, "Let's go in the bedroom and talk."

I started to get worried. As we were walking out of the kitchen, I asked him, "Is everything okay with your job?" I had never gotten over the anxiety from how he had lost his previous job.

He quickly said, "No, no. My job is fine. Don't worry about my job."

As we went into the bedroom, he shut the door behind us, and we sat on the bed. I waited for him to say something. He looked scared to death, was fidgety, and couldn't say a word. Normally he is a pretty calm person and does not get nervous about things. He started blowing air through his lips, like he was trying to keep from hyperventilating, and then said, "I knew this would be hard, but I didn't know it would be this hard."

I started freaking out. I said, "Are you sure your job is okay? Are you sick? Are you dying of cancer or something?"

He wouldn't answer. I started pacing; my heart was pounding. Heat rushed up my body to my head and I felt like I was going to pass out. "You have to tell me, now. Would it help if I stopped looking at you?"

He said maybe it would. I took a deep breath, sat down on the bed with my face to the wall and my back to Scott. He said something about my needing to hear him out and try not to react after the first sentence. I said okay, and finally he said, "I am gay."

Life could no longer be the same

I totally did not see that one coming, but I was so relieved that he had finally said it that I let out a sigh of relief. Through stressed laughing I said, "At least you haven't lost your job and you're not dying of cancer." We both chuckled at that. I don't remember everything he said and everything I asked, but I do remember that the thought kept going through my mind, "Where do we go from here?"

We talked about his experience with coming out to himself, the fact that he did not choose to be this way, that he had always tried to suppress and ignore these feelings, that he had been faithful to me and never had relations with any men. We talked about how he had been reading Carol Lynn Pearson's book *No More Goodbyes* (that was what was in the bag that he got out of the car). He told me he had been so scared to tell me and didn't want to hurt me, but simply could not bear to keep it from me any longer; it had only been about 10 days since he had really figured it out himself.

The main point he seemed to want to convey is that life could no longer be the same, and that he could not make any promises to me that he would be with me for the rest of our lives or forever, because he did not know what the future might bring, and he didn't want to risk feeling the need to break such a promise later.

I'm not sure exactly how I felt. I can't really remember. I was numb. I was in shock.

We finally decided we should go to bed.

After a few minutes we decided we should watch some TV to help get our minds away from the subject so that we could try to sleep. I have no memory of what we watched.

When we turned the TV off and tried to sleep, I couldn't. I had no idea what all of this really meant. Was my marriage now over? If he's always been gay, and we have survived this long, can't we keep living like this forever and pretend that nothing has changed? Does his being gay mean that he has never been attracted to me at all? In high school, through his mission, through our 13 years of marriage, was I nothing more than a friend?

He snored off and on through the night, so I think he slept more than I did. I cried softly into my pillow, my mind kept going through all of these questions. I had never been so confused or felt so helpless.

Where do we go from here?

Around 3:00 a.m. I got up, found my scriptures and went in the living room. I read my patriarchal blessing. I read his patriarchal blessing. I read the Book of Mormon. All three things brought me comfort. I went back to bed around 4:00 a.m. and finally slept for a while.

Then at 6:00 when the light started to come in the window, I woke up. The thoughts and questions filled my mind again. I desperately needed to sleep, but I couldn't. Maybe some music would help me relax. I picked up my pocket PC and starting perusing my MP3s. The words of a song went through my head. "Where do we go from here?" I remembered that Brooke White had sung it on American Idol; it was from the movie version of *Evita*. As Scott was sleeping, I listened to the song:

> Where do we go from here?
> This isn't where we intended to be
> We had it all, you believed in me
> I believed in you
>
> Certainties disappear
> What do we do for our dream to survive?
> How do we keep all our passions alive,
> As we used to do?
>
> Deep in my heart I'm concealing
> Things that I'm longing to say
> Scared to confess what I'm feeling
> Frightened you'll slip away
>
> You must love me
> You must love me
>
> Why are you at my side?
> How can I be any use to you now?
> Give me a chance and I'll let you see how
> Nothing has changed
>
> You must love me[23]

My quiet tears turned into audible sobs. I couldn't believe how perfect the words were. I had to hear it again. I sobbed harder. I didn't want to wake Scott, so I went to the kitchen to get some

---

[23]Lyrics by Tim Rice, music by Andrew Lloyd Webber.

ibuprofen for my pounding headache. I got a cup from the cupboard, then turned to head toward the fridge for water.

I jumped. Scott was coming down the hall and into the kitchen. I was sure he had been asleep. Seeing him, I felt like he was a different person, like I had no idea who he really was, a stranger in my house. He had tears streaming down his face. He tentatively came to me and hugged me and said, "The second time through that song was too much to bear." We hugged for a long time, crying together. He loosened his grip, looked me in the eyes and said, "I didn't choose this. You understand that, right?" I nodded to comfort him. But in my heart, I did not know. And I kept thinking, "Where do we go from here?"

They had no idea what had happened

The day after Scott came out to me, I was very tired due to lack of sleep, and very emotional. I attended a Relief Society breakfast. I wasn't sure I should go, but I decided I needed to try to get away for a bit. I piled on the makeup to hide my puffy eyes. I had some light conversations with some good friends, and no one asked me if I'd been crying or if something was wrong. Talking to one of them about it weeks later, she did notice that I was quiet and preoccupied that morning, but decided it best not to ask. She was probably inspired.

I left the breakfast early to attend our oldest son's ice skating lesson with the rest of the family. I was consumed with my thoughts. I sat there watching my husband, still feeling like I really did not know him.

After the lesson, we decided to take the kids to see the movie Wall-E. It ended up being a bad choice for me as I cried at the blossoming romance in the movie, keenly aware that the romance in my life was not what I thought it was.

The next evening we went to Scott's parents' house for our typical Sunday night visit. As we sat at the kitchen table, playing games with his parents and his sister and husband, I was keenly aware of the fact that I usually shared my struggles with these dear people, but right now I could not. I desperately wanted them to know so that they could love and support us like we needed them to. I was very uncomfortable and distracted. During the game, I looked at the cards in my hand, trying hard to concentrate on my strategy. Out of my lips came the words, "Where do I go from here?"

Scott and his sister have this habit of breaking into song whenever anything prompts them to do so. Immediately, his sister started singing, "Where do we go from here? This isn't where we intended to be ..." She started gazing into her husband's eyes as she sang. I turned on my PDA and hit play, because the song was there ready to go. Everyone was surprised, but didn't ask about it as the sister continued to sing. Before too long, I couldn't take it anymore and I burst into tears, turned to Scott and apologized, and abruptly left the table to cry loudly in another room.

Of course, everyone was shocked and had no idea what had happened. Scott made some kind of excuse for me. They all know I am an emotional person, so I'm sure it wasn't too disconcerting. I quickly gained my composure and returned to the game, pretending nothing had happened. No one said anything.

When we got home, I told Scott that I needed him to tell his sister so that I could have her to talk to and lean on. We started to make plans for how and when to tell her.

I could not lose my best friend

The next day we got up early to go to the temple. Once we got there, we realized that it was Monday, so the temple wasn't open. Later that day I started reading *No More Goodbyes* by Carol Lynn Pearson. I cried and cried through each agonizing story of self-hate and suicide. The stories were not sugar-coated. They were a reality I never knew existed. I read the quote on the first page of the section about mixed-orientation marriages: "Should I smile because we're friends, or cry because that's all we'll ever be?"

The reality of my marriage hit me like a brick. I went into the next room and shared the quote with Scott, but as I tried to read it I broke into tears and could not finish. That is when I started to really understand. That is when I started to really hurt, for him, for me, and for us. I decided I needed a break from the book. It had been a very emotional day.

The next morning I again woke up early and could not sleep. We were again planning to attend the temple that morning. I decided to read. I went in our closet and sat on the floor to read so that turning on the light would not wake Scott. I read about failed mixed-orientation marriages, and I came to the conclusion that our marriage was officially not going to make it. I kept reading and cried and cried. Scott got up and showered. I wanted to keep reading, but I knew I needed to get ready, so I closed the book and dressed for the temple.

Scott could tell I was really upset but did not know exactly why. I was quiet during the ride to the temple. Scott was afraid to ask me to share what I was thinking and feeling. We attended a session. It brought some comfort, but still, my mind was tormented with the reality of my life and fear for what it meant. I could not be alone with four children to raise. I could not lose my best friend. I *could not do it*. Why me? What was really going to happen to us?

In the dressing room, one of the temple workers was the mother of a high school friend. She greeted me happily and asked about how our family was doing. I said we were fine, even though I desperately wanted to share with her what I was going through. I had not been able to share it with anyone but my Heavenly Father, which was good, but not enough. A few weeks later I found out through the grapevine that this lady had a gay son who had left the Church. I couldn't help but think that maybe I was being prompted to tell her the truth about my life.

On the ride home, Scott was brave enough to ask me what I was thinking and feeling. I let it all out, and it felt good. I wished I had told him how I was feeling before we went to the temple. He told me some of his ideas of what felt right for the future, with a disclaimer that he had no idea what the future would actually bring. Some of his ideas were not very comforting, but he said that he could not imagine a future without me in it.

All would somehow be well

When I got home, I found some courage and began reading again. The next chapter happened to focus on positive mixed-orientation marriages and how some people are able to make them work out. Oh, how I wished I had kept reading before the temple, that I had gone with this comfort in my heart from Carol Lynn Pearson: "I speak for romantic love. I speak, too, for trusting the mystery, for forgiveness, and for believing that love in all its forms once created can never be undone. And that not only in eternity, but here, hidden under the grey, all is well, and all manner of things shall be well."

Peace began to fill my heart, and I began to heal and to trust my Heavenly Father that he had brought Scott and I together for a purpose, and no matter what the future might bring, we would have each other as best friends, and all would somehow be well.

It was really nice to have the summer to process everything before I had to go back to school. Scott and I both began to devour the words of other gay Mormons on the Internet. Scott already had a blog and I decided to start my own blog at the end of August to help me write out my feelings and experiences, mainly for myself, but also for others who found themselves on a similar path.

We began to come out to important people in our lives, starting with Scott's sister and then with his dad. After praying about it, we talked to our own children. We have never regretted that decision. We have continued to be completely honest with them through everything since, and even though it has not always been easy for them, it definitely has been the right thing to do, and they have been amazing.

Shortly after that, Scott wrote a letter to all of his ten siblings and step-siblings. The responses were varied, with those who were most active in the Church having the hardest time, and with others being incredibly supportive. I gradually began telling people in my family when the time seemed right.

I feel strongly that the gospel is true

Eventually our bishop found out what was going on in our lives, despite the fact that we had both decided that we did not want him to know. Scott had not done anything wrong, so there was no need for repentance, and therefore no reason for him to know. We don't know who called and told him, but his approach only deepened our agonizing struggle with the Church. We had already been having a hard time with the Church's participation in the gay marriage ban in California, and with homophobic comments that came up during lessons at church.

As fast Sunday approached, we both felt prompted that Scott should share his story with our ward by bearing his testimony in sacrament meeting. The reactions and consequences of that decision is a whole story for a different book, but neither of us can deny the Spirit we felt that told us it was the right thing to do at that time.

Scott was able to baptize and confirm our third child. A few months later, we were unable to renew our temple recommends, because our leaders questioned whether we could say that we sustained our leaders. But they did give Scott permission to ordain our second child and oldest son to the office of a deacon. Then we both took some time off from church attendance while we continued to send our children.

Now we have each chosen different paths. I am back to full activity with the children, with temple recommend in hand, and Scott has recently had his name removed from the records of the Church. We are both content with our choices, and I have learned to accept the fact that I have a different perspective than I used to, which makes church much different for me than it used to be. But I feel strongly that the gospel is true, despite some confusion among members (and leaders) about homosexuality.

I need the gospel in my life, and I believe that members of the Church need me and my children to help them more fully understand both sexual orientation and unconditional love. Sometimes I am sad at Scott's decision and I wonder what eternity will bring for his soul, but I believe God is merciful and that He knows what is in Scott's heart and will reward him accordingly in the life to come. I believe that the Atonement might be even more powerful than we can even imagine. I hope that someday he will come back to the Church, but I am fully aware that it will most likely never happen. So, we continue to try to accept each other's beliefs and decisions without judgment.

We will all be okay

Meanwhile, things have also changed drastically in our relationship. My worst fears of two and a half years ago are coming to pass, but I am strong and handling it well, ever grateful for the blessings in my life. I am certain that the prayers of our many friends and family are carrying me through. It has been incredibly difficult and painful for both of us as Scott has decided that he cannot continue to live pretending he is something that he is not.

During the past year, as we were unexpectedly pregnant with our fifth child, Scott began to let go of me emotionally, one step at a time. A month following the birth of our son, at the end of July this year, he wrote me a note to let me know that he couldn't do it anymore, that he would move downstairs for now, and then we could slowly proceed to work through details of a divorce. Writing and sending the message to me caused him his first real panic attack because he did not want to hurt me, but knew it would.

And yes, it was extremely hard on me, and I have been through many different phases of anger and depression and resentment and confusion. But I have also handled it with grace, with smiles and laughter, and I hope that everything will work out for the best for both of us. I still have times when I hope he will not find the love of his dreams, and that he will decide that having a romantic relationship with me has trade-offs that are just as good as anything else he could find in the long run. But I know he firmly believes that will never happen, that the chapter of his life that includes an intimate relationship with me is now over.

And so begins the chapter of raising the children together as friends but nothing more. He continues to sleep in the basement, and we are making plans to finish a more permanent arrangement for him down there so that he can stay indefinitely to help with the children and household. He goes on dates from time to time, attempting to find true love. Meanwhile, I am feeling a little bit negative about relationships in general and so will put off pursuing my own new romantic interests until I am ready.

We have no idea what the future will bring, of course, but I'm sure we will do the best we can to keep a friendly relationship and maintain some sort of family structure, for the sake of the children if nothing else. And no matter what happens, we will all be okay, for I believe that we truly have angels watching over us.

Scott Nicholson

*"It is the chiefest point of happiness
that a man is willing to be what he is."*
– Desiderius Erasmus

I grew up in Sandy, Utah in a devout Mormon family. I accepted
as truth the things that I was taught about homosexuality: it was
an abomination, a willful perversion of the natural order of things,
second only to murder in offensiveness to God. This understanding
led to an adolescence filled with mental gymnastics: I knew that *I*
wasn't a bad person, therefore I couldn't be gay. Any evidence to the
contrary had to have another explanation.

When the young men in my scout troop passed around a "swimsuit
edition" at a week-long summer camp, I felt nothing but disinterest
and perhaps a bit of revulsion. Of course that was simply because I
viewed women as sacred and worthy of respect, and because it wasn't
proper to take pleasure in the exposed flesh of the models in the
magazine.

When I found myself gazing in longing at a handsome young man
at school it was only because I was jealous of his good looks, muscles,
and charm. I wanted to be like him, and so it was only natural that
I would feel drawn to him. I ignored the fact that I never felt drawn
to a young woman that way.

When I grew close to a certain mission companion and felt an almost unreasonable happiness in his company, it was only because I had found true Christ-like brotherly love. The bliss that I felt as I ran my fingers through his hair when I gave him a haircut every few weeks was just the joy of being able to give service to a fellow missionary.

I had other explanations for my attractions to men: I can't take my eyes off him because he reminds me of someone I know, and I'm trying to figure out who. Or I'm anxious to get to know him because we will be serving together in some calling in the near future. Or maybe I even knew him in the pre-existence.

As for the physical arousal that I experienced at the sight of a well-built man at a public pool, or a shirtless man glistening with sweat as he labored in his yard — that was a little harder to come up with convincing explanations for, so I simply ignored it. I convinced myself that it was the normal reaction of a pubescent young man teeming with hormones, again ignoring the fact that girls never made me feel that way.

It had to be with her

When a lovely young woman asked me to the first girl's choice dance of my senior year, I was flattered at the attention. I found her easy to talk to, and over several dates we became good friends — even best friends. I certainly felt differently about her than I had ever felt about a girl. Perhaps that was what being "in love" feels like? After five months of dating, I even decided that I was ready to kiss her.

Sarah and I dated steadily through our senior year of high school. When she went away to college she seemed to miss me more than I missed her and to need me more than I needed her. But that just meant that I needed to try harder to demonstrate my affection and to make her feel loved and desired.

This imbalance was also evident as I served my mission: she wrote to me at least twice as often as I replied. But I still considered her a dear friend, and so I was alarmed when she wrote that a man at the college she was attending was interested in her. I recognized that the relationship I had built with her was not something that I could easily re-create with another woman, and that if I was to have any hope of marrying and creating a family, it had to be with her. I responded with a heartfelt letter stating as much, and when my parents came to pick me up from my mission I confided to my dad that I might need a loan when we returned to Utah, so that I could buy an engagement ring.

Less than three months after I returned from my mission, I married Sarah, my high school sweetheart.

Please tell me you're not gay

The honeymoon went as expected, and the beginning of our married life was certainly not devoid of physical expressions of affection. My mission president had been adamantly against birth control, so we used none. Consequently we had only been married a couple of months when we found ourselves expecting our first child. Over the next thirteen years three more children joined our household, and we became the image of a perfect young Mormon family. We both served faithfully in various callings, attended our meetings regularly, and were from all outward appearances as happy as could be.

Over those thirteen years, though, I was simply not as interested in intimacy as she expected me to be. That lack of interest took its toll. She often felt rejected or undesirable, and though it pained me greatly to know that I was hurting her, I still wasn't very good at forcing myself to pretend to interest that didn't exist — at least not for more than short periods of time.

I reasoned that my lack of interest in sex was the result of stress. Or maybe it was a side effect of the antidepressants that I was on at one point or another? I even considered the possibility of a testosterone deficiency. Sarah encouraged me several times to talk to the doctor about our issues and request a check of hormone levels. In the meantime I would still find myself aroused by a hot guy at the pool or curiously drawn to the handsome young man who had recently moved into the ward with his new wife.

More than once, the conflict over our intimate relationship came to a head, resulting in tearful discussions as we tried to determine the root cause of the problem. One particular discussion will forever remain ingrained in my mind:

I wanted Sarah to understand that the problem was with me, not with her. I wanted her to understand that my lack of desire did not mean that she was undesirable. I explained to her that in the many hours I spent on the Internet each day (as a freelance web developer and in my role as an IT consultant for the company that I worked for) I would occasionally come across images of women who were scantily clad or even entirely naked. These images, I said, "did nothing for me."

"If they were pictures of hot *guys* with few or no clothes on would they do something for you?"

"..."

I couldn't answer her, because as soon as she asked the question I knew that the answer was "yes". She understood my silence for what it was, and began to panic.

"Tell me you're not gay... Please tell me you're not gay!"

As she repeated herself over and over I finally did just what she was asking me to do:

"I'm not gay."

Apparently satisfied, Sarah rolled over and went to sleep, but sleep didn't come easily to me that night.

A profound spiritual experience

Over the next six months I devoured everything I could find on the subject of homosexuality. What did science say about it? What did the Church say?

I read literally hundreds of accounts from gay Mormons on the Internet. Most of them ended up leaving the Church to pursue a romantic relationship, but some had chosen to remain active and celibate. Like me, many had married before coming to terms with their orientation, or in the hopes that marriage would "cure" them. Some few of these still remained married, but it seemed that the majority were ultimately unable or unwilling to do so.

I examined my own life, trying to do so without prejudice or preconceptions — to be completely open and honest with myself. Eventually my studies and self-examination led to the unavoidable conclusion:

I am gay.

The first time I "spoke" those words in my head I had the most profound spiritual experience I have ever had. I was overwhelmed with feelings of affirmation and acceptance and love. I had discovered a true part of myself, and decades of self-deception were undone in an instant. I knew peace as I had never known it before.

Where do we go from here?

Of course I had to share this experience and new knowledge with Sarah, and I immediately began to plan how I might do so. I had no idea how she would react. In the stories I had read of others in similar situations the reactions of the straight spouses had ranged from tears to anger to outright rejection, and I mentally prepared myself for the worst.

About ten days after I "came out" to myself I sat down with Sarah and after five minutes of silence as I mustered up my courage, I spoke the words aloud for the first time:

"I'm gay."

Her immediate reaction was relief. My obvious anxiety had led her to assume the worst: Had I lost my job? Did I have terminal cancer? Oh ... I was just gay? Whew!

As the reality of what I had told her set in, though, the tears began to flow. All that had once seemed so certain about our future together was now called into question. Where do we go from here?

I told her that I was unable to make any firm commitments. With my new understanding of who I was, so many things were uncertain that I could not in good conscience promise her that nothing would change. I didn't want to make any promises that I might later break. All we could do, I told her, was take one day at a time and see how things played out.

Over the first week or two after I came out to Sarah she went through an amazing transformation. As she heard my story and read the stories of other gay Mormons, she was blessed with a great compassion for those who struggle with the conflict between sexuality and spirituality.

In the weeks that followed, as we came out to friends and family, she stood by my side. When others expressed concern at my unwillingness to firmly recommit to our marriage and unreservedly declare my intention to remain with Sarah, she was the one who defended my position.

Against the advice of others, together we came out to our older children, who were 11 and 12 years old at the time. They were unfazed by the news, and would grow to love the gay friends we later met and socialized with.

244 Gay Mormons?: LDS Experiences of Same-Gender Attraction

I bore my testimony

In November of 2008, on the first Sunday of the month (Fast Sunday) I woke with my heart pounding. I felt very strongly that I should come out in testimony meeting that day. I had considered the possibility of coming out to members of our ward at some point, but in my mind it had always been something that I might choose to do in the distant future. I stayed in bed for a good thirty minutes, pondering what I might say and what the consequences might be.

Sarah had been up before me, and eventually she interrupted her preparations for the day to come talk to me:

"I keep feeling like you need to come out in sacrament meeting today ..."

With two independent promptings, I became certain that it was the right thing to do. I took our almost-eight-year-old in for a baptismal interview with the bishop that morning, and when the interview concluded I told the bishop what I intended to do. He was concerned about the possible consequences but indicated that he wouldn't stop me.

By the time the testimony portion of the meeting started my heart was beating so hard that I could scarcely hear the first person who got up. I had written notes, so that I would not forget anything that I intended to say. Grasping this paper, I slowly walked to the pulpit. Shaking, I bore my testimony of God's love for His children. I explained that I knew He loved me because He had told me so when, after several years of denial and struggle, I had accepted that I am gay.

The response over the next few weeks was generally better than I expected. Some members of the ward went out of their way to demonstrate that their opinion of me had not changed. Some seemed to take steps to avoid me in the halls at church. But most members continued to treat me as they always had.

Only one or two people actually approached me to talk specifically about homosexuality, and I was grateful for their interest and acceptance. In my mind, one of the primary reasons for coming out to the ward had been to increase understanding of homosexuality and to demonstrate that being gay didn't inherently make me a bad person.

Troubling questions

Despite the generally positive reaction to my coming out, I grew increasingly uncomfortable at church. It was an interesting coincidence: within days of my coming to terms with my orientation, the Church released a letter encouraging members to give of their time and means to ensure the passage of Proposition 8, a ballot measure that would amend the California Constitution to define marriage as only between a man and a woman. Members of the Church found themselves faced with questions about the nature of homosexuality, about equality and fairness, and about faith and obedience.

The political environment compounded my own struggles. I was raised to believe that obedience to Church leaders' counsel — regardless of personal beliefs or feelings — would bring blessings. Yet in my interactions with other gay men and lesbians I met many who had been in long-term relationships. One couple in particular had been together for over fifteen years, longer than Sarah and I had been married at that point. They had twin boys, seven years old. They were a family in every sense of the word. My heart and my mind were repulsed by the idea that their love and their relationship should not be granted the same respect and legal recognition as my marriage to Sarah.

My willingness to accept the counsel of our leaders was further tested by what I had discovered in my months of research and self-examination. The statements about homosexuality that came from Church leaders had been unanimous in the 50s and 60s: homosexuality was a perversion; it was not an inherent trait, but a consciously-chosen "lifestyle" that could, with faith and obedience, be abandoned.

But that rhetoric had softened considerably in more recent decades, to the point where the Church recognized that these feelings and attractions might indeed be inherent. Gay members of the Church were no longer excommunicated simply for coming out. This change was welcome, of course. But it raised questions that troubled me. Since these leaders, who I revered as prophets, had been wrong about the nature of homosexuality, what else might they be wrong about? And might the Church's current position on homosexuality and on same-gender marriage still be based on the personal biases and perceptions of our leaders, as it had become apparent those earlier statements had been?

I became disillusioned

Several weeks of struggle and prayer led me to a firm and undeniable conclusion: The relationships of these friends who I had come to know and love were no more condemned by God than my own relationship with Sarah. Family and love were among the highest tenets of the gospel I had been raised to believe, and those were not lacking in these same-gender relationships. God valued these families every bit as much as He valued mine, and the Church's efforts to deny these families legal recognition were misguided and not inspired.

Sarah and I both became proponents of legalized same-gender marriage, and we paid the price for our advocacy. Sharp comments in Relief Society meeting were directly (though not explicitly) aimed at Sarah, as the instructor decried the unfaithfulness of those who questioned the leaders of the Church on the matter of gay marriage. A high council speaker called members of the Church who opposed Proposition 8 "wolves in sheep's clothing" and compared them to the unfaithful third of the host of heaven who followed Lucifer. Homophobic comments in elders quorum cut me, especially considering that many of these men knew that I was one of "those people" they were referring to.

Eventually we were denied our temple recommends by a bishop and stake president who firmly believed that *sustaining* the prophet meant obeying every word that came with the signature of a member of the First Presidency or Quorum of the Twelve attached. Over the course of several meetings with the stake president (and an appeal to our Area President which was returned with a curt message to "follow the counsel of your local leaders") I became disillusioned by what seemed to me an extreme emphasis on obedience over personal revelation. Church attendance had become increasingly uncomfortable anyway, and I eventually determined that I simply could not believe in the principles that my local leaders insisted were true.

I stopped attending Church meetings and remained an inactive member of the Church for several months. Eventually our stake president called my father to inform him that they were considering disciplinary proceedings against me, presumably for apostasy, since I was not shy in sharing my belief that the Church was wrong in its opposition to gay marriage. Not wishing to fight for membership in a church that (from my perspective) didn't want me anyway, I formally resigned.

I do have feelings for her

In the meantime, my relationship with Sarah had been the subject of considerable experimentation and had changed significantly as a result.

Before I came out to Sarah, we had considered the question of whether we were done having children. Pregnancy had always been difficult for her, and it seemed that it got harder with each child. After coming out and recognizing that our future together was anything but certain, I determined that it would not be responsible to bring another child into the family. Sarah agreed, and I had a vasectomy.

Six months after the doctor pronounced me "clear" (sterile) we found ourselves expecting our fifth child. The news of her pregnancy was difficult for me; I knew that it would strain the already uncertain relationship Sarah and I had.

To be clear, I love Sarah. She is not only the mother of my children, who I love dearly; she has also been my best friend for seventeen years. Even if my feelings for her have never been romantic in nature, I do have feelings for her.

I continued to try to find some way of making our relationship work, but I found myself no longer able and willing to completely deny myself the emotional and physical intimacy that I longed for as a gay man. Since my early adolescence, I had tried to ignore the emptiness that I felt. I now hoped that I could find some way to satisfy those needs well enough within the parameters of a faithful marriage.

I made many gay friends, and most of them love Sarah at least as much as they love me. I appreciated the emotional aspects of my friendships with them. Regular massages from a male therapist were helpful; these were not at all sexual or erotic in nature, but still comforting. When that seemed insufficient, with Sarah's permission I tried "platonic" cuddling with a friend. That too was nice and good, but the emptiness was still there.

We will still be a family

Eventually, despite all of my efforts and all of her tolerance and understanding and compassion, I came to understand that I would never feel complete in a relationship with a woman. I felt I had two options: I could remain with Sarah and resign myself to a life half-lived, or I could part from her and seek fulfillment and happiness.

I deliberated over this decision for many agonizing months. I did not want to hurt my best friend. I knew that my family needed me, all the more so when the baby was born, who I welcomed lovingly into our family. I could not in good conscience simply abandon them or leave them to fend for themselves while I ran off in pursuit of happiness.

The solution that I eventually came up with is non-traditional, and to many it has seemed less than ideal. Sarah and I remain married, for the time being. We call ourselves "separated", but I continue to live in the same house. This allows us to raise the children together and to more efficiently budget our pooled resources, avoiding the additional costs of renting a separate apartment. I have started dating, and hope that eventually I will fall in love with a man who is willing to become a part of our family, whatever shape it may take at that point.

And we *will* still be a family. I've learned that the narrow definitions that people often place on this word don't really have much meaning or application in the real world. To me, a family is simply a group of people who love each other enough to be there through thick and thin. It may have a father and a mother and children, or it may lack one or another of those elements. It may have two fathers or two mothers, or an aunt or grandfather who fills the role of "parent". The parents may or may not be legally married. The children may or may not be biologically related to the parents or to each other. There may be additional members who have married or been adopted into the family unit. As long as there is love and support and help and acceptance, there is family.

I'm grateful that the choices that I have made in life have given me a family. I would almost certainly not have made those same choices if I had been able to accept my homosexuality at an earlier age. I don't recommend the same choices to young gay people who are coming out in a world that is far more hospitable to gay people than it once was. But I'm happy with the life I have led so far and where it has led me, and I look forward to the future with a peace and happiness that I didn't know was possible just a few short years ago.

Allen Miller

"... [M]en are, that they might have joy."
– 2 Nephi 2:25

I've known I was "different" since my earliest memories. There was something about my play, my interests, and my relationships with other children that set me apart from boys my age at the earliest stages of life.

In kindergarten, I had an overwhelming crush on the little boy next door. I wanted nothing more than to be with him, to play, to talk, to sit, and to explore. One mid-summer afternoon when this boy and I were alone behind the garage, my desire to show my affection and commitment overwhelmed me. I grabbed him impulsively on both shoulders, pulled him close to me and planted a kiss squarely on his lips. My satisfaction and sense of connection quickly evaporated as he, in return, slugged me in the stomach and ran home crying.

Several years later after spending a week with my aunt and uncle, it came time for me to return home. The week had been wonderful, primarily because my fifteen-year-old cousin who I idolized let me follow him everywhere. I wished with all my heart that I might be able to stay. At my departure, as I stood with my parents, my aunt, my uncle, and my cousin, tears rolled down my cheeks. I ran to my cousin, threw my arms around his neck and kissed him with all the passion my eight-year-old heart could muster.

In less than a second, I felt my father's glare and his careening knuckle across my skull. "What are you doing, stupid boy? Men never kiss men!" he growled.

These experiences and others like them delivered an indelible message to me about who and what I was. The bottom line — I wasn't like everyone else. At a time in my life when all I wanted was to fit in, I didn't. I didn't think like the other boys, talk like the other boys, or act like the other boys. The desires of my heart in fact were totally different from those expected of boys my age. Despite my best efforts to convince myself otherwise, I was different. I knew it, and everyone else suspected it. The best thing for me, I thought, was to bury the truth or ignore it.

The situation came to a head some years later at summer camp. One night as we were waiting to fall asleep, my best friend told me that he figured I liked boys instead of girls. In a casual supportive way, he told me about another friend who liked boys too, and suggested I should get to know him. This well-intentioned advice turned my world upside down. The secret I had tried for so long to ignore was obvious to him. And if it was obvious to him, I reasoned, it must be obvious to everyone.

Overwhelmed by fear, I quickly recognized that I was faced with a choice. I could withdraw from the world and hide in fear or I could confront my fears by facing the world head-on. I decided that I would do whatever it took to be like every male I knew. I would play the rough games, date an endless number of girls, and keep my eyes unfocused whenever I ventured into the locker room.

We asked them about the Church

When I was fifteen, my family moved from Central California to Montana. I would leave my doubts behind me and begin a new life — a manly life of living on a ranch, riding horses, herding cattle, irrigating grain fields, and bucking hay bales. It would all work together to transform me into the type of man I really wanted to be.

Upon arriving in Montana, my brother and I quickly became accustomed to the routine of a teenage ranch hand. Throwing our lot in with our closest neighbors, we were in the fields early and worked continuously until sunset. The experience was new, invigorating, and bonding. We quickly became close friends with two of the neighbor boys closest to our age.

Late one Saturday evening after a grueling day of bucking seventy-five-pound hay bales, we walked with our new friends to their home for dinner. As the stars sparkled overhead and the breeze touched us with the first signs of fall, I casually asked them to tell us about their religion and what it meant to them.

My own religious experience was varied and not very deep. Matters of faith were important to me, but my family for the most part was not religious. I had been baptized a Methodist, and had regularly attended Catholic and Episcopalian services without real commitment. Even at my young age, I had my own beliefs about God and faith, beliefs that varied significantly from any Christian denomination with which I was familiar.

In response to my request, our friends began a long and fascinating tale about a man named Joseph Smith, about the appearance of God the Father and Jesus Christ to him as a young boy, about golden plates and the Book of Mormon, and about the fact that through the Restoration men and women could actually become gods.

As we listened to their story, my brother and I were at first fascinated, then excited, and finally convinced. The message our friends shared made sense. For the first time, religion seemed to fit together like a jigsaw puzzle. My questions were answered, and the message rang true to me.

Some four hours later, early on a brisk Montana morning, my brother and I walked the fields from our friends' house to our own, changed forever for good. I knew without a doubt that what I had heard had come from God, that His truth had been restored to the earth and that it was my good fortune to have found it.

An intense inner struggle

As my testimony grew and my commitment to the gospel increased, I continued to hope that the objects of my sexual desire would gradually alter as well. I recognized that it was by small means that great things were brought to pass, so I wasn't expecting a change in the twinkling of an eye.

To prove my faith and worthiness, I did everything in my power to control my thoughts, my emotions, and my physiological responses. I dated girls. I talked of marriage. I tried every avenue to move the target of my affection from male to female.

But the change never came. It was about this time, in my late teens, that I began to grasp the gravity of my situation. I learned that God in his perfection never would create a human being destined to possess such vile and repulsive desires. And as a result, I was condemned. The surety of my ultimate damnation was overwhelming, sometimes depressing. My only hope was the faith I had in my ultimate recovery and redemption. If I kept the commandments, if I went on a mission, if I married in the temple, and if I raised a righteous posterity, the change would come. All would be well.

My mission was a challenging experience. Not only was I confronted with a new language and culture, I was required to live day-in and day-out with male companions, some of whom were impossibly kind and impossibly beautiful. In the emotional heat and physical exhaustion of the work, it was all I could do to remain faithful and focused, but I did.

Maybe I am normal

Two months after returning from my mission, I met my future wife. It was love at first sight for her and total infatuation for me. For the first time in my life, a woman actually took my breath away. She served in the Relief Society presidency in our BYU ward while I served as the ward executive secretary. We meshed perfectly. We talked together, laughed together, and planned together. We held each other, kissed passionately and enjoyed the closeness that young love affords.

One Sunday as we stood sharing a hymnbook, I glanced at her hand next to mine and realized that I had fallen in love. It was a sign that perhaps the cure had come. Admittedly, I still checked out nearly every man I saw despite my best efforts to the contrary, but the fact that I was in love with a woman stood as witness that my desires might actually change.

My relationship with the beautiful and good woman could not have been closer. We shared everything, our hopes, our dreams, our ambitions. She quickly became my best friend and I quickly became hers. Five months later we were married, and I entered the marriage believing that the issue that had plagued my life was behind me. But it wasn't.

There's something you need to know

The first few years of our marriage were demanding. My wife taught school and bore five children one after the other, while I finished my undergraduate and graduate programs and then focused on my career. Our love for one another deepened, and we built a strong family on a foundation of commitment and trust. My wife and I were the best of friends, dedicated to one another, our children, and the gospel. But I wasn't happy.

Those feelings and desires that were supposed to dissipate if I lived righteously and focused on my family still remained. Despite my attentive and faithful effort to change, I continued to experience fantasies of men, and to yearn for their bodies, their touch, and their love.

Initially, my raging hormones and vivid imagination had made intimacy somewhat satisfying for me and my wife, but as time passed, I realized that while my devotion to my wife was real, it was more akin to the feelings one has for a best and precious friend. It was enriching, but not fulfilling.

We had been married for nearly five years when I first confessed the secret of my life. In a fit of frustration and loneliness, I whispered as I lay beside her at the end of a long and difficult day, "Sweetie, I'm gay." My wife was surprised. "Do you want a divorce?" she asked. "No," I said simply. "Then this shouldn't be a problem," she responded with a yawn. "You love me, right?" "Yes," I said, "I love you." "Then it will all work out," she concluded and fell gently into my arms and an easy sleep.

For me, sleep never came that long and difficult night. I held her close, watching her breathe as I realized that regardless of my love for her and her love for me, my soul would remain empty and the void unfilled. I would never feel the tender caress or the gentle kiss of someone I could fully love. My heart would continue to beat its unending rhythm of despair, and despite my wife's devotion to me, I would be alone.

After what seemed an eternity, the dawn cast a single ray through the curtained window and with that ray, my despair eased. The morning light whispered hope, and the comforting words of my grandfather came to mind: "Life is hard," he would say. "Accept it. It's how you play the hand you're dealt that really matters."

It was then that I realized that although I had little power over the subject of my desires, I did have power over how those desires would impact my life. For the sake of my family, I decided then and there to play my hand with optimism and courage, with devotion and love. That's what my wife needed and that's what my children deserved.

What have I said?

It was about this time that I made a major shift in my view of homosexuality. To this point, I saw myself as innately cursed, filled with an evil that must be controlled and dominated at the peril of my soul. As a result, my self-image and confidence suffered greatly. I more than once considered taking my life as a better option than the life I was required to live. If I were assured damnation because of what I was, damnation might as well come sooner than later.

One day while I was praying about this issue and asking Heavenly Father for guidance, a thought came to me. What if instead of being cursed, I was suffering from a genetic or biological disorder, like Down syndrome or cystic fibrosis? I came to the conclusion that if I couldn't be healed in this life, I would be healed in the next. While this insight was not altogether satisfying, it helped me climb out of the pit of despair and self-hatred where I often found myself trapped.

During this period of my life I was very focused on my career. My job with a multi-national corporation required me to make frequent and extended trips throughout the world. These trips were typically exhausting physically, mentally, and emotionally. Despite my hormones, the stress of travel, and the constant temptation, I remained faithful to my wife.

Sometimes, however, it was not as easy to remain faithful to my secret. One day after returning from an arduous and highly contentious trip to the Middle East, I was having lunch with several fellow executives. I was exhausted, suffering from jet lag, and wanted nothing more than to leave work for some much needed rest. Our waiter brought us menus, and I was smitten. His face and body were beautiful, his movements fluid, and his voice was like music, a cello. Without thinking, as he began clearing our dishes at the end of the meal, I shook my head faintly and said, "Isn't he the most beautiful man you have ever seen?"

Immediately, I froze, realizing that I had just outed myself to some of the most powerful men in the company. I was terrified. And with my terror came a solution. I began to laugh. Fortunately, my companions understood the "joke" and immediately laughed with me. A crisis was averted. Minutes later we all arose from the table and excused ourselves. I went immediately to the restroom where I spent fifteen minutes vomiting, the penalty incurred from the fear and stress I had experienced as a result of letting down my guard.

Life is a roller coaster

Trying to live as a straight man in a gay man's body can be overwhelming. At times I would feel that I had everything in control while at other times I would be emotionally devastated by the impossible situation I was trying to manage. My wife and children brought me joy, but I always felt a void in my heart that could not be filled.

The hardest part was the duplicity, the deceit that permeated my life. While I lived openly with my wife, I lived a lie to the world. More than almost anything, the human soul yearns for integrity and honesty. Because of my choices, I had denied myself that comfort. The burden that resulted was at times unbearable.

Interestingly, our extended family and friends thought our lives were perfect. My wife and I were the epitome of the Mormon couple. We treated each other with kindness and consideration, were devoted spouses, and rarely argued. People saw us as happy and content. Our five children were bright, beautiful, and well-behaved. Eventually, they all served missions, graduated from BYU and married in the temple. We were everything the typical Mormon would desire.

People sometimes said, "If only I had a family like yours!" My wife and I would laugh and say, "If you knew what our family was really like, there's no way you'd trade places with us." My wife was understanding and continued to be supportive. Because we were both devoted to our relationship and to our children, we made a firm commitment to do what it took to make things work. I figured that regardless of how empty and alone I might feel at the core, it was my responsibility to soldier on and "man up". As the years passed, this became more and more difficult.

The revelation

In 2000, my life reached an impasse. My professional and Church activities provided a sense of accomplishment and success, but my homosexuality was always the elephant in the corner. Regardless of the good I did or the degree of my accomplishments, I felt like a failure, worthless and ultimately unworthy. These feelings were so overwhelming that I would often curl in a ball, pull a blanket over my head and sob in despair.

It was at this time that I again tried counseling. The counselor helped me develop patterns of coping, and the results led me to the most important revelation of my life. One evening as I despaired for help from God, a tender mercy finally dawned, soft sweet thoughts that touched my heart and filled my soul with joy. The feelings whispered gently, yet clearly:

> Allen, I love you. I made you who you are. You are my son, my gay son, and that is well. As with all my sons, you are fashioned in my image and are the zenith of my creation. I want you to know that you are good because of who you are, not despite what you are. Most importantly, my son, I accept you as you are.

Because of that experience, I finally came to terms with myself. If Heavenly Father created me and accepts me as a gay son, how could I do any less? For the first time in my life, I knew I was whole and could stand before God without feeling guilt for my nature.

The week following this experience I was called to serve as a bishop. It felt as if through this calling the Lord had sealed my revelation with his divine imprimatur. As I was preparing to serve, fasting and praying about my responsibilities, a vision came to my mind: I saw people with heavy burdens and struggles, sitting there in the chapel surrounded by the love of God, and I heard the Lord's voice just as clearly as anything in my life, saying, "Feed my sheep. Feed my sheep." It was a tremendous spiritual experience. Inside I knew what I struggled with, and it made me much more receptive to helping these people who were struggling with their own burdens. Serving them was a life-changing experience.

Coming out

I felt in my soul that my life as I knew it could not go on forever. I believed that by nature I was a person of integrity. Living a life of duplicity was gut-wrenching. When I was asked in the temple recommend interview, "Are you living the law of chastity?" I could answer yes with a clear conscience. But when I was asked if I were honest in my dealings with my fellow men, I wanted to scream, "No. I'm living a lie every day." The deception became impossible and created a terrible dilemma: Where do I go from here? Do I continue with the status quo, or do I take courage and do what I knew in my heart was right?

My wife's perspective was consistent. We would continue to tackle the issue one day at a time. This approach had worked for our entire marriage. My wife and I got a copy of Carol Lynn Pearson's book, *No More Goodbyes*. When we read these stories, we thought, "Here is our life." It was the first time we had seen anything like this. We both cried through the whole book. Finally we were not alone.

When our last child moved from home, I hit the wall. I could no longer live a lie. I could no longer pose as a straight man in a gay man's body. I could no longer be someone I wasn't. It was then that I decided to face things straight on. I told my wife that it was time for me to step out, to be free of the chains that had bound me my entire life. It was time for me to be who I really was.

While I didn't want to destroy our family and cause her and our children pain and heartache, I needed to fill the emotional void that had left me empty. I had to live the life of the man I actually was. I had to open the closet door and deal with my homosexuality straight on without equivocation or deception.

My wife and I knew that this decision would change our lives forever and that once initiated, it would offer no opportunity to return to the way it was before. Despite the fear, I was confident I had to move forward. And there was no going back. All would be well, regardless of where the path we chose might lead.

Gradually, I started making gay friends and becoming involved in the gay community. Through the guidance of the Spirit, I was directed to a group of guys that became my rock and my guide. They provided the love, support, and direction that made a difficult transition manageable.

My wife and I told family and friends about our situation, and we found love and support. When it came time to decide to end our marriage, the decision came simply for both of us. I thought I would feel terrible. Instead it felt like a thousand pounds had evaporated from my shoulders. I just felt peace and happiness.

Where I am today

Exactly twelve months ago, I was barely managing my marriage and struggling terribly with the thought of divorce. The path I walked was rocky, clouded over, and difficult, but the perpetual glow of the distant horizon beckoned me and called me to move, to adapt, to change. And so, despite my fear, I did.

With some confidence and a little faith, I stepped off the ledge of the mountain I'd been climbing my entire life, into the void that surrounded me, half expecting to tumble viciously to the razor-sharp rocks below. Instead, to my surprise, I found myself floating, soaring, free from the pull of the earth, savoring the thrill and exhilaration that could come only from one's first flight into the heavens. The pain, the anger, the sense of dishonesty and duplicity that had perennially dogged my life and held me down, were gone. Peace and a primal sense of joy rooted themselves firmly in their place and raised me up to dwell with the stars.

For the first time, I felt the sun completely, warming me from the inside out. I saw the world clearly, without blur or blemish. I smelled the sweet fragrance of life. A friend asked me last week if I would consider going back to the life I had lived before. In response, I simply smiled and shook my head. If man's purpose is to find joy, I have found it and regardless of the cost, I will never let it go.

Warren Bailey

"Life is about learning. Not being perfect. So, learn all you must, but don't beat yourself up for the lessons."

I grew up in Seattle in a devout Mormon family of 10 children. We went to church every Sunday and participated in all the activities. We were a very close-knit ward, and I made a lot of good friends there and at school, with both girls and boys. We all played together, and it was easy to be friends with everyone.

When I was around nine or ten, I discovered that I really enjoyed taking baths with my friend "Drew". It wasn't sexual, but I just really enjoyed being alone with him in the bathroom. It went on for a while, until he told his mother and she said we probably shouldn't do that anymore. I remember feeling sad, because I had really enjoyed it.

He asked me to do a lot of things

An elderly man named David Herget lived just behind our house. He was in the ward and got to know our family through church. He was diabetic and would ask for help mowing his lawn, vacuuming his house, or washing his car. Since he lived so close, it was really easy for me to just hop over the fence and help him out. When I was 11 years old, I started going over and mowing his lawn whenever he needed it.

I had been doing that for a couple months, when one time he asked me to come inside to see something. I told him I'd be there in a minute. When I walked inside, he wasn't there. I kind of shouted out, "Where are you?" He said to come back to his computer room. When I got back there, he had me come over and sit on his lap at the computer, which I thought was kind of weird. Then he turned on his desktop and started playing a video that showed two boys and an adult doing sexual things with each other. And that's where it started.

At that point I didn't really know what porn was. I had never really heard of it or encountered it. Over the next four years, he asked me to do a lot of things with him that I didn't really want to do. When I appeared to be feeling bad about it or not wanting to continue it, he would tell me it was okay, that he loved me, and that boys my age were always doing things like this. If I still resisted, he would ask me why. And I didn't really have an answer for him, so he just took that as a sign that I was okay with it, and he would go ahead and do whatever it was he was doing.

There were two other boys in the ward who would come over to help out around David's house or yard, and he started putting us together, doing things with him or with each other. All of this was exciting and new. There were a lot of feelings that I was experiencing, that at the time I shouldn't have been experiencing, but I didn't know that until later. Subconsciously I knew that it wasn't the way that it was supposed to be, but I didn't want it to end. I didn't really understand the implications of it. I liked having that kind of attention from someone. It was something I had never experienced before, and it was addicting. David often said that if I told anyone, then I would get in big trouble and that he would kill himself.

There were really no boundaries in the relationship. It intensified as the years went by, and the other boys and I eventually started doing things outside of his supervision. The sexual intimacy going on between us became what defined my relationship with David and with the other boys.

Everything was fine

When I turned 15, the parents of one of the boys found out about what had been going on for all these years. They called my parents late one night at 12:31 a.m., and I had a feeling that this was what it was about. I went to sleep, not wanting to worry about it. The next morning, my mom was crying. She told me what they had told them and asked me if it was true. I said yes. My older sister was in the room, so she found out at the same time.

I pretended like everything was fine. I knew that everything wasn't okay, but that it would be okay in the future. So I went to school that day, and I didn't have any trouble in classes or anything like that. But during my cultural geography class, I walked out into the hall to get a drink, and I saw my sister in the hall sobbing, talking with a friend. I just ignored it and went back to class.

During the day, one of my sisters' friends came up to me and asked if anything had been going on at home. I said that everything was fine. When I went home, I acted like everything was normal. I was suppressing most of my emotions. I didn't want to think about what would happen, so I just decided not to worry about it. So I felt fine. I didn't have any anxiety or nervousness or sadness at the time.

Police and therapists

After all of the parents found out about the abuse, the police were called. They didn't want us to have to testify in court, so they decided to do a sting operation: they would try to lure David to implicate himself so they could arrest him.

During this time, he was still walking around interacting with all of our families. It was very difficult for my mother to let him into our home and let him interact with us after she knew what had been going on.

After about three weeks, the sting operation was successful: David emailed one of the other boys pretending to be me, asking for sexual favors from the other boy. The police used that as cause enough to arrest him and put him in jail. Three days later he committed suicide in his cell.

They told me that it wasn't my fault, and that I shouldn't feel guilty for him dying. And I didn't feel guilty about it. After he committed suicide, my parents kept asking me questions, but I gave very limited responses.

All three of us boys were sent to the same therapist. He didn't really talk about the issue or give me tools to cope with the effects of the abuse. Instead he would talk about irrelevant things. He gave me the talk about "the birds and the bees" for some reason, as if I didn't already know. He talked about his experience learning about swear words and how to use them. I didn't see how that was supposed to be helpful to me in any way.

After all this, it was difficult for me to just change my habits, to not have the affection and intimacy that I had been having. I became sexually active with other boys that I knew through school, church, or extracurricular activities. I craved that kind of attention from someone, because after David was taken away, it was something that I found I needed very much.

I wanted to move on

In February 2007, on Valentine's Day I asked "Lisa", a girl from school, to be my girlfriend, and she said yes. I had never gone on a date with her, but she was very intelligent, and I found that to be a very attractive trait. We just talked a lot, and after school I would help her with the school newspaper, which she was chief editor of. We enjoyed each other's company and would watch movies together and hang out. We held hands in the hallway at school. But there wasn't really much of a dynamic to our relationship. I didn't really spend that much time with her. About four months into our relationship, it became tiring, and we officially broke it off in May 2007.

In the summer of 2007, my family and I moved to Pocatello, Idaho. Here all of my self-destructive habits and needs dissipated, because I had no way of fulfilling them. I spent my time making new friends and becoming social within my new high school. But I continued to have a strong attraction to men, physically, mentally, and emotionally. After about two years in Pocatello, I sought help from therapists again. I found one that was very helpful. He taught me to be honest with my emotions and with myself. He told me that I would probably always have same-sex attractions (SSA), but that it was not the end of the world, that it was not a horrible thing to deal with. I discovered that it really didn't matter whether or not my feelings of SSA were caused by the abuse. He also taught me not to allow what has happened in my past to define how I feel about my future or how I feel about myself.

After I got done with high school I turned 18, which gave me one year to prepare to go on a mission. The plan I had outlined was to audition and be a part of the music mission in Nauvoo, Illinois during summer 2009 and then leave on my full-time mission within a couple months after that. In December 2008, I talked to my branch president about what had happened in my past and what I was feeling. He decided he was going to "cure" me of these feelings and proceeded to treat me like I was a child. He wanted me to get rid of all of my SSA feelings and the abuse aftermath within one year, which I told him was pretty much impossible. I had him talk with my therapist, but he still didn't change his views. It was very frustrating, because I wanted to move on with my life and pursue an education at BYU-Idaho, but he wasn't willing to give me the necessary ecclesiastical endorsement unless I was completely done with the SSA feelings and the abuse aftermath. And that made it pretty much impossible for me to attend the college.

For the year and a half since I had moved to Pocatello, I hadn't done anything sexually, but in January 2009, I became involved with another guy and we had sex. After that, I did not feel like I was worthy to go on a music mission or a full-time mission, and I confided with my branch president what had happened. Of course, my parents were expecting me to go. When I told them that I wouldn't be able to go on the music mission, they were okay with that, but later when I told them that I wouldn't be able to go on the full-time mission on time, it was harder for them to accept. My dad wanted to know why. At this point he still didn't know about my SSA.

I got exhausted with it

That same month, I asked "Julie" to be my girlfriend. I hadn't dated her before, but we had been friends for a year and half, and I knew that she liked me and I liked her. She was a very pretty girl and fun to be around. She fit my sense of humor really well. We spent a lot of time together. After a month and a half, I got tired of the relationship, and I broke it off. But we're still really good friends.

I realized later that I really wasn't attracted to Lisa or Julie. It was more that I was attracted to the idea of being in a relationship. I liked holding hands, cuddling, and kissing. The relationship was an excuse to be able to do those things. I wasn't really attracted to them as a person, and I didn't really see them as any kind of long-term companion.

It was something that was very enjoyable at first, but there just wasn't any emotional or romantic attraction to them in the relationship, and I got exhausted with it. I realized that it also was not fair to them to continue with it, because they were attracted to me as an individual and I wasn't to them. Generally I only find girls at most mildly physically attractive, and I've almost never been emotionally or psychologically attracted to them on any level.

Support from friends and family

In the summer of 2009, my therapist told me about an organization called North Star. Through North Star, I was able to meet a lot of LDS people who experience SSA. It has helped me by giving me a group of people to relate to and talk to, making it easier to deal with this issue in a healthy way.

In October 2009, I told my mom that I was attracted to men. She kind of already knew. She told me that when she started having children, the Spirit had told her that she would have a child that experienced SSA. She explained how much she loved me and how much she would support me in anything I decided to do even if it went against what she personally believed was a good choice.

In January 2010, my father found out. I don't think he understood it extremely well, but he was okay with me having these feelings. Later in July 2010, my mother told all of my older siblings that I struggled with this. I was fine with that. Several of my siblings have made it clear that they will support me in whatever I decide to do in my life. My mother gave me the idea that in order to figure out what I wanted to do, I could try dating girls and guys, to give me experience so I could decide what I wanted to do.

I tried to keep myself busy

I took a job as a phlebotomist and moved to Idaho Falls. My former branch president continued to have me drive back and forth to Pocatello (45 minutes away) to meet with him every weekend; he would not heed my request to transfer my records up to my new branch in Idaho Falls. After six months, I got one of the stake presidents in Idaho Falls involved, my records were transferred, and I was finally able to move on.

After that, I continued to be active in the Church, and I tried to keep myself busy in order to keep from forming bad habits. I told my new branch president about my feelings, and he has been pretty understanding and compassionate. He told me that he didn't know much about the issue, so he didn't think he would be able to help me much, and that was okay.

After an incident with a guy that summer, I kind of retreated within myself and became emotionally distant to everyone, my friends, family, and coworkers. It was a way of coping with my failure to keep myself sexually clean. I would have been able to walk away from my family and friends without any kind of regret or emotional stress if that's what I had decided. But I kept up my relationships with them because I knew that they were supposed to be there, even though I didn't feel any emotional tie to them or anyone else.

In September 2010, I went to Journey into Manhood. It gave me a chance to face the problems I had been having with my emotions and my past in a healthy, safe environment. This in turn gave me insights into my biggest issues that I was working on. It kind of took me out of that emotionless rut that I had been stuck in for the summer. It helped me realize that one of my biggest issues with relationships is that I had trouble trusting people with me as a person. I had trouble trusting them with my past and allowing them to help me with my issues now. By being able to realize that about myself, I was able to find an emotional connection back to reality and was able to regain the emotional ties with my family and friends.

Everything happens for a reason

As of right now, I hold a calling in my current branch and continue to be an active LDS member. I believe and love the gospel very much and the influence it has on my life. I still struggle very much with attraction to men. But it's not something that I allow to have a lot of influence in my life. And I don't allow it to affect the relationships that I have at church, at work, or in general, really.

I don't know if I'll ever be able to go on a mission, or if I'll have to wait a while. But I know that if I can't go, then God will figure out another way for me to learn what I'm supposed to learn on my mission. God has a "plan B" for everything.

I don't believe in being too preoccupied with the fact that I am attracted to men. I don't allow it to change my perception of religion or of what I believe. The bottom line is that I'm attracted to men, and that's it. I'm not "gay"; I'm attracted to men. Society has a lot of preconceived notions on the word "gay". It's the same with "straight" or other labels like "emo" — they all have implications which depend on the perspective of the person using the word. Just because I'm attracted to guys doesn't mean I have to adhere to any kind of mold or preconceived notions about who I am.

I've never been in any kind of romantic relationship with another male. In general, I've never had a boyfriend or dated a guy. I've been on dates with guys and girls. Sometimes I feel like if I were to get into a relationship with another man, then I would feel like I was going against what I have been taught all my life. In the past I have felt that there wasn't any point in being in a relationship with another man. However, I have realized that good things can come from a healthy relationship between two people of the same gender, just as they can from an opposite-gender relationship. For me personally, I don't believe that any sexual interaction would be healthy for me in any kind of relationship. If I decided to have a boyfriend or have a girlfriend it would have to be with someone who was very grounded, who didn't need to have sexual intimacy as a part of their relationship with me, and who just wanted to take things very slowly and not worry about where the relationship was going to go.

To those who struggle with SSA and have to deal with hurtful comments from their peers and family, I would say this: continue to be as understanding and compassionate to them as you would like people to be to you.

I believe that everything happens for a reason. Whether people are born with SSA or whether they pick it up somewhere along the way, I believe it happens for a reason. The Church does not claim to have a lot of clear information on homosexuality and how it fits in with the gospel, but I do believe that it is possible to live a fulfilling and peaceful life if you experience these feelings. I believe that God will continue to be there for everyone whether they're an LDS member or not. I believe that religions can have very misunderstood beliefs on homosexuality, but I believe they will become clearer in the future.

Dan Olsen

"For God hath not given us the spirit of fear; but
of power, and of **love**, *and of a sound mind."*
– Timothy 1:7

My story starts off like that of many other faithful youth in the Church: I was born while my parents were attending BYU. I was baptized when I was eight years old. I received the priesthood when I was twelve. Growing up, I lived an innocent life. I never had any real desire to date or interact with the opposite sex until high school.

In high school, I was asked to some girls choice dances, and I felt I needed to at least ask girls out for prom and homecoming. When I was 17, one of these girls liked me. After our second date I received a rose and a letter from her, explaining how sorry she was for not cuddling or holding hands with me. I was just bewildered. I hadn't noticed anything wrong on the date. Why was she so concerned about physical contact? I wondered if I had done something wrong. I offered to make up for it by taking her out to dinner and a movie. During the movie, I let her hold my hand and let her put her arm around me, and she gave me a long hug at the end of the night. All of it was awkward and unpleasant, and I assumed this meant I must not really like her.

My first semester at BYU was an incredible spiritual experience. I made some great friends, adjusted to living on my own, and got ready to leave on a mission in January. Because of my focus on a mission, most girls considered me "off-limits", and I didn't see any reason to try to change that.

I just wanted to be good friends with him

Serving my mission was an experience that I will forever be grateful for. I served in what I liked to call "the bottom of the world" in southern Chile. I met some fantastic people, and grew and learned in ways I never imagined.

About halfway through my mission I was assigned to be with an extremely likable companion. We both worked hard and had several baptisms, due in large part to his charming personality. He was genuinely concerned about people, he liked to hug, and he was pretty much the perfect missionary. He and I became close friends. Towards the end of our companionship I remember thinking to myself, "all I have to do is find someone exactly like him, only a girl, to be my wife."

A second experience involved someone I will call Elder "Blaire". For six weeks my companion and I shared an apartment with him and his companion. I always looked forward to being with him at the end of the day. We found all sorts of excuses to go do work together, even though we weren't companions. When circumstances prevented us from living in the same apartment anymore, I wrote in my journal:

> I'm really going to miss Elder Blaire, it would be awesome
> if we could be companions.

When he was feeling down, I would be concerned for him. Several times I fasted for him when I was particularly worried.

> Well, one of the more important things I wanted to write
> about was Elder Blaire ... I had the opportunity to talk
> with him about a lot of stuff. He told me that two people
> never meet for coincidence ... he's a really great guy and
> I look up to him a lot. (Apr 18)

One night, over the phone Elder Blaire said some things that were really offensive to me. I'm a very easy-going person and almost never get angry or upset, but that phone call shook me so much that the other three elders in our apartment immediately knew something was very wrong. After that, if Elder Blaire called, I tossed the phone to my companion to answer, and I avoided any meetings with him.

After a few months one of the APs stepped in and forced us to meet together. I said whatever needed to be said to get out of that meeting as quickly as possible, and the few conversations we had after that were brief and to the point.

On the last day of his mission, as part of my normal responsibilities I drove him and the other departing missionaries to the bus terminal, where they would have a 12-hour overnight ride before catching a plane home. All of the office missionaries were giving the typical handshake and left-arm hug to say goodbye to each of the departing elders. When I finally made it to Elder Blaire he ended up giving me a full-on hug. It was a big strong hug and we were both instantly in tears. In that moment I knew that it didn't matter what had happened in the past; I just wanted to be good friends with him.

A future full of uncertainty

As I returned to BYU after my mission, I fell into the same dating patterns that were familiar from high school. Occasionally my roommates were able to pressure me into a group date, and I even went to a homecoming dance once, to fill in for a friend who was sick.

I was very disappointed when I was unable to gain admittance to the BYU film program. Hitting that wall was a tough experience, especially when I felt like this was what I was supposed to be doing. After several months of soul searching, I decided to move to California to finish my education there.

In many ways the move to California was a pivotal moment in my life. I was so distraught about the situation that I spent the first two hours of the drive home in tears. Left behind was my BYU degree, friends, opportunities, and the perfect path I had been on up until that point. Ahead lay a future full of uncertainty.

It would take only a year to graduate. One of the last classes I took was a job placement class, where we often had "mock" interviews (in front of the entire class) with real people working in the industry. During one particular interview I was asked about my ability to speak Spanish, and I quickly explained that I had lived in Chile for a few years. Unsatisfied with this minimal explanation, my teacher stopped me and asked me to explain the details of the experience. I did, and the interviewer expressed that he admired such service. Several months later, when I applied for a position at his company, he remembered my story, and I had the elusive "in" that is often so difficult to find in the film world.

You can't keep ignoring them

With my career on a steady course, my focus once again returned to the standard Church formula: priesthood, mission, college, wife. It was pretty obvious to myself and everyone around me which item on that list was missing. I was active in my ward, serving as the ward clerk, but never made close friends there. I was conscious of the fact that I was supposed to be working on marriage but was completely oblivious to what the girls around me were doing.

One Sunday the wife of one of our bishopric members pulled me aside for a chat: In effect, she said, "Dan, you need to pay attention. There are several sisters who clearly like you, and you can't keep ignoring them. Sister so-and-so is particularly interested in you, and I think it's very important that you do something about it. You can't get married if you don't ever take any action. It's your responsibility to make the efforts to ask these girls out."

I was stunned. Not a word left my mouth during the entire conversation, just a series of mumbles and nods. Eventually, I did go on several dates with one of these girls. We had fun, but I never even managed to get as far as hand holding. My attempts at further dates were simply met with no response, and so I moved on to other things. Looking back, I can't help but help wonder if she sensed my obvious lack of attraction.

Something I had never understood before

Over the course of the next year I spent a lot of time contemplating where I was going in life. I was starting to become conscious of the fact that I might be attracted to guys. That said, I had convinced myself that there was no way I could be gay. In my mind, gays were people who liked cross-dressing, promiscuous sex, drugs, and alcohol — all things that I wanted no part of.

I remember being aware that the movie *Brokeback Mountain* was playing in theaters. Out of curiosity, I wanted to go see it, but I was too terrified of what that could mean. What would I say if someone saw me in the theater? But my increasing curiosity lead me to download the movie *Latter Days*. Even in the safety of my own room I was too scared to watch most of the film. I fast forwarded through large sections of the movie, and permanently deleted it a few days later.

Eventually I stumbled onto a short film online: It started out with two friends walking through the Irish country side. I'll call them Peter and Nathan. They ended up sitting down next to some train tracks and Nathan pulled out a knife and started throwing it in the ground. Suddenly Nathan grabbed Peter's wrist and forced his palm against the ground. Peter tried to twist his hand away, but Nathan looked him in the eyes and said, "Just trust me. I'll put my hand over yours so that if I miss, I'll get cut first." Taking the knife in his fist, Nathan began to stab back and forth between their fingers. He started slowly at first, but he eventually started going faster and faster. Soon his hand was moving back and forth in a blur of stabs until there was a loud train whistle and suddenly a train was rushing by, inches from where they were sitting. As the last section of the train moved on, the film ended with a shot of their two hands, intertwined together.

Seeing that moment was like breaking through a brick wall for me. For the first time in my life I understood why someone might want to hold hands with another person. I was filled with longing for a new type of emotional connection — something I had never understood before, brought on by a simple shot of two hands. But it was very clear to me that a relationship like the one I longed for would never be possible within the current constraints of the Church. The entire experience was pushed into a dark corner of my mind.

A year later I moved back in with my parents for a few months before I could find another apartment to rent on my own. After living with them for three weeks, my car was stolen and things started to spiral out of control. It was the beginning of a mid-life crisis that would change me forever. The cloud of despair that had settled over my life was only amplified as I looked around me for people to help. Beyond a few attempts at failed relationships, I had never shared a meaningful intimate connection with another human being. Not once, in my entire 27 years of existence.

People who were just like me

During this time period I was still keeping in touch with several friends who were living in Provo, and I also regularly followed news events that involved the Church. I learned of an art exhibit at BYU that dealt with homosexuality. The exhibit, created by BYU student Michael Wiltbank, consisted of pairs of photographs; each one was a close-up of a face, with the person looking directly at the camera. In each pair, one of the individuals was gay, and the other was someone who supported them. The catch was that there were no labels, so it was impossible to tell which of the individuals were gay. Within one week the project was taken down by school officials, but then re-hung after a surprisingly large controversy. Several news organizations from other parts of the country picked up the story, and both the Salt Lake Tribune and the Deseret News featured stories on the exhibit.

This was the story that helped me realize that there were other gay Mormons out there, many of whom were just like me. They were not the strange and twisted individuals that I had always been told homosexuals were. They were not drug addicts, alcoholics, or sex-crazed maniacs. These were faithful individuals, struggling to deal with a difficult conflict that often involved the rejection of both their families and their community. As I watched the controversy surrounding the exhibit unfold, I became aware of a small community of gay Mormon blogs. At first I was too scared to even comment on them, but eventually I started reading, then commenting, and finally I felt like I was actually ready to talk with some of them.

I found out about a small monthly party hosted by Scott and Sarah Nicholson, a mixed-orientation couple, and I decided to drive to Utah to attend. I can still remember how nervous I was as I drove to their home. I told my sister I was just going to hang out with some "friends from college". That night, for the first time I met people who were just like me. Some of them were going to BYU, and some of them even had a boyfriend. It was the first time I had ever admitted to someone in person that I was gay. It was also the first place that I could hear stories about how people's bishops had reacted, what their family's response was, and what their plans were for the future. I drove home that evening on an emotional high, excited for the opportunities that my future could hold. One of my first acquaintances from the blogosphere was there that night, and he left me a CD with some of his favorite songs on it. My theme for the night, and one that I listened to more than a few times on the way home, was "No Day But Today".

Time, hope, and love on our side

When I returned home to California, there was continuing discussion over Proposition 8, the constitutional amendment that had recently added one line to the state's constitution:

> "Only marriage between a man and a woman is valid or recognized in California."

As I pondered the ramifications of my recent experiences, Proposition 8 continued to be a common theme and topic at church every week, even two months after the election had ended. I was careful to keep my silence and avoid any association with the issue. Having just barely started to deal with my own feelings, I wasn't ready to have a conflict with the Church, and I badly wanted the issue to just disappear. Things got worse as Proposition 8 soon became the default answer for examples of how to follow the prophet, ways Satan tries to confuse us, and the wickedness of the world in the last days. A common statement I heard at church was that gay people were incapable of true love. On several occasions my local Church leaders compared gay activists to extremists and even terrorists. During a special fifth Sunday lesson on Sodom and Gomorrah, one member suggested that all of the gay people in San Francisco should just be exiled to an island someplace.

On top of this, both of my parents seemed to be concerned about the lack of dating in my life. My dad was starting to mention the idea of a dating quota that I could fill every month instead of paying rent. A few days later my mother asked me if there was anyone I was interested in dating, or if I just wasn't interested in dating at all. I was convinced that she was beginning to suspect I was gay, and it worried me.

Eventually my desire to live a more open and honest life led me to consider finding a way to share this part of myself with my parents. I decided to give them an absolutely amazing book by Carol Lynn Pearson titled *No More Goodbyes*. On the day I moved out of my parents' home, I left a copy on their bed, along with the following letter:

Dear Mom & Dad,

I wanted to have this conversation in person, but I don't trust myself to properly convey my emotions, and how serious I am about this topic. First, I want to thank you for being wonderful parents. You raised me with an excellent understanding of right and wrong, and even more importantly, you have always been there for me. You supported me on my mission more than any other parent that I have ever known. When the whole Film/Media Arts mess at BYU rolled around, you were patient and supportive while I bumbled around trying to figure out what to do next. And after that, your advice and support helped me start a new career which I really do love. For all of this and so much more I will be eternally grateful.

During the last 6 months I have spent lots of time prayerfully considering my future. I believe that it is now time for me to be a little more honest with you and the rest of the family. Mom & Dad I am gay. Please allow me to explain what this means, as there are so many misconceptions about this term (especially within the church). For starters; I am not, have never been, and will never be attracted to women. This is not a sudden change or something I have just realized, but rather, this is me being open and honest about a part of me that I have had to hide for far too long. Please realize that I am the same person that you have always known. Being gay does not mean that I live or support the "gay lifestyle". That is to say that I am still the same clean, honest, and good person that you have known and been proud of for all these years.

One of the biggest questions racing through your minds right now is probably what this means for me and my relationship with the church. I love the church. It has given me so many experiences, friends, & treasures which I will never be able to replace. At the same time, the experiences of the last year have shown me that there is no place for people like me in the church. Again, let me assure that I am not making these decisions or statements lightly. As I have pondered and prayed about where to take my life, I have been impressed that God loves me just the way I am. He created me in His image, and wants me to live a life of happiness & love. A life which will be dedicated to a man that I can love and serve for time and all eternity.

As I have agonized over whether I should share this information with you, and what your reaction would be, one of last year's Christmas presents has provided me with some small amount of comfort. Mom may not have read the letters that Dad gave us, but towards the end was a phrase that I have repeated over and over again in my mind. "Please know that we love you with all our hearts and will sacrifice anything we have to help and support you." I pray that this statement remains in effect.

Part of me wants to think that you have been guessing at this for some time. However, I am also realistic enough to realize that a letter like this probably comes as a great surprise to you. Please, please, please take the time to read through the book I left you. When you are ready, I'll be happy to answer any questions you have. Please don't feel like you have to hide this, or keep it a secret from anyone. At this point I am more than ready to be open and honest about this part of myself.

Love, Your Son

I left my parent's home that night fully prepared for the fact that I might never return. Considering my parent's activity in the Church, along with their significant donations to Proposition 8, I was convinced that this was a very real possibility. I was nervous but also excited about the new path I was about to embark on. The next morning my parents got on the phone together and called me. They explained that they had started to read the book, and they wanted to make sure I knew that they would always love me, and that they always wanted me to remain as part of the family. It was a huge relief.

A week later we met for dinner so that we could talk about some of the concerns they were dealing with. Among the many questions they asked me were things like, How long have you known? Have you told your bishop? Have you told anyone else in the family? Why didn't you tell us sooner? What are your plans for the future? I was completely honest with my answers and explained that I had already been on a few dates and saw myself eventually dedicating the rest of my life to a husband and my own family. Again my parents made it clear that no matter what, they wanted me to feel comfortable and welcome as part of the family. My family's reaction has far surpassed any expectations I had. Things aren't perfect, but there is time, hope, and love on our side. Some bridges will have to be built or crossed when I get to them.

Finding joy in the journey

The most difficult part of coming out was establishing a new community and group of friends. Because of the events I witnessed at church during the Proposition 8 campaign, I may never really feel comfortable during a church service again. I have only been to church once since coming out, and that was a Christmas present for Mom. But the end of my church attendance meant that I also lost the biggest social support system I had ever known. Suddenly I had almost no friends living nearby, and no community to turn to in order to find new ones. It was a painful, lonely situation that took me more than six months to resolve.

Thankfully, I have been able to reach out to many great individuals who I can now count as friends. Through my blog I met many other people like me, some of whom have also become close friends that I am really grateful for. I also stumbled onto a group of guys here in southern California called Guys Like Us. The group was formed to create spaces for gay, bisexual, trans, curious, and queer guys where they can interact, make friends, and socialize in an environment that doesn't involve clubs and alcohol. It was a perfect match, leading to even more friends, and a support system similar to many young adult activities in the Church.

So where does that leave me today? I still believe in God, and I still miss a lot of things about the Church. But as much as my heart aches from the spiritual damage of being separated from the Church, I believe that finding a husband and starting my own family is more important. There will admittedly be sacrifices I have to make along the way. I may have to miss my sister's temple marriage. I don't know if my parents will agree or fully support such a decision. One day I might even have to go through the process of excommunication. But whatever the sacrifices are, I am convinced that my future husband will be worth it, and to put it in familiar terms, I am busy finding joy in the journey.

Matt Sutton

"We would subject ourselves to the yoke of bondage if it were requisite with the justice of God, or if he should command us so to do. But behold he doth not command us that we shall subject ourselves to our enemies, but that we should put our trust in him, and he will deliver us."
– Alma 61:12-13

Growing up, my father was Catholic and my mother was LDS. I really embraced Mormonism from very early on. I would encourage my family to have family prayer, and I would push my mom to be on time for church. I knew I wanted to go on a mission when I grew up.

As a small child, I remember I would play with my sister's Barbie dolls, and my favorite toy was "Puppy Surprise". One time I asked my mom, "Why can't boys marry boys?" It didn't make sense to me. In fourth or fifth grade, girls were talking about how they were in love with the actor Jonathan Taylor Thomas, and I had a secret crush on him too.

When I went through puberty, that's when I really knew that I was not attracted to girls but to guys. It was troubling for me. I had always been taught that it was wrong to be gay, that it was a perversion. I couldn't understand what was going on.

For the next few years, I would read the scriptures all the time. I thought there was something horribly wrong with me. Night after night, I would cry and pray to Heavenly Father that he would change me, that I could be attracted to girls. I pled with God and made bargains that I would do anything for that. I became really depressed. I was scared of life, but I was also terrified of death, because I thought that I would go to hell.

One year at Scout camp, while I was playing Truth or Dare with another boy, one thing led to another, and we did immoral things. Afterwards, I felt a lot of remorse and shame. We both felt guilty about it, but I didn't feel like I could talk to the bishop. A while later, a similar thing happened with another boy. I felt terrible about myself and carried a burden of shame.

"You're just confused."

One day I had been praying really hard, and I felt Heavenly Father speaking to me, telling me that I was okay, that there was nothing wrong with me, that I was a beautiful child to Him the way He had made me. So I started to accept myself, but I still felt really bad.

When I was about 16, I started drinking, and one time my mom caught me. I told her I was going to talk to the bishop to tell him about that, and I did, but I also told him everything else. Soon afterwards, the other boy's dad talked to my mom and told her everything. She confronted me about it. I told her I was gay, but she said, "No you're not. You don't know. You're just confused. You're not that way." She started saying very derogatory things about gays and what a sinful life they lead. I felt worse than ever.

Then my mom put me in counseling with a family therapist, a member of the Church. He said they were going to help me to change. They treated me like I had a mental problem. I don't remember everything they said, but I just remember being in tears. I hated it. I remember the trauma that it caused me, because they were trying and trying to change me. And I had already tried to change myself for so long, and I knew I couldn't not be gay. I had finally started to accept myself, and they weren't going to allow that.

I just wanted to escape

Somehow the word got out and people at church found out I was gay. I felt like the woman in the book *The Scarlet Letter*. It seemed like everyone was looking at me and talking about me like I was some whore. I had always loved the Church, but I felt like everyone there hated me. I felt like even my mom was ashamed. She said, "What will people at church think about this?" And she would blame herself and say things like, "I don't know what I did to make this happen." That voice of shame, the disappointment in her voice, was awful. It stuck with me for a long time afterwards.

After that, my mom started punishing me. She took away my cell phone and wouldn't let me use the house phone. She would lock it up or take it with her when she went to work, and the modem too so I couldn't use the Internet.

I remember one time before school, I found the phone out on the counter, so I crawled under the counter to use it. Just then, my brother saw me, and he told my mom. And then my mom came in and jerked the phone away and yelled at me.

They kept putting me into counseling, trying to change me, and finally I refused to keep going. I said that if I went, I wasn't going to tell him anything, that she would just be wasting her money. At the beginning I thought they were really going to try to help me, but it was only making me more depressed. Not only did I hate myself, I hated everyone around me, at church, and in my family. I felt like everyone was so disappointed in me, so disgusted with me because I was gay. And I knew I couldn't not be gay, so there was nothing I could do about it.

So I just gave up. I didn't want to do anything anymore. I stopped going to church. I would hardly ever talk to my mom or anyone in my family. I got into drinking and a lot of drugs. I just wanted to escape. I couldn't live with myself, my family, and my surroundings.

Throughout this time, my one true friend was Rachel, a girl I had known from seminary. She was the only person that I felt I could talk to, the only one I could trust. Supposedly I wasn't allowed to leave the house, but sometimes I would run outside and meet Rachel on a side street, just to hang out and be together.

I started praying again

During this time, I got really lost, going down the wrong path for a while. When I was 18, I ended up getting arrested for possession of drugs. After that, my mom started being really supportive of me. She wasn't trying to question me because I was gay; she stopped focusing on that. It was the first time I felt like she loved me. And it was weird because I had just been arrested, but somehow it brought us closer together.

But I still didn't want to have anything to do with the Church, and I continued down the wrong path for about two years, until I went into rehab when I was 20. After I got sober, I realized I wanted a relationship with God really bad. I went to a lot of non-denominational Christian churches, and I started praying again.

I got into an AA program, focusing on building a relationship with a higher power. It was still the same God I always believed in. I still believed that Joseph Smith had restored the gospel in this dispensation. But I felt like I just couldn't go back to the LDS church. So I was trying to find a different church, but none of them could compare with what I knew, because I really had a testimony that the Church was true.

I had a spiritual awakening

After that, I got into a long-term relationship with a guy. We lived together for about two years. I was happy. I felt comfortable in the way I was living, and in my relationship with God. I knew living together before marriage was wrong, but there was no option for gay marriage, and we agreed that we were engaged, whenever marriage became an option. But I wanted to be with him and was really devoted to him. So I was comfortable with that.

But when that relationship ended, I fell back off the wagon and started drinking again and getting involved in drugs and immoral behaviors. I just didn't know where my life was going. And I ended up getting arrested again. That Friday I got fired from my job, where I had been working for about three years.

When I got home, I was hysterical. Then the officers came with a warrant to arrest me for violating my probation, and they put me in jail. I had no idea when I would get out. I was really terrified. I got down on my knees, praying and praying. Something happened to me when I was in there. About the third or fourth day I was there, I had a spiritual awakening. I felt like finally I was surrendering to God. I knew that I was tired of living the way I had, tired of running from everything in my life, from the fact I was gay, and from the religion that I believed was true. I wanted to stand up and start living life the way that I felt was right, and to be part of my religion no matter what it did to me.

Coming back to the Church

I got out of jail on Friday a week later. I felt that God was talking to me, putting questions into my mind, "If I believe the doctrine of the Church is true, why am I not going? Because of what people will say about me? Why am I more afraid of man than of God?" So that Sunday, I went back to church.

At first, I only stayed for sacrament meeting, but I kept going. I started making YouTube videos sharing my experience, and trying to reach out to other people. I needed a support system. I needed to learn from other people how they dealt with their struggles, and what they had found to be true. I was feeling more and more comfortable exploring my relationship with God, getting back into the Church, and trying to catch up on everything I had missed.

I asked my home teacher to come over and give me a blessing. He knew of my struggles and was someone who I felt had never judged me. He was a very caring, loving, humble man, and I looked up to him. He blessed me to be able to have the support I needed to transition and get back active in the Church. He suggested I could go and talk to the bishop.

I wanted to go and start the repentance process, but I really struggled with that for about two months. I prayed every day, "Heavenly Father, show me what to do?" And I just didn't know. Because I knew that I was gay, and I was really worried that they were going to try to change me, to try to make me straight, and that this whole mess was going to start over again.

I started reading Church articles and scriptures about repentance, and finally I went and talked to the bishop. I told him everything. He said something like, "I have a friend who was living the 'homosexual lifestyle' for a long time, and then he decided that this wasn't the way that he wanted to live, and he went through the repentance process, and after some counseling, as of last year, he was married in the temple." And I was thinking, "Oh my gosh. They're going to try to change me again! I can't do this." I told him I was just going to try being celibate, that I had tried changing and wasn't going to put myself through the depression of doing that again. And he was okay with that. But because of my past actions, they had a disciplinary council, and I got disfellowshipped. But I continued to go to all the meetings.

I've been praying a lot

Since then, things have been going really good. My mom is a best friend to me now. I share everything with her, the relationships that I've had, my concerns, and my struggles. She has been very supportive of me and has even gone out of her way to be there to support other parents dealing with similar issues.

I'm going to church every week now and trying to be a better person. But I'm starting to feel like there's still something wrong. I believe everything to be true, about the doctrine of the gospel, but there's a part of me that thinks, "How could I be alone my whole life?" I can't imagine not being able to have a family. I see all these little kids and people that are happily married, and I want to be able to have a family of my own. And I'm thinking that I honestly believe that that's what Heavenly Father wants for me too, to be happy and to have a family.

I know this is against the Church rules and everything, but I just don't feel that it's wrong. I feel like, if Heavenly Father loves me so much, why would he condemn me for not wanting to live a lonely life without a family? It just doesn't make sense to me. I wonder if it is social norms that have clouded us in the Church and stopped us from seeing that Heavenly Father wouldn't do this. I've been praying a lot about that, and I hope someday to have an answer.

Bridey Jensen

"For I am persuaded, that neither death, nor life, nor angels, nor principalities, nor powers, nor things present, nor things to come, nor height, nor depth, nor any other creature, shall be able to separate us from the love of God, which is in Christ Jesus our Lord."
– Romans 8:38–39

I was born in the Church. From the time I was in elementary school, I knew there was something different about me, but I didn't know what it was. As I grew up, my friends were noticing guys and saying, "He's so cute. I have a crush on him." During my freshman year of high school, I began to think, "Wait a minute. I don't have a crush on anyone."

I just thought I didn't like guys yet but that eventually I would. When girls would ask, "Who do you like?", I would name a guy in my ward, because I had learned that if I said I didn't like anyone they would say, "Oh you have to like someone."

There were girls that I became really emotionally attached to. And I couldn't understand why they didn't feel the same way. I wasn't thinking of it as romantic; I just knew I really liked being around them.

There was a girl "Becky" that I had known from the time we were in Primary. In middle school, I loved being around her, and I thought she was cute. We were both really touchy-feely, huggy people. In high school, I didn't like it when she started dating guys. Although I wouldn't admit it, I was jealous.

My sophomore year is when it hit me that the feelings my friends had for guys were the kinds of feelings that I had for girls. Once I became aware of that, for a while I kind of pulled back from everything, from my friends. I told myself, "I'm not that kind of person."

This wasn't going away

My junior year I was really close friends with a girl "Kim". We were in the marching band together, and it was really great. Then all of a sudden, people started making up rumors about us. It was hard, because she kind of freaked out and said we couldn't spend so much time together.

My senior year I started spending a lot of time with "Karen", a girl that I had been friends with since the fifth grade. I just wanted to be close to her. When we were on the band bus, I always wanted to sit with her. We always went to lunch together. We were in most of the same classes and sat next to each other. In those moments I remember feelings of really liking her. Then one day, on a band trip, she told me something personal and was really emotional about it. I remember sitting and thinking, "If you let me, I would take care of you. I would love you." And it caught me off guard. That's when it hit me, that I really liked her, that I loved her. I think that was the first time I realized that this wasn't going away, that it wasn't something that I could just ignore.

I don't remember ever being attracted to guys. For a while I was really wanting guys to ask me out, because I thought maybe I just needed to meet a guy. And some of them did ask me out, but they always just felt like friends. I think the closest I ever got to actually liking a guy was a boy my senior year. He was in the band and was also LDS. He was really comfortable with himself and made other people feel comfortable too. People would say he was really cute, and he was. He was funny and talked to me all the time. Instead of going to prom, the two of us went to a movie and dinner and hung out. I don't remember ever wanting to be physically close to him, but he was a really great friend.

I knew I wasn't a bad person

The summer before I came to BYU, I didn't know what I was supposed to do. From church, I always had the idea that being gay was not okay. It was bad, it was wrong, and people would hate me for it. I was worried about it. One time I was in the car with a good friend, a member of the Church. I was really quiet, and she asked, "What's up?" I said, "I'm attracted to women." I realized this was probably not the most subtle way to bring it up. Her initial response was, "No you're not." And I was like, "Yeah, I am." As we drove, the conversation mostly consisted of her suggesting that I have a weak testimony, and that if I chose this, they would kick me out of the Church and BYU. At the end of all that, she said, "I love you," and I went home. I think it was then that I realized that I didn't need to talk to the bishop, because I hadn't done anything. I wasn't a bad person. But even though I knew I wasn't a bad person, I was really frightened by the things she said about how the Church would react.

After that, I told another girl, a member of the Church, and her response was like, "Oh, congratulations! I'm so happy for you that you've come out, that you're finding who you are, and that you're not afraid of it." It felt like the wrong reaction. I just wanted to have someone tell me it was okay to be me. I didn't want to be patted on the back for any of this; I was still not okay with everything.

The other person I told was Becky. Her response was perfect: she wanted to know if I was okay and asked, "Is there anything I can do?" I said, "No not really," and she said, "Oh, okay." I loved hanging out with her; I could just be me. One time I told her that I thought she was really cute and I wanted to kiss her, and her reaction was like, "I think you're cute too, and if I was gay I would probably want to kiss you, but here we are." And it wasn't awkward. She didn't make a big deal out of it.

I could still be a good Mormon

So I came to college at BYU and lived in Helaman Halls. I was terrified that people would find out. It got to the point where I was doing everything right, going to BYU, reading my scriptures, being nice to people, and I was just getting tired because nothing was changing. I was convinced that although I wasn't a bad person, I must have done something wrong and that's why I was gay, because why else would this be happening? I knew I didn't choose this. And so that went on for a while. I felt bad, and I stopped wanting to come to church.

My roommate noticed and asked why I didn't like coming to church. I burst into tears and told her I liked girls and that I didn't know what to do. She didn't really say anything, but she just held me as I cried. I felt bad because I was pretty sure that she had never encountered this. After that, we never really talked about it, but it felt good that the person I was living with didn't think I was a bad person.

That's when I met "Megan", another girl in my hall. One night we were up late talking and doing homework, when she confided something really personal to me. I felt like if she trusted me that much then I could trust her, so I told her that I liked girls. She said, "Oh, okay." She didn't freak out. We talked about it. I didn't know if she really understood it, but she didn't have a problem with it. After I told her, she started to become more touchy-feely and hang around me more.

A few weeks later, during the Conference weekend in October, Megan and I were at her grandma's house. While at BYU, no boys had asked me out, and I had a daunting feeling that since I didn't like guys, I would never be able to get married and never be able to be happy. I was wanting somebody to tell me that I was okay, that I wasn't undesirable. We were the only two there, and while we were watching Conference, I asked her, "If you were gay, would you like me?" In response, she leaned over and kissed me. I was surprised, but it made me feel really happy. For a few weeks after this, we were kind of dating. She's the one who called it that. I was afraid to call it that. It felt really happy. No one else knew except her and my roommate.

She didn't feel bad about it, but I started to worry. I went and told my bishop. I made her go too. I think he was the first person that made me feel like I wasn't a bad Mormon, because he was the first one to say, "You can feel whatever you want," that it was only behavior that could become an issue. He let me know I wasn't a bad person. It felt awesome. After that, Megan still wanted to do stuff, and I felt bad that I didn't want to. But my bishop had given me the confidence that I could still be a good Mormon and feel the way I did, so I was firm in saying, "Nope, we can't do this anymore."

So I knew it probably wouldn't go away, but that this was okay, that I could still be a good person. I really started wanting to be a good member of the Church and do everything right. But I still really liked Megan, so it was hard. The thing that really confused me is that later she told me she had kind of just been doing it for fun. (She liked guys, and she's married now.) When she told me that, it kind of left me feeling alone again.

You have to fix this

My sophomore year I moved in with Megan's roommate "Liz". I told her about everything, and she was fine with it. We went through a lot of tough stuff together, and I became really close to her. I felt myself starting to have a crush on her. When she went out with guys, I would get jealous. It was difficult, because subconsciously I was waiting for her to realize that she liked me back.

Eventually she got a serious boyfriend, and I hated it. To me it seemed like he wasn't all that great, that he didn't really understand her, and yet she chose to be with him most of the time. During my junior year, I eventually told her, "I really like you and have for a long time." For me it felt great. Finally I was being honest with my best friend. And at first she was like, "Okay. You're not going to do anything, right?" It had kind of been an understanding in our friendship that as long as I never hit on her, it would be okay. But this seemed to change everything. Everything I did now — if I hugged her, or if I wanted to sit next to her in a movie, she started to second-guess it, "Are you doing this because you're my friend or because you like me?" And it just got to be too much. Things kind of fell apart, and we don't really talk anymore.

That put me on a track of thinking, "Okay, if I could just make everything better with myself then things would be better." So I started going to church all the time, going to the temple, doing everything with the intention of showing God that I was a good person. God can do anything, right? So if I did everything, read my scriptures, and was a good Mormon, and asked God to make me straight, he would, right? I had read the scriptures that say, "Knock and it shall be opened," and "Ask and ye shall receive."

I prayed so hard. After a few months, about the time Liz stopped hanging out with me, I just remember feeling, "God, You have to fix this. What can I do?" I felt like God didn't love me anymore. What was the point of the Church being true if it couldn't help me? People would talk about how all the answers are in the scriptures, and I would think, "But it doesn't tell you what to do if you're gay!"

I felt like God wasn't hearing my prayers, or if he was, he was ignoring them. It was devastating. It pushed me into a horrible depression. My grades plummeted. I went to the BYU Counseling Center and to LDS Family Services. One of the counselors helped me with the depression, but after I told her, "I'm gay," she didn't know how to help me with that.

It felt like I should be here

The depression kept getting worse, and I wasn't functioning anymore. I could barely get out of bed. It got so bad that I had to leave school during Christmas, and I went back home. There I talked to an LDS therapist referred by my stake president. She really helped me get out of the depression, and the medicine helped. And then, when it came to the topic of how I still had feelings for girls, she didn't really know what to do about that. So I stopped going. But I was feeling a lot better.

There was a point that summer that I was feeling really good, and I decided to put in my mission papers. To make the long story short, my bishop thought I was totally fine — he knew about everything. My stake president also thought I was fine, so we submitted the papers. Because of the past depression, they sent someone to interview me, and I told him everything, about how I was attracted to girls and had been really depressed about it. A month or so later, my stake president called me in and told me that he had gotten a letter stating that I wasn't going to be able to go on my mission. It sent me back into a depression, because I felt like I was trying to do something good but couldn't even do that.

A couple weeks later, though, I started humoring the thought, "I could go back to school." Within a week, everything was falling into place. I was reaccepted to BYU. I got a spot back in the marching band. I found a place to live with a friend. It felt really good. The only thing that has ever felt good like that has been to come to BYU.

I came back, and within a few weeks of searching on the Internet for every possible combination of words "gay", "BYU", "groups", I found a blog that said something about a "gay group at BYU". I looked it up, and that's how I found out about Understanding Same-Gender Attraction (USGA) and met Brent. The first time I came, it was absolutely amazing to me! Up to that point I had thought I was alone. It was such a relief to find this group, where people understood, and where we could talk. It helped me feel a lot more open and comfortable with myself.

I feel optimistic

If there is anything this whole experience has taught me, it is to be understanding and to just love people. For the longest time I was just miserable and really hated myself. I remember thinking I just wanted somebody to tell me that it was okay to be myself. I've learned that a lot of people need that. I've learned that it's really easy to love people for who they are, when you think about it, when you realize that they're a child of God. We say that all the time, but it became real for me through this whole thing.

I don't think it has really changed the way I feel about the Church. I've never disbelieved in the Church. But I think I've gotten to a point where it has sometimes become hard to see where I fit in it. I don't hate it. I don't think it's not true or anything like that. I just feel like I am still struggling with two very important parts of myself. I haven't reached the point yet where they're not mutually exclusive. I do hope to reach that point somehow.

For the longest time, I felt awful about myself because of what I was taught in the Church growing up, that homosexuality was bad, an evil choice. When I couldn't get rid of it, it gave me the idea that I was being punished for something. And I know that the Church says now that it doesn't make you a bad person, but I sometimes feel the members in general haven't changed a whole lot with how they feel towards it. When I go, it still makes me feel a little scared, even though I know I'm not a bad person. People have said things about homosexuals being bad people, and they act like that's what the Church teaches, when they don't really understand.

So here I am at BYU. I still go to church. I may not go every single week, but it's enough to stay active. I don't really know what will happen in the future, but I feel optimistic.

Sam "Hughes"

"If we have no peace, it is because we have forgotten that we belong to each other."
– Mother Teresa

I was raised as a Southern Baptist in Arizona. From early on, one of the first Bible stories I heard, after the creation, was how God destroyed Sodom and Gomorrah. I was taught that they were evil because they were "homosexual", but I didn't know what that meant. I asked my parents, but they wouldn't tell me; they just said that it meant they were evil people and so God destroyed them.

When I was five or six, I began to feel attractions to boys. It wasn't sexual; it was just that I liked them and wanted to be with them, more than I did with girls. In kindergarten, I remember one cute boy in the class; over the next couple years, I developed a crush on him.

About that time, I found out that "homosexuals" were people who liked people of the same gender. I began to feel tremendous guilt. It was a terrifying realization. As a little boy, I didn't know why I had these feelings. I just knew that God was very angry at me.

I began to deny I had the feelings and prayed they would go away. At the same time I was also dealing with feelings of depression and anxiety resulting from having been molested as a child. I had never told anyone about that, not even my parents. Meanwhile, I read my Bible, memorized scriptures, and did all the things I was supposed to do.

I wanted to tell someone

In junior high when I was 11 or 12 there was an athletic boy who I thought was very good-looking. I played the flute in band, and he played the trumpet. He was very intelligent, and the girls loved him. He was such a nice guy, and I wanted to be with him. It hurt that he didn't like me the way I liked him. I wished I could hold his hand. I didn't think of it as homosexual. It was more of an emotional thing.

AIDS was a big issue. We used to listen to a radio program by Dr. Dobson, and on it people would talk about how gays could be "reprogrammed", "fixed", or made whole again. But the more I tried to fix myself, the more anxiety I felt. I was terrified about these feelings and that people might figure out I wasn't attracted to girls. I was terrified of telling my parents. I tried to suppress the feelings but it only made them stronger.

I wanted to tell someone, but I didn't know who I could talk to. The message I was getting from the radio and at church was that gay people were evil: they should be put in prison or killed. I was scared that if people found out, the police might come and take me away to jail.

There were times when it seemed like the feelings had gone away. But when I went through puberty and sexual desires began to emerge, the feelings only intensified. I realized this wasn't just a phase, that it wasn't going to go away. That meant I had to take even more drastic steps to crush it.

I began to date a lot of girls. I started running and lifting weights. I did all these things with a focus on becoming "straight". But by the time I was 15, I realized it wasn't working. My idea of God was an angry fire-and-brimstone God who would never love me. I felt I had no worth, because I had been molested and because I was homosexual. I felt like I had no value and that God wanted me dead. I decided I couldn't keep living, that it wasn't worth it. If this is all life was, I decided I couldn't do it anymore.

I attempted suicide by taking pills, ten times the lethal dose. I got extremely sick, threw up, and passed out. My mom found me, took me to the hospital, where they pumped my stomach and saved my life. I was in the psychiatric ward for five days after that. A psychiatrist asked me why I had tried to hurt myself. I just said I was depressed and scared. I was too terrified to tell him the truth. He diagnosed me with generalized anxiety disorder, put me on medication, and sent me home. For a while I thought maybe I was fixed and life was going to be okay.

Six months later, the depression came back. I realized I couldn't go on like this. I tried even harder to use religion to fix myself. I read the Bible even more and got involved in the Christian groups in my school. I began to witness to people, telling them about my faith as a Southern Baptist and doing community service. I began to memorize whole chapters of scripture.

It got to the point where if I had an attraction, whether emotional or physical, I would recall a scripture, and it would temporarily block out the thought of the attraction. It gave me hope for a while, but long-term the feelings were getting stronger and more intense. I would smile on the outside but inside I felt terrible.

I went on a few dates with girls in high school. It was awkward, but I just did it, hoping things would change. There was a time when I felt some small sexual desire for a few girls — not really anything emotional, just sexual, and it was very fleeting. But it gave me hope that maybe I could be fixed.

But by the time I was 18, although I still wanted to change myself, I realized that I probably couldn't. At the same time, I began to be disillusioned with the church, because of the hypocrisy I saw there. And so I left.

I felt conflicted

After a year, I began to visit different churches. I liked the Catholic Church. It felt very inviting and warm. I began going to mass with a friend. Eventually I decided I wanted to become Catholic, and I met with a priest to talk about what I needed to do. I loved the Church.

It had been hard on my parents when I left the Southern Baptist church and became non-religious, but it was harder still when I joined the Catholic Church. After a while, they came around a bit though: they still believed I was going to hell for going to a different church, but they realized I was doing good things and living what I was supposed to be doing overall.

One time I went to a party with other Catholics, and I was shocked to see people drinking. As a Baptist I had believed it was huge sin to drink. Eventually, though, I became okay with it and would drink some wine with them.

After two years, the scandal broke out about how Catholic priests had been molesting children. From the media reports, gradually I became more aware of it and troubled by it.

At this point, I was going to a counselor because of my depression. She would say things like how gay people are destroying our culture and society and how giving them rights would make things worse. I knew I couldn't talk to her about my feelings, but I talked to her about the abuse from my childhood, and she helped me with that. She would say, "Stand in front of the mirror and say: 'You have value. God loves you.'"

At the same time, I felt conflicted. I talked to the priest at church and asked him about the abuse scandal. He said it was an issue they were going to have to deal with at the Vatican, that it was a localized issue, that they didn't really need to worry about it. It hurt that he seemed to just brush it off. Meanwhile new reports of abuse were coming in from all over the nation, and I was disappointed by the Church's response. There were some archdioceses that dealt with it well, but there was a lot of denial. I felt that the way they handled it was anything but appropriate. It made me angry that they weren't punishing these people, turning them into the police, or defrocking them, and that they weren't really doing much to help victims heal.

And that's when I realized, after a few months, that I couldn't do this, that I couldn't be part of this church anymore. I tried to stick with it for a while, but then I would see things on TV that would remind me about the issue again. I honestly believed the Pope would address it; he was so well respected, and people thought he would fix it, but he didn't. It angered me. Every time the Church tried to cover something up, it felt like I was being raped again.

"If ye shall ask with a sincere heart"

It was very painful to leave the Catholic Church. I went back to being nonreligious for a couple months, but then I began to look at the LDS church. I had a lot of negative stereotypes about Mormons. But I also had known friends at school that were Mormon, who I knew were good kids. I decided to try calling the missionaries, using the number on a pass-along card from a friend.

I met with them, and after the first discussion, I felt like I couldn't swallow the Joseph Smith story. But something inside just said,

"Keep listening." A couple weeks later they came back, and they talked about repentance, baptism, the Holy Ghost, and doing good works. I decided I could accept that. And so we had a third discussion, and they introduced the Book of Mormon. I became comfortable with it and decided if I accepted the Bible, then I could also accept the Book of Mormon. They asked me to read Moroni 10:4 and to pray to find out if the Church was true.

The next day, I went with some friends to a non-denominational church. I was in the back seat, reading this scripture from the Book of Mormon, and thinking, "This is kind of a stupid way to find out if a church is true," but I said a prayer in my heart, "If this is true, what do I do?"

I wasn't prepared for the answer. It wasn't audible, but it was instantaneous, quiet, very clear, and very powerful: "It's true. Follow it." That completely freaked me out, because I wasn't prepared for that. I remember shutting the Book of Mormon and thinking, "I can't take this." The next week, I called the missionaries and told them what had happened, and they were excited and said, "Now we need to talk about baptism."

We talked about the next steps and what would be expected if I joined the Church. I learned about the Word of Wisdom. At that point, I had already pretty much given up drinking, so that wasn't a problem. But giving up coffee and tea sounded crazy. I decided to go ahead and give it up, though, and we set a baptism date for three weeks later.

I was conflicted because I felt like I should join the Church, and it was exciting, but at the same time I was terrified of what my family would think. I told my parents that I was going to be Mormon, and their response was, "How could you do this? Why are you walking away from God? We raised you better than this." They warned me not to get baptized. My friends warned me not to get baptized. But I got baptized anyway. I was 25 years old.

God would never make someone gay

Part of the reason I joined the Church was that I thought they might be able to help me not to be gay. I jumped into the Church with both feet. I did a lot of callings and service projects. I read the scriptures, memorized, and prayed. As soon as I could, I got a Limited-Use Recommend to do baptisms at the temple.

But the more I tried to suppress my feelings for guys, the more intense they became. I began having nightmares where, in my dream, someone had outed me and told everyone I was gay. Although I had not told anyone about my feelings, I was very anxious that people might find out somehow.

Finally, one time during an interview with my bishop, he asked me, "Do you struggle with same-gender attraction?" I hadn't heard that term and so I asked what it meant. He said, "Homosexuality," and at first I denied it, but over the course of the next few weeks, he brought it up a few more times, and I finally began to admit it. He said that it was okay, that they could fix this, that I could overcome my same-gender feelings. That gave me a lot of hope. I thought if they could fix me, then that meant I wasn't really gay. He referred me to a new counselor.

The counselor told me that God would never make someone gay, that it wasn't my fault that I had these feelings, but that if I dwelt on them it would be a sin. During this time I was going to the temple once or twice a week, doing baptisms. My counselor knew I had been molested, and he treated me as a victim and told me that was why I had these feelings. And I believed him; it was something I had been told before as well. I met with him regularly for six months. Eventually I started to realize it wasn't working, that it was just making the feelings for guys more intense, and that I still didn't feel anything for girls. I explained this to the counselor, but he said this was something I'd have to work with for a few more weeks and then it would heal, if I kept going to the temple, reading the scriptures, praying, and dating girls.

But the more I did these things, the more I realized it wasn't working. I decided not to go anymore. The visits with the counselor were only making me feel more anxious and lonely. I felt betrayed. I felt like I had been lied to. It was very disillusioning when I had done *everything* I was supposed to do, and yet my feelings for guys had only grown stronger.

So I gave up on the counselor and decided I would have to just try to fix myself. I got endowed and for more than four years, I continued active in the Church. Occasionally I had some small feelings for girls, again primarily sexual, not emotional. I thought as long as I had any feelings at all for girls that must mean I'm not gay. At one point I was going on dates with girls four or five times per week, in addition to going to the temple regularly. Sometimes I would go on several dates with one girl, but there was no emotional connection. I would try being intimate, holding hands and even making out with girls. It was part of my self-therapy, but it felt very awkward, and internally it felt completely wrong and unnatural.

I thought I was the only one

One day the thought occurred to me that maybe if I was surrounded by Mormons, straight conservative Mormons, that it might help me. I had some friends in Utah, and the economy was good, so I decided to move there.

In 2008, the California Supreme Court ruled that the ban on gay marriage was unconstitutional; that piqued my interest. The Church then got involved in supporting Proposition 8, to reinstate the ban. At the time, my bishop knew I struggled with same-gender attraction. I was the elders quorum secretary in my ward. The bishop called me in to meet with the elders quorum president and said we needed to help support Proposition 8. He assigned me to call people in the ward and work with the Relief Society. I willingly did everything he asked, but inside I was miserable. I felt, if this is who I am, and it can't be fixed, then maybe I *am* gay. I continued to do what the Church asked, but by the time Proposition 8 made it to the ballot, I realized that I ought to be supporting rights for people like me. Quietly, I was hoping that Proposition 8 wouldn't pass.

In the meantime, people would make comments in sacrament meeting, "We've got to stop these gay people. They're destroying our families and our world, and God has commanded us to take a stand." It really hurt, to feel like I was being demonized although I had tried for years to do everything I was supposed to.

Then one day, in a conversation, a friend mentioned something about a gay Mormon that he knew. I said, "Really? They're gay *and* Mormon?" I thought I was the only one in all of Utah. He put me in touch with this person, and from him I found out about the "Matis firesides". At the first fireside I attended, there were over 200 people. It was a huge relief to realize I wasn't alone. I made some good friends, and it was one of the best things that could have ever happened to me.

After that, I started telling a few friends that I was gay. I was surprised at how many people in the Church were supportive, and there were quite a few who said they already knew I was gay and were just waiting for me to come out.

Turn from this evil

It has been difficult for my family to accept that I am gay. Last December, I sent my Mom an email, hoping she would understand that I'm trying to be a good person:

Dear Mom,

As you already know, I struggle with Same Gender Attraction (SGA) and would consider myself to be a gay man. I know that I didn't choose to have these feelings or desires and from the age of 5 knew that I was differant than other boys my age. I have tried over the years to "erase" these feelings and tendencies to no avail. I have gone to 3 differant counsellors, read my Bible, done thousands of hours of volunteer service around the nation, memorized dozens of scriptures, said hundreds of prayers asking God to make me "straight", and tried to supress my feelings by telling myself that I'm not gay and that I was confused and could and would change, and yet no matter what I have done the feelings of Same Gender Attraction (SGA) have only gotten much more intense.

One of the resons that I chose to join the Church of Jesus Christ of Latter-Day Saints was because I knew that they had conservative beliefs regarding homosexuality, and I believed that my becoming a active member of the Church that it would help to change or reprogram my mind and emotions. I have been told by several Bishops that I could and must change or be damned to Hell, and I immersed myself into Church and Civic callings to attempt to take my mind off these feelings of Same Gender Attraction in the hope of changing my feelings toward men. Over the past year I have come to the realization that I'm a gay man and that isn't going to ever change at least not in this life.

I know that you believe that God would never create someone gay, and that it's a perversion and that for my own sake I must change my feelings and actions. I know that you will probably not be willing to change your mind regarding this belief, but for my sake please seriously consider be more willing to treat me with respect and compassion with my "struggle". I love you and want to continue to have a good relationship with you, and hope that we can work through this issue together.

Love, Sam

I felt like I was doing everything I could to reach out for reconciliation, trying to establish some common ground. It was very painful to read this response:

Dear Son,

While I can certainly understand your predicament with dealing with same gender attraction, you wont find any compassion from me in this regard. You and I already know that the Bible clearly teaches that homosexuality is a sin and that those who engage in it will be condemned by God for doing so ...

I firmly believe that if you had not been sexually abused that you would not be a homosexual, and that with enough prayer, faith, and counseling you can be healed from this sexual perversion that you are suffering from. Your father and I taught you right from wrong, and you know in your heart that God would never create someone "gay" ...

I know that you have told me that you support changing the laws of the nation to allow for so called same sex marriages, but as you already know, marriage is only valid with one man and one woman for life, that is how God created it, and that wont change regardless of what the politicians or judges say and rule ...

As Americans and more importantly as Christians we have a moral and ethical responsibility before God to defend the family and encourage the following of Christian morals and values, and you supporting so called "equal rights" for homosexuals is only encouraging the wrath of a divine and holy God on our nation and on your life as well Son. You say that you have tried hard to change your perversion and my advice is that you try much much harder: pray more, fast often, go to a Bible believing church, pay your tithing, memorize many scriptures, beat on the doors of Heaven and humbly ask God for mercy that He might save you from this evil that is sweeping the globe.

I don't want to hear about how you support giving evil perverted people any civil rights as they are the ones who will ultimately bring down the wrath of God on our nation and world for their evil ways. The U.S. Supreme Court has only facilitated this evil by decriminalizing it here in the U.S., but that does not make it right in the eyes of God, as his law still stands and justly demands that such activity be severely and quickly punished and that those who engage in it should be put to death as an example to those who might be tempted to follow the same path of perversion ...

I have talked with my pastor ... about your problem and his advice as a man of God is to have you find a Christian counselor and go through the steps that He suggests to reprogram your heart and mind, God can and wants to heal you and than after that bring a godly woman into your life and give you a family and children that you were created to have, love and provide for.

[He] also advised me to tell you that if you continue to publicly support homosexuals that I as a Christian mother will have no choice but to cut you off from my life even though I love you. I have the Christian duty to protect myself and the rest of the family, and friends, as well as my community from this evil perversion that you as my son are trapped in, It is my heart felt prayer that you will find mercy in the eyes of God and will turn from this evil and back to Him who can save your soul from the eternal fires of Hell.

Love, Mom

More compassion and empathy is what is going to heal relationships and help keep people alive instead of killing themselves. It is possible to be civil and compassionate without agreeing about everything.

I'm still on a journey

In the last year and a half I have accepted that I am how I was supposed to be created. I've realized that it's okay for me to love a guy, and that people like me ought to have the same rights as everyone else. I've got feedback from some people telling me I'm apostate, that I'm not listening to the prophet. But I've also got a lot of positive feedback.

Initially I fell in love with the Church. I loved everything about it. It shook my faith when they couldn't "fix" me after promising it was possible, and after I had put so much into it. But I'm still searching for a God of love that I can believe in. I haven't found it yet — I don't know if I'll ever find it in the Christian faith — but I want to. I'm still on a journey. I still go to church and read the scriptures. It's part of who I am as a religious person.

It's my hope that someday the Church will let people like me love who we love and not publicly oppose equal rights for us. I'm not asking to be able to marry a man in the temple; I just want to be able to be loved, accepted, and respected for who I am. I hope to find someone I can fall in love with and marry and have the same rights, protections, and responsibilities that a heterosexual couple enjoys. I hope that the Christian conservative community and the gay community can put down their arms and instead of fighting each other, work together and embrace each other, not as gays and straights but as human beings.

There is more that unites us as humans than divides us. We all drink the same water and breathe the same air. Yes there will be things that divide us, and things that make us unique. But let's look at what unites us, and let's celebrate our diversity. When you better your community you better yourself. My goal is to do that wherever I am.

The biggest lesson I've learned is this: When you can learn to accept yourself for who you are, life is no longer something you have to live, it is something you want to live. And when you can love yourself, then you can love other people, and that is when you find true happiness.

John "Peterson"

*"Even though large tracts of Europe and many old
and famous States have fallen or may fall ... we
shall defend our island, whatever the cost may be
... we shall never surrender ..."*
– Winston Churchill

My same-gender attractions go back before puberty. I wouldn't
have had the vocabulary to tell a person that I was attracted to
guys, but after puberty it was definitely a sexual attraction. I had
attractions to girls as well. One year in high school, I asked four girls
to the prom, but they all turned me down!

Growing up my parents viewed homosexuality or same-sex attraction as a mental illness. My father couldn't contain his disgust and
loathing for people who dealt with the issue. My father never knew
that he was talking about his own son. I learned at an early age to
keep my mouth shut. I was unable to reach out for help, so I was left
with fasting and prayer. I found that I couldn't pray it away. I could
read my scriptures and do everything that I knew how to do, but it
couldn't change how I felt. I didn't tell anyone; I was afraid of losing
my friends.

I believed then and believe today that if my father knew that I
dealt with the issue, it would mean an end to our relationship.

I dated, served a mission, and went to BYU. When I was 23, I
went inactive. I never told anyone why. There has never been a day
in my life where I felt like people who deal with same-sex attraction
were welcome in the Church.

When I was 30, I guess I felt the clock ticking. I wanted a
family, and I had never lost my testimony of the truthfulness of the
Restoration. I came back to church and got married; my wife was
one of the girls who turned me down at the prom years ago! I am

currently in my twelfth year of marriage. We have two kids: one boy and one girl.

I've never specifically talked with my wife about the issue. This past year I made a friend who has a lot in common with me. He wasn't obviously gay, but my wife seemed to be jealous of my friendship with him. Before Christmas 2010, my wife and I went out to Temple Square with him and his kids. At one point, my wife went and had a private conversation with him. While we were in the car on the way home, she told me she had decided she was okay with my relationship with my friend, "no matter what that relationship might be." That is the extent of our talking about it.

I married probably the only person in the world that would put up with me. That evening before Christmas I was so filled with love for her and grateful that I married her. It was the first time in my life that someone close to me had expressed Christ-like love to me in that area of my life. As far as attraction goes, I never found anyone more attractive in my life than I found my wife that night. It was a really beautiful experience. I am happily married and active in the Church and I expect to continue to be both.

I hope anyone who reads this will have compassion for those who are "the least of these". You may find there are people closer than you think who are affected by this issue.

Jesse "Dawkins"

"You wear a mask for so long, you forget who you were beneath it."

I was born in Baltimore, Maryland in 1979, the youngest of five kids. My parents separated and divorced after I was born. My mom attended college and would sometimes take me to her classes, which was a great learning experience. My siblings and I would go treasure hunting in the woods behind our house. During our early youth we did not grow up with TV or video games. At age nine, my family moved to Tacoma, Washington. There I found new friends and lived a carefree life.

As a child I enjoyed watching the PBS painter, Bob Ross. From him I learned a passion for art. I did most of the Christmas and Halloween decorating in my family. In addition, I loved to bake cookies, cinnamon rolls, and pies at night when my mom was gone working night shifts as a nurse. Later in my teenage years, my passion and interests moved to backpacking, investing, and watching CNBC endlessly.

My "normal" carefree childhood began to evaporate late in elementary school when I began to understand that I might be different. In fifth grade my school hired a new Physical Education teacher. He was young and would wear form-fitting athletic clothing. During gym class I would overhear girls talking and giggling about how cute he was, and honestly I wanted to join in, but I stayed silent. At that time I did not fully understand what was happening to me or what a "normal" boy at my age should be feeling, but I at least knew that it was not "normal" for a male to verbally express how attractive another male is.

My goal was to become straight

Between the age of 11 and 12, it became apparent that I was only physically attracted to men. I could tell if women were beautiful, or soft on the eyes, but I did not find them attractive. I began to feel ashamed. I prayed every night for years, many times with tears, begging God to change me. I began to question if God existed, because why would He make me this way? I would plead for God to let me know He existed. I became self-conscious about how people would perceive me. After playing the clarinet for three years, I stopped, partly because it seemed "gay". I began to join in verbal gay-bashing, in order to deflect any questioning of my sexuality.

As I became more aware that I might be gay, I desperately tried to find information on homosexuality. In my mom's library, I found a book with a story about a returned missionary who, after a period of homosexual activity, returned to the Church and ended up marrying a woman. The book taught that homosexuality was unnatural and that it was an addiction to overcome. I determined that my goal was to become straight, and that it was possible if I would pray, fast, read the scriptures, and attend church.

One time while I was attending Scouts, a young men's leader was joking around and made fun of Ellen Degeneres, calling her "Ellen Degenerate". This was just after Ellen came out on her show. The moment my young men's leader said the word "degenerate", it became clear to me that if I did not change from being homosexual to straight then I too would be deemed as degenerate. Around this same time I concluded that I could never have a happy life if I accepted my homosexuality. I saw gay activists on the TV and they seemed unhappy. Where I lived, I only knew of one gay person, a man from my ward who had come out, contracted HIV, and died from AIDS.

I did not want to leave his side

One day while at the bus stop, two kids were picking on me. My friend "Adam" came up and told them to lay off. I ran behind some bushes. Adam came and asked me if I was all right. I was humiliated, but I was also grateful for his help and friendship.

Adam was a year older than me. He was tall and had dark hair, blue eyes, and a smile and laugh that could light up a room. Being around him made me want to be better. He was one of the most caring people I had known. One day I found out that his father had committed suicide. I attended the funeral and gave him a hug. I had tears streaming down my face when his sisters tried to sing a song for their dad and couldn't finish.

One night Adam and I watched a movie at his aunt's house. There was some nudity in it, and I covered my eyes during those parts. While driving home, Adam started to open up about a lot of issues that he had not told anyone about. He was crying, so he parked the car on the side of a rural road. He said that I was an example to him in a lot of ways, including how I had covered my eyes during the movie. I was very uncomfortable with him thinking I was an example to him. I thought, what if he knew who I really was? I wanted to give him a hug, but I was too scared that it would be too intimate.

He drove to the church parking lot and then jumped out and gave me a big bear hug. We laid on the hood of his car and watched the stars. I did not want to leave his side that night. I felt at peace just being with him.

You would always be there

Later that year, Adam told me that he was a month late turning in a major class project. The teacher had informed him that if he did not turn it in by the next week he would fail his class. I left him alone at my desk in my bedroom and told him to start writing. Every half-hour or so, I would take what he wrote and type it up in my family's library. After several hours our teamwork paid off and he finished. He felt like a huge weight had been lifted off of his shoulders. It began to snow, so we walked around the neighborhood. While horsing around, I had him carry me a little ways. I then had him look back at the one set of prints and told him that it feels sometimes that his friendship and example help me get through the days. It reminded us of the poem "Footprints in the Sand". While in college I wrote a poem about that night:

Footprints in the Snow
Whispery flakes lazily fell in the night's luminous grey sky
Silencing a chaotic world
It was our escape for a night as we walked side by side in silence
In a deserted world of ice
We spoke of our dreams while walking in our enchanted
Surroundings, where we could never believe in mediocrity.
I had you carry me that night to show you the single set of
Prints that represented the friendship you gave to me.
For your example supported me through life's ferocious winds
That strived to scatter my dreams.
For we became each other's anchors that silent night
In our broken homes that lent us no direction or peace.
We spoke of our Godly potential in those prints, yet at our
Age, we naively questioned its attainability.
You left me that night at my driveways end pondering
On the next day's rains that would melt my heaven away.
Yet I knew as I opened the door to my chaotic world
And went to my room, that you my first true friend
Would always be there to catch me when the winds blew.

I felt like I could do anything when I was around him; it felt like I could fly. Then I would remind myself that my love and obsession for him was wrong, which would bring me back down to the ground. I was mentally wearing myself thin.

I had no one to speak to about the issue. I felt alone. I contemplated for a while whether I should tell Adam:

> I feel so empty. I have no life. I feel terrible. Tomorrow I'm going to tell Adam about my problem. I feel like I'm going to burst. I want to yell. I feel like a burden on Adam. I feel that I'm throwing my problems on Adam when he has tremendous ones to deal with already. I just want to tell Adam everything and get it all out and get on with my life. I pray it won't mess up Adam's life. I need to tell the Bishop. I feel dead inside. I feel like a machine.

You will be able to receive forgiveness

The next day I tried to tell Adam, but I was petrified. For many months I considered speaking to my bishop. Finally in December of 1995 I got up the courage. Adam gave me a ride to the church:

> I went into the Bishops office, and after sitting down the Bishop just came right out and asked what I wanted to talk about. I was shocked I didn't know what to say. I just finally said I have a sin that I'd like to receive council on. Then the Bishop said to me there are some sins that you don't have to talk to me about and there are sins you need to talk to me about, because they will affect your standing in the church. He asked in a joking manor.. You haven't killed anyone? Then he said before I could say anything that he needs to know what the sin is. I slouched back in the seat about ready to cry with hundreds of thoughts going through my mind. I moved my lips but no sound came out. I began to feel like I was losing consciousness and everything went fuzzy and my head became light. I felt like I wasn't really saying it, but I said in a whispery hesitant tone, "What about homosexual thoughts?" I quickly interjected that I had not had the thoughts for 4 months and that I did not have issues currently with the thoughts."

That was a lie of course, but at the time I felt like mitigating the thoughts meant I did not have them. I did not want to look even worse in the bishop's eyes.

> After telling the bishop I could see almost no emotion in his face, but I could see a little surprise in his eyes. While I was still wondering how I got the strength to tell him, the bishop first asked me if I've had any sexual relations. I said NO!!! Then he asked about if I've had sexual fantasies. I sheepishly lowered my eyes and said Yes. He asked if any young boys were involved and I said NO in disgust!! I said that it just began at puberty and it just never clicked and that I understood I was supposed to lust after young ladies. I desperately said that I truly am going to marry in the temple and raise a family. The bishop said that since I've not had homosexual thoughts for the past

four months and that I've not gone into anything deeper, that it did not affect my church status.

He asked about my social life. I told him it was much better than it used to be. I said that once I got involved that most of the thoughts went away. He said that in these teen years that many things go on in your mind and Homosexual thoughts happen to most young men in which they can't control, but they don't let the thoughts take up a chair and fester in their minds. He said that if I stick to the Lord and have a strong moral social life and keep my standards high, that the thoughts wont totally go away, but that you will be able to receive forgiveness if you do it in faith.

For a short while I felt like I had relieved some of the burden I had carried around for years.

I wish this could be the end of it

Several months later, in a Physical Education class, Adam and some other guys were talking about a crude scene from a movie and laughing. When I turned to leave I noticed that Adam was behind me and was the loudest one laughing. I stomped off self-righteously. I stopped going to his house for a ride to seminary each morning, and after a while he stopped attending seminary. I even switched my P.E. class with my Spanish class, so I would not have to see him every day. I stopped acknowledging him at church and school. Soon he began taking more Sunday shifts at work and stopped going to church for a while. Because I did not know how to deal with my feelings for Adam, I used his innocent laugh as an excuse to cut all ties with him.

Bitterness surrounds me. It engulfs me. It fills me. It destroys me. O how I wish this bitter cup never was put on my table. O how I wish I never drank it. For today I took another step in trying to get Adam out of my daily life and I have achieved it. I changed my 1st period conditioning to 5th period. O I wish this could be the end of it, but it isn't, for I can never truly get Adam out of my mind.

About a year later, I gave a talk at Church on pride, unrighteous judgment, and forgiveness. While waiting for my turn to speak, I was nervous. Right before I was to speak, Adam walked in and sat in the back of the chapel. Without mentioning Adam, I told the story about how guys in my gym class had talked about crude, inappropriate things. I explained how my pride, judgment, and self-righteousness had led me to change my class schedule. In a way, I was trying to apologize to Adam. I quoted the scripture about the mote and the beam in the eye. Later that day, Adam and I spoke, and I formally apologized. He graciously accepted, and he also apologized, which I profusely told him was not necessary.

I felt like a huge failure

Gradually, it began to sink in that my orientation had not changed at all from age 12 to 17. It had only become stronger. I still had no interest in females. Over the past year, I had gone to a formal Valentine's dance and a swing dance because the girls asked me out. In both cases, in the car after the dance, the girls had moved in for a kiss. Once I noticed their head moving towards mine, I had desperately opened the car door and said good night.

After six months of thinking about it, I decided to serve a mission. It was what I had been taught my whole life was the right thing to do. I served my mission in the Philippines. I held out hope that I would be attracted to women after I served an honorable mission.

On my 21st birthday in the last area of my mission, I began to read *The Miracle of Forgiveness*. My heart sank as I read statements that a person's sexuality can change through faith in God. I sat slouched in my chair perplexed why after eight years of prayer and faith nothing had changed. I couldn't understand why I was only attracted to men instead of women. I felt hopeless. I felt like a huge failure. The last several weeks of my mission, I did what was expected of me, but I had no passion for the work. I numbed myself, so I would not have to think of the future, because when I tried to guess what post-mission life held for me, I only saw loneliness.

I do have a desire to change

After my mission, I moved to Provo and got a job. I lived with five other guys in a basement apartment that we called "Down Under".

I was often depressed, and I began to take long drives up Provo Canyon to Kamas and back until 3–5 a.m. I felt discouraged that I had not changed. My life felt stagnant. Many times I thought of driving off a cliff or into a rock wall, but luckily it was just thoughts that filled my mind on those serene lonely drives.

> I spoke to the Bishop on Tuesday, I told him just about everything. We spoke for over 30 minutes. I didn't cry, I just told him. It took a while to verbally say it. I felt emotionally and spiritually numb. After I told him I was gay, he fumbled around in some binders for a little bit. He was honest with me and said that he cannot promise the feelings will ever go away. His main advice was to balance my life more socially, spiritually, and financially ... I still have not set up a plan; however I did set up another appointment. So I need to get to work to show God and the bishop that I do have a desire to change and to follow his council. (October 28, 2001)

That year, I did go on several dates. I went on a date with each of my sister's three roommates. My sister told me that one of her roommates liked me. According to my sister, her roommate loved it when I visited, because she loved my cologne and how well I treated my sister. Later, after it became clear that I was not going to continue dating her roommate, my sister informed me that her roommate had cried over me. I felt bad hearing that. I felt bad that I had even gone on dates with her when I knew that it could only lead to friendship. I hated hurting girls, but I was trying to fulfill the part that society and my church expected me to play.

One of my roommates in "Down Under" was gay, yet he never admitted he was gay; it wasn't necessary to even talk about it. He was hilarious and a little bit soft, but amazingly talented. He was in a comedy club at BYU and the girls swooned over him. He had a subscription to Martha Stewart magazine. I would jokingly make fun of him, but then when no one was looking, I would read about decorating and cooking tips from the "Homemaking Goddess" Martha Stewart. He confused me. On the one hand, I was jealous of how he had accepted who he was and how it had helped him expand his artistic talents. During high school, I had stopped nurturing my artistic talents because it made me look gay. On the other hand, I judged him because it seemed like he wasn't even trying to become straight. But I realized he might not be the amazing talented person he was if he had hid in the closet and buried his talents like I had.

My secret, cursed abyss

One of my roommates was "Jake". He was a quiet, yet humorous guy that worked out and played the guitar and could sing well. He was a smart pre-med student with a 3.98 GPA, and he had an adorable face. At first I wasn't interested in him, but this changed after we had lived together for a while. Every weekend we played games together. We cooked for each other. We would make funny noises to each other when we played games. I am sure my other roommates thought we were crazy, but they joined in too. When I started attending UVSC, for hours I would quietly study on one couch while Jake would study on the other. I felt so peaceful just being with him. Many times I would wake up and look up at him sleeping with his messy hair, and I just felt content. While in college I wrote this poem:

> **Curse**
> A swelling love, an unwanted curse, yet desired
> Forbidden to quench its fiery desire
> Love desired, yet set aside to hide
> Unknown to a person of perfection who's a mystery to my soul
> Who chases perfection, to me unattainable.
> A forbidden love that scorches the soul
> Knowing it shall never be known
> A love that destroys perfection
> That must be suppressed
> To consume my soul, leaving me hollow
> Never to be filled by a perfections kiss
> Left to the colds bitter loneliness
> Hidden in my secret, cursed abyss

I just want to say I love you

Over the next five years, I continued to go through cycles of false hope, frustration, and depression:

> My mind just keeps going in circles ... I will have to force myself to desire anything else and hope I will like it ... I've been fighting myself for the past month knowing what I should feel and trying to make my heart feel that and nothing more. Now I know why I don't love many people or care for them, because I am too scared to show who I am. (January 27, 2002)

I want to run, yell and break something, because I am so frustrated. The debate of forcing myself to love and care for a gender that at this time I don't frustrates me. I have to wipe away these natural feelings and plant a new seed in myself so different feelings grow. (February 8, 2002)

I find it interesting how I can have so much hope one day and then in several days all the hope is gone. I just have an overwhelming need for a close guy friend that I can just open up to. It's as if all I really want is a best friend. Since I haven't had one since I was 16 my mind and heart takes it overboard and interprets it as something far more than it is. Almost every day I just want to say I love you or I love your guts to my roommates, however I can't because I feel like that would take me out of bounds. I think I know what love is, however I've never learned exactly how to show it. Lately when I'm agitated or in a ways jealous or lonely I just play the guitar and it takes my focus off of insignificant things and helps me to get over it. (March 9, 2002)

I was able to get off of work early at 5:00 am and I made it to the 6 am temple session. I am just glad I was able to make it. I just hope it will help me to be able to want to marry. It will be a miracle if that ever happens. (September 23, 2002)

It was painful as I saw every guy I loved and cared about eventually get a girlfriend, marry, and drop me out of his life:

What do I feel I ask myself? I feel happy and I hope every perfection that is brought in my life marries and is happy. I learn much from them and I hope their examples, especially in getting married will help me develop a desire of such. (October 20, 2002)

I spoke to the bishop several weeks ago. My mindset is so much different than the last time I spoke to him. The last time I felt like I had hope of marrying. Now I have no hope of marrying ... Sometimes I just want to sleep and never wake up. (April 1, 2003)

I have been thinking crazy thoughts as of late. I think I have no hope of marrying, so I get depressed and think

I have no purpose in my life, so I think of just ending it now. It would make things so much less painful. Just think of having to endure never being intimate physically or emotionally with anyone. It will be a lonely life with friends here and there but we always move on or they do ... Maybe I still don't know what friendship is. However, yes, many times for the past two weeks I have entertained thoughts of how to end this all. They are selfish thoughts, because living I can do so much more ... I wonder if I should go to a shrink and get some pills and counseling. I am too prideful to do such a thing. (April 3, 2003)

Every day I am at a crossroad. I am paralyzed to succeed in my life. My procrastination and negative thoughts poison my future. I need to be positive. Having a positive attitude will help me to overcome the hurdles of life. It will make it easier for me to begin a project that may seem hard to accomplish. I sang at the retirement home today ... It was fulfilling and I hope to become more involved so I may become happier. Service may bring some stress into my life, yet in the end, it will relieve me of more burdens than it will add. (November 21, 2004)

Bush is trying to pass this marriage amendment again ... It is a very divisive political issue ... It is sad for people with same sex attraction that settling down with one person is not encouraged by the government. It is unhealthy in the straight and gay community to be jumping around. (June 5, 2006)

I did not attend church again today. My new home teaching companion called me and left a message ... I know I need to get back into church to be happy again, but where do I go from there? I won't marry and I will fall for someone, or be interested in someone that I could never date. I would add more friends to my list that once they marry they will never keep in contact. I feel hopeless. I feel that for 2 or 3 more years I may sort of fit in, but after awhile I will fall out because everyone my age will be married. (June 18, 2006)

I've been thinking lately about church and becoming social again. It will be hard to get back into church when I feel out of place with the whole Plan of Salvation. Should I speak to the bishop? What would be the point? He can't straighten me up. I can use him as help to make sure I don't fall over the fence that I am sitting on top of; leaning to the wrong side. I do need to become social. It will help me feel happier and it may even help me become less depressed and more motivated to fulfill my goals, such as the GMAT. I know that church helps even though my testimony is weak. I need to read my scriptures also. (June 20, 2006)

I wonder how many straight people understand how much of a blessing those feelings they have are. So many people think that it is a choice. It is not a choice. If it were, I would rather be straight and love a woman and be able to go after those feelings that would help me not just lay on the couch everyday depressed. I honestly hate those people that feel that I would rather be depressed all day and want to take my own life (I don't have the guts) because I chose to be gay. I don't choose to be gay and I don't have the choice to be straight, so I choose to be a virgin hermit that will not socialize so I don't continue to meet amazing people that will make me more depressed because I can't develop a deeper relationship. (July 31, 2006)

I just needed someone to vent to

One time, after attending a Penn State vs. Ohio State football game, during the long car ride back to Washington D.C., I told a friend "Mark" what was going on in my life:

My heart was pounding ... I said, "ever since I was around 9 I had known I was different", and it just flowed out. I did not cry. I was just shaking and my heart was pounding. I do not remember all the details. Mark did say that after our last conversation on the phone ... he had suspected that I dealt with "same-sex" attraction and he had re-searched it. [He] had pulled up some talks. Of course I wondered if the way I act makes it so obvious to others that I am gay. We talked for around 2 hours about this. Mark asked me if I had read all of the talks and I said I had, but that they are all the same. They say that gays are fine in the church as long as they do not act on their feelings. I explained that that is a hard thing to accept that I will have to be alone the rest of my life and hope I will be mentally changed in heaven. I said that luckily I have not done anything "bad", because I have not put myself in places where I might be tempted ... I spoke to him about how this issue has directed and changed my whole life. I did not join sports partly due to being scared to be outed in front of others. I always feel like I have to act one way to make sure others do not suspect, and now I question God as I have my whole life due to this issue ...

Mark really pushed that I would be fine in the church as long as I did not act on it. I was somewhat irritated by those comments. I said it is not just the physical part that I will be missing, but also the emotional part of having someone to go home to be with ... Mark also said the church has many other programs such as support groups where you meet with other LDS men dealing with the same issues. (The church does not sponsor these programs) ... I openly said no way to that. I do not remember if I made it clear to Mark how I have never been aroused by a woman in my whole life so should I be going to some gay AA group for something that I am and is not harmful to others? I did not make it clear that ... he did not understand and did not need to patronize me with how to help or how to "cure" me. I just needed someone to vent to. I also apologized for how I felt I was always lying to him about why I did not date or why I did not believe in marriage.

Mark sort of opened up to me about his straight life issues ... He told me he had proposed to an amazing woman, but that he already knew from the temple the answer would be no and she had felt the same thing. They still went together to the family Florida trip and he joked they still kissed a lot on their parting week. That last sentence just ripped my heart out because I have never kissed and I could not fully understand his "straight life". I guess I should have been more understanding.

I spoke a lot of how my faith in God has waned and that I honestly do not believe in God anymore. I said "I could not understand how a God with a plan of Eternal Families could put 2-5% of his children down on earth lacking the fundamental key to be able to at least marry." Mark also went on a tangent about doing service, like helping with microloan programs. Mark gave me a hug. For me it was awkward because I truly did not know what he felt of me as a person ... I went inside at 4 a.m. laid on my bed, then quickly fell asleep spent physically and emotionally. (December 9, 2007)

An overwhelmingly uncomfortable silence

The next summer Mark was in Utah for an internship. I had been intermittently less active for several years by this time. However, it was much easier to attend church when he was in town. I gave him the following letter the day before he left Utah.

> "It was nice to attend church again. It has been a long time since I have attended. I hope that I will attend more often. I do have to admit it is hard ... A big struggle with me at church is when I meet these amazing, spiritual, good looking men that of course, a person would want to be friends with, or be around them ... Annoyingly, my mind thought that way about the Elders Quorum teacher. During the lesson, my mind got into a nice war with itself. I of course knew that it was wrong to think that there could be anything else than friendship, but it just pops in and it ticks me off. But it gets my mind debating about what place I have in a singles ward and what happens when I turn 30 or when I turn 35. What will my place be?" (May 27, 2008)

The week before Mark left Utah, he took me on a date as the third wheel. He drove me and his date to visit "Troy", one of his former mission companions. Troy had a beautiful home and a wife and child. He seemed like a stereotypical wholesome Mormon. After our visit, we drove Troy to the airport so Mark could say goodbye to his old buddy. While driving, I had a conversation with Troy in the back seat. Troy asked me where I lived. I told him I lived in the Avenues in Salt Lake City. He then said, "You better watch out for those faggots."

An overwhelmingly uncomfortable silence hung in the car. My mind was racing trying to understand how I might respond to such a statement. I finally broke the cold silence by asking Troy questions about his family. I do not think he understood that I was gay, even after the awkward silence. Mark later wrote to me in an email,

> I was also bothered by "Troy's" comment. In fact, I was pretty embarrassed for him — you probably noticed the awkward silence too :-) ... Sometimes his backwoods Idaho roots do come to the surface with comments like that :-)

I felt such a burden off my back

In August 2008, I was in downtown New York on a business trip, and my sister flew in from upstate to visit me for the weekend. For the past several weeks she had been dropping some hints that she knew that I was gay. She had tried to say things that would make me feel like she would be okay if I were gay. I had decided that this visit would be a good time to tell her that I was gay and to explain my situation.

After a long Saturday touring New York with her, we went back to the hotel and watched some of the China summer Olympics. After a while she asked me to turn off the TV because she wanted us to talk. I turned it off and began to prepare myself to confirm to her that her assumptions were correct that I was gay. However, instead she revealed to me that she may be lesbian. I was flabbergasted! That thought had never entered my mind.

As we talked about our situations, it dawned on me that this was the first open conversation I had ever had with a gay person. From the time I knew I was gay, at about age 10, I had purposely steered clear of talking to people I suspected were gay. But now here I was, talking with my sister. I knew she had lived a great life. She had served a mission in Russia, and had done everything that was expected of her in the Church, yet the first time she fell in love was at age 30 and she had fallen for a women. I felt such a burden off of my back to actually speak with a person that was gay and not just with a straight friend, family member, or bishop.

My whole paradigm changed

My understanding of homosexuality changed after my sister came out to me. When I arrived home, I reread a lot of the teachings of the Church, and I realized that the teachings I had been taught about homosexuality were incorrect and were based on false stereotypes. I began to feel betrayed. I felt like I had wasted almost 20 years of my life trying to be something that was impossible for me to be. I began to perceive the people that I had loved and respected to be in deep and almost purposeful ignorance about homosexuality.

I finally accepted that being gay did not make me broken. I accepted that I was not innately evil. I realized that if any of the amazing guys that I had been attracted to had reciprocated my interest, then I would have been in a committed monogamous relationship. I had never wanted to live the stereotypical "gay lifestyle" that I had been taught was what gays innately want to "act out". I knew I wanted and aspired to have the same type of relationship that many straight Mormons desire to have. I had been so homophobic. That is why it took me so long to see that what I wanted was not wrong, but was healthy and right for someone in my situation.

Since my teenage years, there has been an emotional and physical void in my life. Now I look forward to the day when I have my first kiss — I hope before I turn 32 — and my first real relationship. I now look forward to the day when I find my knight in shining armor, and can settle down with someone for life. I am excited to find someone that will never treat me like an afterthought in this life. I look forward to being able to exchange vows with the man I love, "I promise to be true to you in good times and in bad, in sickness and in health. I will love you and honor you all the days of my life."

"Topher Moore"

"Don't ask what the world needs. Ask what makes you come alive, and go do it. Because what the world needs is people who have come alive."
– Howard Thurman

I grew up as an only child in southern California. My family didn't subscribe to any religion specifically. We would go on camping trips with my cousins, and I would sometimes go and stay for a couple weeks with my cousin "Cindy" and her girlfriend. They loved each other, and Cindy was the closest person that I had in my life growing up. We would talk on the phone often.

In my family, I was always a "little adult". My parents would take me to their adult parties, and I saw my first stripper when I was eight. In middle school, when I realized that I was into guys instead of girls, I recognized that meant I was gay. In my mind, it wasn't really a bad thing. I wasn't ready to tell anyone, though, because I was afraid of what people would think. I knew that kids in school who seemed "femmy" were made fun of. When I was 12 or 13, Cindy invited to me to Pride in Los Angeles — not because she thought I was gay, but just because it was something she was doing and thought I would have fun. My mom didn't want me to go. She was worried about the gay community being targeted by hateful people; she thought it was unsafe. It wasn't a big deal to me; I wasn't sure if I wanted to go anyway.

Maybe I could make it work?

I met "Wendy" the first class of the first day of freshman year in high school. We worked together in class and would pass notes to each other. Part way through the semester, eventually one of her notes said, "I like you." I was hopeful that I was wrong about having to be gay; if a girl was interested in me, maybe I could make it work?

We dated for a week or two at a time on and off for about the next six years. She would date other people in between, and I would date other girls in between, but we would always come back together. But then we would never work well together, so we would break up. We were just better being friends than dating.

While we were doing this flirtatious friendship thing our freshman year, she invited me to her church, and I said I would go. When I found out she was Mormon, though, I changed my mind and decided not to go. The only experience I had had with the Church was about five years earlier, when I went to the San Diego Temple open house with my mom; it was a cool experience and a beautiful, amazing building, but the members there seemed frustrated with us. There were probably more people than expected and not enough volunteers to help out. In elementary school, there were two LDS girls who had constantly teased me and bullied me. From the experiences I had had with Church members, I just felt that they were stuck up and cliquish.

Over the next couple years, though, Wendy continued inviting me to things. She asked me to help set up for a blue and gold banquet at the Church, and so I went. When I got there, there was nothing to do, but Wendy walked me around the building, and I remember thinking the chapel was really cool. There were lots of kids at the banquet, and I felt very comfortable. I realized maybe this religion wasn't as crazy as I thought.

It was just too weird for me

One time I asked Wendy to tell me about her church. She was like, "Well, there was a boy and he went to a grove of trees and prayed and God and Jesus Christ told him to start the church." But she didn't give me any background, and when she said "church", I thought she was talking about the actual building. So I was picturing a 14-year old boy at a grove of trees somewhere in our city in southern California, and God telling him to build a church building. It just seemed weird. I didn't even believe there was a God.

But I started going to more activities like Church dances, and Wendy performed in a road show, so I went and watched her. Eventually she was able to get me to commit to taking missionary discussions in her home, not that I would ever get baptized, but just to learn more about her. So I took the discussions, and I wouldn't commit to anything at all. The whole thought of praying just seemed weird. I was like, "Why would you pray?" The concept just seemed so abstract to me. I felt like I would be talking to myself. I would have classified myself as insane if I thought someone was listening. It was just too weird for me.

But I read all the assignments they gave me. When they asked me to live the Word of Wisdom, I said no, that I wasn't going to change my lifestyle just for something I didn't believe in — even though the only thing I drank was an iced tea once a month or something. I was basically already living the Word of Wisdom, but it seemed silly to commit to it.

An inward understanding

One of the last discussions was about fasting. One of the missionaries was a "greenie", and he told me, "My mom used to tell me as a kid that if you're fasting and you get hungry, that means you're not praying enough." For whatever reason, I decided that I would give fasting a try. I wanted to say that I had tried everything that they told me to do. So one school day I fasted. Around lunchtime my stomach was growling, and I remembered the words of this missionary. So I just offered a simple prayer, "God, if you want me to join this church, let me know."

At that moment, I was filled with a knowledge that I had never felt before, that there was more, that there was a God. I'm a logical guy, and it wasn't like a warm fuzzy feeling or anything. It was just this inward understanding of truth. That was when my testimony was born. That was when I knew I would get baptized. I was 16 years old.

That same day, I wrote Wendy a letter and gave it to her, telling her about my experience and that I was ready to be baptized. So then I started going to church every week. I was fully committed to living all of the gospel principles. One struggle that I had was that the Church was fighting against gay marriage, with Proposition 22 going on in California at the time. I didn't know why a church that talked so much about love would try to stop people from having rights. But I got past it.

I loved the Church

A couple weeks before I was to be baptized, I met with the missionaries and they gave me a run-down of what the baptismal interview was going to be like. I was nervous about it, but they said it was easy, "There are only three questions they'll ask: have you participated in an abortion, have you ever committed a serious crime, and are you gay?"

I started freaking out, but I pretended like everything would be okay. I told Wendy's mom that I was nervous, and she said, "Why? Are you gay?" And I was like, "No, of course not." I was planning on getting married in the temple, and I hadn't done anything with a guy, so I was trying to justify to myself that I wasn't gay. But going into the interview, I didn't know how I was going to answer the question. Then, in the interview the actual question was, "Have you ever been in a homosexual relationship?" I had definitely never had a relationship with a guy, so I answered and everything was fine.

A week after I got baptized, I was called as first assistant in the priests quorum. I got super active really quick. I loved the Church and got involved with everything. I organized a youth conference. I introduced a couple of my friends to the Church, and they got baptized. I would talk to everybody about the Church and try to get them to take the discussions. My license plate said "CTRMAN", and I would explain to people about how it meant "Choose the Right".

I became friends with all the missionaries in the mission. I literally knew every missionary. If the APs found out that two missionaries were fighting, they would send me, and we'd go get ice cream and I'd end up doing mediation with them. The mission president loved me.

I was kind of torn

During my senior year, I was a co-leader of the peer counseling program at my school. Our school piloted a program called "Challenge Day", so I became really involved with the organization and attended trainings in San Francisco. The general message was, "Love who you are, and be who you are", while at the same time the Church was teaching me, "God doesn't want you to act on these feelings that you have." So I was kind of torn. That was the first time that my testimony was really tested.

One day at work, I walked past a guy, and he asked me what time it was. I was on break, so we started talking. He was a caricature artist, and he suggested, "Hey, you should come let me draw you sometime." After work I let him draw me, and while he was drawing, out of the blue he asked me when I knew I was gay. I got uncomfortable very quickly, and he started talking about when he knew he was gay. I didn't really know how to answer. I did allude to the fact that I was indeed attracted to guys. He invited me to come hang out sometime at his place.

To make the long story short, I did come over, and I put myself in a bad situation. We played Truth or Dare, and we ended up messing around. I kept telling him that I didn't want to. I should have just left, but I let him keep pushing me into doing stuff. We didn't do much, but we did more than we should have.

I felt really bad afterwards. I was pretty sure I was going to get excommunicated. I went and talked to the stake president, and he referred me to my bishop. I ended up just having informal Church discipline. The bishop was very disappointed and had me stop taking the sacrament for a couple months. I would have to wait a full year before I could go on my mission.

The bishop also encouraged me to go to LDS Family Services in San Diego. I wanted to show that I was willing to do whatever I could to repent, so I went. They gave me a book to read, and then we talked about my dad and how he was an alcoholic, and that's when I became convinced that this was why I became gay: My dad wasn't around, so since he wasn't around, I needed male affection or bonding, and the theory was that when a young man goes through puberty, then those longings are associated with sexual feelings and desires, thus creating the gay version of myself, who God of course would never make that way. It made sense at the time.

I asked Heavenly Father what I could do

I felt like I really needed to commit to get ready to go on a mission. I had to get away from the stuff that was making that a hard decision. That's when I decided to move to Utah. I had friends there, missionaries who had served in my area.

So I moved out to Utah and did really well. I went through the temple, received the Melchizedek Priesthood, put my papers in, and got my call. I had talked to my parents about the Church, and they weren't big fans. But they were excited that at least I was going to a church, because they didn't like the fact that I hadn't believed in God. They seemed to think Mormonism would just be a phase for me.

When they learned I was going on a mission, though, they realized it wasn't just a phase, and I could tell they weren't real happy about it, but it wasn't too bad.

On the mission, it seemed like a lot of the other elders were not focused on the work. It was frustrating to me that they were missing out on the opportunities to do real missionary work. The gay thing wasn't a huge deal. I never felt like I was attracted to any of my companions.

I did have a lot of anxiety issues, though. A doctor on my mission put me on some medication. I just had a feeling that I could never be good enough. I had a lot of conflict in my companionships. If my senior companion said, "Let's go tracting today," I would say, "How about we visit some members and help them build stronger testimonies so they'll share with their friends?" And then we would do it and have huge success. I was a missionary that my companions hated serving with, although afterwards they loved me, and we have stayed really good friends.

There were nights where I was so anxious that I stayed up all night wanting to die. Eventually I asked Heavenly Father what I could do. It was getting to the point where I was not sleeping and was sick. At 14 months I received a really strong answer that I should go home. I wrote a letter to my mission president, and I went home a week later. It seemed crazy how quick it happened. It was an honorable release. I tried to go on a service mission after that, but they basically told me, "As far as the Lord is concerned, you served an equivalent mission to anyone that served a full two years."

Everything seemed perfect

When I went home, I ended up working at the San Diego Temple. I loved it, and later when I moved back to Utah, I ended up working in the Provo Temple too. I always belonged to a ward and was really active, although I felt disconnected.

Around age 24, I started dating a girl "Kelly". She was a bit overweight and was very humble. She worked with people with disabilities and cared a lot about people. I thought, "Maybe this is the type of girl that I would date."

We never kissed, but we did cuddle a lot. It was very comfortable. It wasn't sexual at all, but we liked to be around each other. We hung out a lot and talked every day. I would talk to her on the phone every night until she fell asleep.

After a couple months, we both decided that we wanted to get married. We had a date set and everything. But I had nightmares over and over again about it; in them, we were going to have to have sex, and I was really nervous.

That's when I let her know I was asexual. I told her, "I'm not someone that needs sex." I said it wasn't a priority, and that our relationship would not be very sexual in nature. Everything still seemed perfect, but we realized we might be going a little too fast, so we decided to step back and take a little break, to evaluate if it was what we wanted. That's when it hit me that it wasn't right for me to marry a girl that I wasn't attracted to. We talked about the fact that I was gay, and we decided not to date anymore.

The weight of the world

About this time I started to understand that I probably would never get married. It would never really work with me being gay. Kelly and I were so close, and it had felt so magical, so it kind of hit me that even with the perfect girl for me, it was still a girl, and it wouldn't really work.

My dad had died, and I had just lost my business; the other two business partners had found out I was gay and had kicked me out. Going to church was stressful, but I felt guilty when I didn't go. I kept trying, though. I just felt like I didn't belong there, like my life didn't fit. I was constantly suicidal. I thought of lots of ways of doing it. I never really made an attempt, but it was a constant desire and ideation.

My bishop recommended I go to LDS Family Services again, so I did. I had given up trying to change who I was, and the real problem was wondering whether God accepted me. I decided to pray about it. I then had an experience where I felt that God loved me for who I was and that He was okay with me being gay. It felt similar to my experience when I knew the Church was true.

It gave me the feeling that I didn't have to stress about whether or not I went to church, because what mattered was my relationship with God and how I lived my life. I started to feel a lot happier after that. My self-confidence increased. It was like the weight of the world fell off my shoulders.

I'm happier than I've ever been

I came to realize that I still judged gay people, and that there was some self-hatred going on. I was okay being gay but still not really comfortable owning that as part of who I am. It felt like I needed to talk to my bishop about it. I emailed him, giving him a history of my life, and then I set up an appointment and met with him. It was fairly quick. He asked if I had a testimony. I explained that I did, but that I also felt like God was okay with me being gay and being who I was. He explained that with those feelings, I must not have a true testimony of the Church, and that I was going against the gospel and its teachings. He told me I could either choose to have my records removed or be excommunicated. I chose to have my records removed.

I still feel like it was God's will that I joined the Church. I truly feel like the Church was a way for me to develop a relationship with God. It was something that was meant for my life, but not for my entire life. I have no hard feelings. I'm happier than I've ever been, and I know God loves me. I find myself bearing my testimony a lot still, maybe even more than when I was a member.

I really believe in personal revelation. I believe that the gospel is designed to lead a group of people, but individual prayer and revelation is what guides individuals. I can relate to Nephi: if God told Nephi that he could kill someone, then God can tell me that I can love someone.

I currently live with three of the most amazing roommates one could ever ask for. I am excited, because I feel like I have this whole new world that has been opened to me! I just need someone to share it with. I don't feel like the story is over yet. I feel like it has just begun.

"Simon Rhyne"

"... who art thou, that thou shouldest be afraid of a man that shall die, and of the son of man which shall be made as grass; And forgettest the Lord thy maker, that hath stretched forth the heavens, and laid the foundations of the earth ... ?"
– Isaiah 51:12–13

I grew up the oldest of eight children in a Salt Lake suburb. My childhood was mostly good. I never experienced physical or sexual abuse. I wouldn't say we were the stereotypical Mormon family, since my parents have always been on the edge of what is culturally acceptable: they were outspoken and active in conservative politics, my mom gave birth to some of my siblings in her bedroom, and my parents taught my siblings and me at home for several years instead of sending us to government schools.

I discovered masturbation on my own at age 13. I first revealed my behavior to my bishop when I was 14, and I tried to stop. When I was around 16, I started viewing pornography in books and grocery store magazines. The images I saw were mostly of women, and I don't recall having strong desires to see images of men. However, during these years, I do recall looking forward to being in settings where I could see other men and boys naked. I looked forward to swimming outings with the Scouts. I don't recall initially feeling guilty about looking. I was simply curious, just as I'm sure many of my friends were. But later there was a comment made by an older boy that made me feel shame for looking.

I attended high school part-time. I remember being fascinated by other guys' legs and enjoyed observing how the newly growing hair made the legs of some guys look attractive. I felt no romantic attractions to any of them but enjoyed the friendships of several men.

I also enjoyed friendships with women and dated several of them, although I never found myself attracted to them. I went on the dates more to please my mother who I recall being pleased that her little boy was in demand. (Most of the dates I went on were girls' choice.)

Once I began college, my dating slowed. After all, I was going on a mission, so why would I want to build a relationship only to have it be a drag on my mission? At least that was the reason I proffered to those who asked. But inwardly, I didn't enjoy dating. I owned my own business and spent lots of time working, attending to my school activities and studies, and spending time with friends.

I need to take responsibility

In the years after my mission, as the Internet proliferated, I discovered it to be an endless source of images. I also discovered that images of naked men had a more powerful effect on me. At 25 I found myself for the first time revealing to my bishop what kind of pornographic images I viewed. As with every subsequent experience with a bishop, he expressed love.

My bishop referred me to LDS Family Services, and I visited several times with a counselor. He told me about a group of men who dealt with similar issues who gathered together to do masculine-type things like play football. I didn't consider myself athletic and wasn't at all interested in joining them. I think that my shame played into it as well: if I showed up, it would mean admitting I experienced attraction to men. It would mean admitting to someone else that, inside, I was not the person I wanted everyone to see.

Over the years, shame has caused me to flounder in isolation. It has kept me from reaching out and connecting with people that most likely would love me notwithstanding my shortcomings. For many years, I only shared my struggles with a handful of people. I believe shame is perhaps Satan's principle tool, along with deception, to keep me from progress and happiness.

And so I continued in practical isolation. Over the years, my bishops encouraged me to date, telling me that when I married, my desires for porn and masturbation would go away. I don't resent them for this. I believe they were doing the best that they could. I don't know if they prayed to know what to tell me or if they simply relied upon their own wisdom. It doesn't matter to me; I'll leave it to God.

What I do wish I would have realized earlier was that I need to take responsibility for my own journey. I can't merely submit myself to a bishop and expect him to deliver me to exaltation. Practically speaking, I wish I had been candid with my bishops about what worked and what didn't. If they encouraged me to do something and the results didn't come, or if they were telling me something I'd already tried, I wish I had been more forthright about asking for other counsel.

A move and a drastic change

At 31, I moved and began attending a family ward. I made an appointment with my new bishop and told him my story. I expected more of what I had been told for the previous ten years: date, go to the temple, etc. But this bishop asked for my temple recommend and told me he wanted me to attend a Church-sponsored 12-step meeting. He was the first to identify my behavior as an addiction. I was shocked. And scared. But I went to a meeting even as I was telling myself that such a meeting was for really sick people. My shame kicked in too, and it was difficult to make an appearance. I was deathly afraid I might be recognized.

When I walked in the meeting I wished I had never gone, because there were two people there that I knew rather well. But I stayed and even shared a little of my struggle, though I didn't dare mention anything about the fact that I looked at male porn. I continued to attend each week. In the months that followed, I began to have longer periods of "sobriety" (no porn or masturbation).

Around this time I first shared my story with a member of my family: my sister. She and I shared a lot and so it seemed natural. She expressed her love and encouragement.

As I began traveling for work, I discovered new ways to feed my addiction. I began hanging around hot tubs, saunas, and locker rooms hoping that other men would come by that I could talk with and maybe see naked. It was all about fantasy. I would have an interaction, and then be lost in my head as I imagined the different things I might have done with the man. Lust is a powerful and intoxicating feeling. Speaking candidly, I loved the feeling. Looking back, I guess I was fortunate that fantasy was enough. I had many opportunities to join men in their hotel rooms, but something prevented me.

Taking charge of my journey

Eventually, I had enough sobriety and was able to get my temple recommend back. Shortly thereafter I moved to the East to attend graduate school. For a few months the newness of my surroundings and the adjustment to a rigorous program kept me from "acting out", but eventually I returned to my old patterns.

I decided to switch from the singles ward to the family ward and met a wonderful bishop. He heard my whole story. When we were done, he asked if it was problematic for him to hug me. Absolutely not a problem! He is the first bishop I recall admitting that he didn't know how to help me. I remember him asking, "What can I do to support you?" He may not have intended it, but he was putting the responsibility for my progress on me instead of on himself. He helped me start a 12-step group in the ward. Anywhere from three to six men attended regularly.

The weeks following his asking that question, I made a concerted effort to apply the Atonement in my life. About two months later, I suddenly realized that I hadn't looked at porn, masturbated, or been in any dangerous sexual situations. I also hadn't been overeating or watching TV nearly as much. I believe that I had been turning to lust, food, and TV to escape from negative feelings which were too much for me to bear. In my effort to apply the Atonement in my life, I fervently prayed every day that Jesus would help me bear the feelings that so easily overwhelmed me: anger, fear, loneliness, boredom, and lust. And He did.

Setbacks and progress

I wasn't having any issues with lusting after men. Or anyone. I felt wonderful. But lust is sneaky and after several months, I began having problems again. I tried praying like I had, but to no avail. I moved to another Eastern state and started working with a new bishop who, while kind, was not as helpful. He didn't know anything about addiction. I attended the Church's 12-step meetings but found them ineffectual. Persons who weren't addicts were welcome if they were supporting a loved one. And the addictions were varied. No one was encouraged to say what they were addicted to. So, the last thing I was going to say was that I was addicted to porn featuring men.

A year later I returned to Utah. I began attending a Church 12-step group which felt different than any of the others I had experienced. These people were social with each other. They went for ice cream after the meeting instead of bolting for their cars. Shortly after I began attending, some of the men put together an overnight hike and campout. Seven of us went together. This experience was one of the highlights of my life for which I will be forever grateful. Up to that time, I had rarely felt so connected with other men. I still had not revealed my whole story, but the honesty and openness that pervaded our campfire discussion generated a love and brotherhood between us that I will always cherish. The date of that hike, June 26, 2009, almost two years ago, marks the beginning of my sobriety.

At that group, I met an older man who took me under his wing. One day he and I went to lunch. I felt that I should share with him what I didn't usually share in 12-step meetings: the type of porn I looked at. To my surprise, he revealed that he struggled with looking at the same stuff. He became a great support to me. He introduced me to Sexaholics Anonymous, a non-denominational 12-step program that I found to be significantly more helpful than the other meetings I had been to. As a result, I have experienced that sex is optional.

Breakthrough

After I shared with this man, I had a pair of experiences at the gym that spun up a lot of lust in me. In each I was showering across from another man. We didn't make eye contact nor did we speak. But we were eyeing each other. I left and found it very difficult not to look at porn or masturbate when I got home. After the first experience, I called some of my 12-step friends and told them that I had been "triggered" at the gym. But I didn't go into any more detail. After the second experience, I realized that I had to do something more than simply say I had been "triggered".

I got on my unfiltered internet connection and started reading recovery stories of other men. I read until about 2 a.m. and went to bed, surprised that I had not turned to porn. The next morning I was still feeling the draw. It was then that I realized that I had to be open and honest about what had happened. I called a friend, and due to shame, I had a difficult time being precise, but I finally got it out. To my surprise, he didn't treat me like a leper but showed kindness and compassion.

I then determined to share in one of my 12-step groups. This was more scary since I was face-to-face with men and I wouldn't know some of them. But I did. It was hard. My voice was low and shaky.

I couldn't look anywhere but down. I cried the rest of the meeting. I thought my friends might distance themselves from me after that. But they didn't. Nothing but love. Nothing but love.

More breakthroughs

Later I attended the Journey into Manhood weekend, which helped me get over the discomfort I felt calling myself a man. The weekend also blessed me with tools to use when I meet or see a man that I feel uncomfortable around, whether due to attraction, fear, etc. I came away from the weekend with a love for my fellow brothers that was almost overwhelming. I realized that they were all valuable just as they are. And so am I.

Soon after, I determined to finally share my story with my father. He listened to me for over an hour as I related my challenges and my progress. Tears don't come easily to me, but my dad can do things that bring them really fast. We've been on good terms for most of my life, but I don't say that we've ever been close. He's not one to volunteer hugs. But after I was finished with my story, he told me that he'd always love me. He had a couple of questions about things that I had said regarding memories of things he had done. We haven't talked much about my issues since then, but I know he still loves me, even if I have to prod him to give me a hug.

All of my immediate family and almost all their spouses know my story. We don't talk about the issues much and sometimes I wish they would ask, because what I have learned about myself fascinates me. More importantly though, it is obvious to me that I am valuable to them.

I still have challenges

In the past year I have learned that there are men here and there that I want to lust after. But I know what to do so that it doesn't turn into an obsession. In the end, I find myself learning that the feelings that come up when I see these men are the result of my being blind to an attribute of my own. They seem to have that attribute in abundance and I'm drawn to it.

For instance, I attended a meeting and couldn't keep my eyes off a younger guy. He kept looking my way too. At the end of the meeting, we talked, exchanged phone numbers, and began talking.

We shared that we were attracted to each other. We've become close friends, even though he lives in another state. Based on other work and reading that I did around that time, I believe that I kept on noticing his looks because I didn't think I was attractive. Since that time, I have made significant progress in believing other men when they tell me I'm attractive. I admit I'm working on accepting that.

A few months ago, I found myself drawn to a tremendously handsome man. Drawn so much that I couldn't be myself around him. I felt awkward and hyper-conscious of everything I did around him. The looks, however, weren't what was causing the problem. I judged him to be gregarious and to have a great ability to draw people in and captivate them. I was intimidated by that. I shared my thoughts with a friend who candidly told me that he thought I had those very abilities but that my abilities were more finely honed and effective. I was shocked. But I think that he's right.

So I view men that I am drawn to as gifts to me. They help me realize where I am blind to the great gifts that God has given me. Sometimes the road to the realization is exquisitely painful. Other times it is great fun. To me, it is important and good to have emotional intimacy with men. I can do this without becoming enmeshed, which I judge to be unhealthy.

"Where do I want to go?"

I don't like going into why I have experienced the feelings that I do. And the reason is simple: I don't know. I perceive that a cultural habit is the need to explain why something is the way it is. I believe that this habit is problematic for two basic reasons: first, the explanation may not be that useful, and second, what sounds plausible may not be true, or, if it is true, it may not be the whole story. As I review my life, I have observed my own tendency to be satisfied by plausible explanations only to find out later that the explanation was just dead wrong. So much of life is not as it seems. Therefore, asking why something is the way it is limits my ability to understand. Better to admit that I don't really know than to fool myself with the appearance of reasonability. I find that a more useful approach is to observe where I am and ask, "Where do I want to go, and how am I going to get there?"

I also dislike labels. I believe they limit me. Moreover, I believe labels cause confusion. Consequently, I don't use the term "gay". In my experience, people use the term to mean different things.

However, I don't gripe when other people use the word. Instead, I try to find out their definition so that I can understand fully what they are saying.

I believe that being drawn or attracted to anyone, man or woman, is perfectly acceptable in God's eyes if the attraction is free from lust. So it doesn't bother me when I enjoy spending time with men more than women. What matters is that I avoid preoccupation or sexual fantasy about the other person, wanting them to lust after me, or developing a desperate sexual or emotional need for the other person, whether man or woman. Most men are attracted to and like spending time with other men. The same thing is true for women. I believe I get into trouble where lust enters the dynamic. But if the dynamic is free from lust, then I can feel good about any such relationship.

A whole love

I know my story sounds like it is more about addiction recovery than about attraction to men, but for me the two are completely inter-twined. At one point I believed that all who are sexually attracted to the same sex must be sex addicts. I don't believe that generalization anymore, but it's my experience that progressive victory over lust brings peace to my relationships with those of my own sex.

I am still more comfortable with men than with women. I haven't dated a woman in about a year and a half. I think I'm just about ready to put a toe back in the water and start simply by building some friendships without necessarily dating.

I actively participate in my ward. I try to build up the men around me. Most of my elders quorum knows that I am a sex addict, but only one or two know that same-sex lust has been part of the story. Eventually I'll tell them, but right now it doesn't seem necessary to do so.

Meanwhile, I seek to support all the men around me. I particularly value the friendships I have made with "straight" men in Sexaholics Anonymous. In a day and age where men are often maligned and denigrated, I am happy to say that I love and support men with a whole love. I say this without shame.

"Jenny Fisher"

"Happiness doesn't depend upon who you are or what you have; it depends solely upon what you think."
– Dale Carnegie

I was born in Orem, Utah in 1992. My mom married my step-dad when I was four years old. They raised me as LDS, but religion was never forced; it was our choice. We moved to California when I was eight. I was very strong in the Church personally, and I tried to be an example for my family. Starting in junior high, for a couple years I was the only one in my family going to church. As the years went on, it became more and more difficult to continue doing this.

After the first month of my sophomore year in high school, I was assigned to sit next to "Melanie" in my math class. After class we would go have lunch together. When I turned 16, she and another friend got me 16 little gifts for my birthday: everything from a frisbee, to a slinky, to play dough. Melanie and I kept getting closer and closer. On April 1, I told her that I found myself wanting to kiss her. Because it was April 1, she was afraid I might be joking. But then a few days later, she opened up that she had been feeling the same way all along.

Throughout this time, I was pretty active and attended seminary and Mutual. Our church was only a block away, which was a blessing. When we had girls camp in our stake, I invited a couple friends along. They had a great time, and our leaders gave them copies of the Book of Mormon afterward. I felt like I was an example and wanted them to understand the light and happiness which the Church brought to my life, that they might feel it too.

That summer, I went on a youth trip to the beach with the young women in my ward. It lasted for several days, and I was texting

Melanie as often as I could. She had given me a playlist of love songs, because she felt as though the songs could put her feelings into words better than she could. I listened to it constantly during the whole trip, and realized my love for her was true, and greater than I originally thought. I missed her terribly.

We were truly in love

When I came home, I gave Melanie a jelly candle that I had made, with sand from the beach on the bottom. I started sleeping over at her house sometimes. We would go on many walks together. One night we found X's drawn in paint in the middle of the road. We stood on one, for probably about half an hour, joking about how "X marks the spot". We both felt the tension and wanted to kiss each other but were too afraid to do so. Another night I was at her house, and we went out on the back porch and talked for hours. Lying beside her that same night, I felt so much tension and anticipation and though our lips were mere centimeters away, we still didn't kiss.

I worked as a lifeguard, and Melanie would often come and visit me. I had to put tons of sunscreen on, and there were places I couldn't reach, so she would help me and make sure I got it all covered. There was one day I went into the restroom to re-apply my sunscreen, and she followed me to help. She had been working up her courage for several days, so after I was all slathered, she just came to me and kissed me. Surprised, and heart aflutter, I kissed her back. That was August 7th. It definitely put me in a twitter the entire day, and that feeling continued as our relationship progressed. We were truly in love, and it was so cute. We had a beautiful relationship. We were amazing and I loved it.

During this time, my friends and I were trying to find ourselves, what we believed in, and what we stood for. Regarding religion particularly, they believed in spiritual energies and in a bit of Buddhism. I liked the ideas of some things they were saying. I grew to believe in a combination of Mormonism and Buddhism.

Just going through a phase?

I would sleep over at Melanie's house every weekend that I could, and so I wouldn't make it to church every time. We were keeping our relationship secret, which made things difficult. As I spent more time with her, not being able to tell my family distanced me from them a lot more. After school I would often just go home with her, and some nights my parents wouldn't know where I was. They took my phone away for great lengths of time, which meant Melanie and I couldn't communicate. This just made the need and desire for us to communicate even greater, so I would get in more trouble trying to find ways to do so. However, because they took my phone, this meant my parents could not communicate with me either. Sometimes I would be gone for the whole weekend, up to three days, and they wouldn't know what to do. One time my mom got particularly upset and threatened to call the cops.

Meanwhile, my step-dad had been in Iraq for the past two years. Without his presence, my mom and I held no limits to our constant bickering. It was a difficult time for all of us. She wasn't able to understand me, and I was treating her really poorly. Without Dad, I knew my mom was really depressed and wanted me there to talk with and comfort and support her. However, I didn't want to be home; I wanted to be out with Melanie. My priorities were shot. Eventually my mom's depression became so bad she backed away from her responsibilities as a mother. I knew I needed to be home to take care of my younger siblings. By this time, it was too late. My efforts to help my mother just ended up with us constantly bickering, and the whole family in tears.

My mom had an idea about what was going on, but it was the last day of my junior year of high school when she found out for sure, by going through my IM chats. I was upset that she had violated my privacy. She thought I was just going through a phase. I tried to explain that the feelings were real, and that it wasn't just Melanie — I had a curiosity towards girls from as early as second grade.

My mom and dad discussed it and decided that the best thing was to send me away for the summer. They said that it wasn't because of my orientation or because of how close I was to Melanie, but just that my mom and I needed to take a break from each other. I argued, begging for mercy and the chance to make things better while still being able to spend my summer with my friends, but to no avail. So a mere two days after my mom went through my IM chats, I was in Kentucky with my aunt and uncle and their four kids for the whole summer.

First time away from home

In many ways, that summer in Kentucky was the best summer of my life. I was 17, and it was refreshing to have a sense of freedom, of being on my own. It was really good for me, helping me develop mentally, emotionally, and independently. I went to church with my aunt and uncle and their family. The branch was like a close-knit family, and I loved it. Everyone was so welcoming, and I was even asked on dates with a few boys in the branch.

I spent a lot of time with my aunt, talking about our families and relatives. She was my mom's sister, the one that I had known growing up. We talked about events from our past, and I helped her with cooking and other things around the house. I also spent a lot of time with my uncle. He taught me how to drive a stick-shift. We would go on runs together, we would go to the grocery store together, and we watched movies every night.

Over the summer, Melanie stopped talking with me. I felt comfortable enough to confide in my uncle about it. Because he was a counselor in the branch presidency, I asked him questions regarding the Church's standpoint and how it related to me. He showed me the article by Elder Holland.[24] We developed a lot of trust between us. He told me things from his past that he hadn't told anyone else, not even his wife.

Every night he would give me a hug before I went to bed, and over time the hugs became longer. He would leave for work at about 5:30 in the morning, and one time he came into my room and woke me up and kissed me before he left. He started messaging me while he was at work, saying things like, "I miss you. I look forward to going on a run when I get back."

His wife was starting to be bothered by what was happening. She talked to him, and he promised that nothing was going to happen. But she started to be on guard and made sure to be around a little more. Every time we watched movies at night, she would also be there. But there was one night when she was extremely tired and so three-quarters of the way through the movie, she decided to go to bed.

After she left, I felt scared, but we finished the movie and I went to bed. Then, at about 2:00 or 3:00 a.m., dressed in his robe, he came into my room, said my name, and told me to wake up. He walked

---

[24] "Helping Those Who Struggle with Same-Gender Attraction", *Ensign*, October 2007, 42–45.

me down to the basement and took my clothes off. He was already prepared with a condom and everything. I didn't know what to do. I was disgusted. It felt so gross. Eventually he had to leave for work, and I went back to my bed and stayed there.

Everyone found out

Soon after, I told my uncle, "This isn't okay. You have to tell someone about this." Over the next week, the guilt got to him, and he told his wife. She was irate and drove me to stay with my other aunt in Ohio, and I was sent home on a plane the next day.

When my uncle's affection towards me increased inappropriately, I hadn't told my parents what was happening, because I knew they wouldn't believe me and would think I was just trying to get home. When I did get home and explained why I hadn't told them as soon as his hugs lengthened, they said, "You're right, that's what we would have thought." They felt guilty about that.

My uncle never did take responsibility or apologize for what he did, and we took him to court. Some of my mom's family took my uncle's side, and we got a nasty email asking, "Why are you guys doing this?" My uncle tried to say that I had "consented", but this was legally impossible because I was 17. He went to jail for less than a month and was released on probation which, if he violates, would send him back to jail for five years. He is also registered as a sex offender.

He had to go to his stake president and step down from his counselor position in the branch presidency. He lived in a small town and because the news was on the front page, they had to move out of there. It's difficult, because they're family, and I love them. It wasn't about vengeance or anything, but it was just upsetting because he never took responsibility for it.

"Why aren't you talking with me?"

After coming home, my parents were definitely there for me. They kept me by their side, comforting me in any way they felt they could. We built up a strong relationship, and I felt I was closer with them than I had been able to be before.

When I got back, I confronted Melanie, asking why she hadn't been talking to me. I knew her answer. I had prepared for it. We argued for a week over text, but ultimately she decided that not only were we done, but that it'd be best if we no longer even talk to each other. She had graduated from high school and was moving away. And moving on. I had been ready for her to leave, but I was not ready for the painful way in which she broke away from me. It was very difficult for me to move on. My depression lasted for almost a year.

A week after I was home, my bishop asked me to come into his office to talk about the situation with my uncle. He suggested that I could have done a lot to prevent what had happened. In fact, this is what was emphasized — no offers of comfort or support. He instructed me to stop taking the sacrament, and to embrace the Atonement. I was appalled at how he seemed to be blaming me and making it my fault. Regardless, though, I stayed strong in the Church.

My parents put me into counseling. However, I ended up talking with the counselor more about Melanie and the issues with the break-up. At the time, I was more pained by that than I was about the situation with my uncle, which I was thinking was just a temporary physical thing. I wasn't thinking about how it would affect me later on in my relationships involving trust and intimacy.

I needed something to keep me busy

That year, I was president of the gay-straight alliance (GSA) at my high school. I also ended up getting in a relationship with a boy "Brian". We grew really close and cared deeply for each other. We helped each other through each of our issues, including the depressions we had been in. We were comfortable with each other and talked about everything, spending every day of the week but Sunday together.

One day in June 2010, Brian dropped me off at my house, and while driving to work, he went off the side of the road and lost control of the car; it spun at least three times and crashed, killing him instantly. I was the last person he saw and talked to, and this had a huge impact in my feelings of guilt. We had made so many plans for that summer, and with his death I was devastated.

I became very active and strong in the singles ward. Since my plans had been shattered, I needed something to keep me busy, to keep me sane. I loved going to church, and I did every activity that the singles ward offered. It brought the structure and organization to my life that I needed to help bring me peace.

That fall I came to school at BYU. I heard a lecture by Bill Bradshaw on the biology of homosexuality, and he mentioned a group called Understanding Same-Gender Attraction (USGA) that meets on BYU campus. I thought, "Finally what I have been looking for." It has definitely made a difference and has been really comforting to see that there are other people in the Church like me, especially at BYU.

The pure love of Christ

When I went home for winter break that year, my mom and I stayed up one night talking. We know that there are differences in our opinions, but she still loves me and respects me. She recognizes that I'm an adult and my decisions and actions are my own. I expressed my thoughts to her, including how I feel about homosexuality pertaining to the Church, which is very much based on the ninth Article of Faith:

> We believe all that God has revealed, all that He does now
> reveal, and we believe that He will yet reveal many great
> and important things pertaining to the Kingdom of God.

One of my BYU professors shared that he has a gay son. I felt comfortable enough to go into his office and talk with him. He has comforted and helped me immensely. We discussed how there are so many gay children being born into the Church, and there must be a reason for it. He and I both think that it is a test of members' faith. It was the same thing with blacks not being able to have the priesthood. The pure love of Christ is loving and accepting of everyone, and a lot of people don't fully understand that. I believe that one important thing God has yet to reveal will involve the acceptance of those who are same-gendered-attracted within the Church.

I know that God loves me

There's a side of me that says, "You could be so happy living with a girlfriend." But I do intend to stay with the Church, and I want to be married in the temple.

I think there's a difference between physical attraction and sexual attraction. There are people who I'm physically attracted to who I wouldn't want to have sex with. I find myself romantically, emotionally, and physically attracted to both men and women, but attracted sexually more so towards women.

I have a friend back home who is asexual. He's not LDS and has had sex before but just isn't sexually attracted. Sometimes I think it would be easier to be asexual, to not have to have feelings of sexual attraction. I've seen how relationships can sometimes be more about hormones and chemistry than they are about real care and affection, and there's pain in that. However, I know that in reality I wouldn't want these feelings to just go away; I know that wouldn't put me any better off.

Since being with Melanie, I haven't been to that same degree of being "in love". With her it was so perfect and amazing, and nothing has really come up to that level. I've been in loving relationships; just nothing yet has felt as impactful as that relationship with her. Right now I'm focused on my education and career. My romantic future is very unclear. Sometimes I have no idea whether I even want to get married. But whatever happens, I know that God loves me for who I am.

"Kyle Rogers"

"Nobody can go back and start a new beginning, but anyone can start today and make a new ending."
– Maria Robinson

When I was five years old, like other boys I played with trucks, cars, and action figures; but I also had a Ken Barbie doll, and I felt differently when I played with Ken. In the evening I would hide the doll under my pillow. At night I would wake up, take out the doll, and slowly undress him and kiss his body. Even then, as young as I was, I remember feeling excited, aroused, and surprised by my own feelings. I did not know what they meant.

By the time I was in fifth grade, I was aware that the other boys around me liked girls, and I thought that I must like them too. I talked about girls and would try to fantasize about their bodies.

In sixth grade, one of my friends told me a story about how he had caught his older brother naked in his room. I couldn't help but feel excited as I imagined this older boy. That's when I began to understand that I was attracted to men, not to girls.

When I entered junior high, I could no longer deny my feelings, but I tried to suppress them, and I didn't dare tell anyone. I vividly remember having crushes on the high school students and trying to become their friends. One of them was "Cory"; he was tall and muscular, and we shared the same P.E. schedule. Every day I would see him walking down the hall, and I would walk right next to him so that our shoulders would be touching; it was a thrilling experience that I looked forward to each day even if, looking back, that was slightly creepy of me!

The only gay person in the world

My sophomore year is when I began to be bullied and ridiculed for being "gay". Even though I had not so much as whispered a word of my sexual orientation to anyone, I was called "gay", "fag", or "queer" at least once a day. I didn't play into the gay stereotype, but since I didn't play sports and was involved in choir and drama, people just assumed. At times, the jocks would "flirt" with me to see if I would reciprocate and hence reveal my true sexuality. There were days when I could easily brush off the name-calling. There were times when I even pretended to laugh with them, as if their hurtful words really didn't affect me. In truth, the bullying and name-calling were the worst. What helped me get through each day was spending time with my friends, singing in the choir, exercising, and striving to maintain a positive attitude no matter what names people called me.

For a while, I had a girlfriend. Honestly, it was very weird. The entire time, it didn't feel right. I kept on trying to have physical feelings toward her, but they never came. Eventually, I couldn't take it anymore and broke things off. It was hard, but we worked through it and continued to be best friends.

There were many times that I would kneel at my bed and ask God to make me "normal". I remember crying and soaking my pillow with hot tears, wondering why God hated me or would give me such a damning trial. It felt like I was the only gay person in the world. In my journal, I wrote an entry to my parents:

> Reading this journal probably killed your hearts ... I have had these feelings since I was very young. I have had these feelings for a very long time. I have prayed fervently for them to stop. I have soak[ed] my pillow with tears crying over this curse. Has it gone away? No. Will it go away? No. Can you accept it? Yes. God is the ultimate judge in the end ... God loves me. I know it.

"You are my son, and I love you"

The first person who I came out to was my first cousin. We had grown up together, and we shared everything together: likes, dislikes, clothes, baseball cards, ideas, and secrets. It took me two years to tell him. I remember very vividly the feelings of anxiety, nervousness, and fear that rippled through my body. When I finally told him, he simply said, "Kyle, it doesn't change how I feel about you. We're like brothers and I will love you forever."

A few years later, when I was in high school, I was still working to build up the courage to tell my mother. I had written a letter for her but hadn't given it to her yet. Then, one day we were watching a documentary about Mormon missionaries, and my mother leaned over to me and said, "I just can't wait until you become a missionary."

My heart stopped. At that time in my life, I believed that someone who was attracted to their own gender could not serve a mission. I went into my bedroom, grabbed the letter, and gave it to my mother. She went into her room and closed the door.

About two hours later, I knocked on her door. I could tell that she had been crying. I lay on her bed, not knowing what to say. Shame, guilt, and fear were ebbing at the edges of my heart. I quickly asked, "Mom ... do you hate me?" She looked me directly in the eyes and lovingly responded, "Kyle ... I could never hate you. You are my son, and I love you."

I sobbed. I was so afraid that my mother would hate or disown me. Later that night, my father gave me some advice. Truth be told, at the time, he had held onto some older ideas about homosexuality, and some of his words were hurtful. But I knew that both my father and mother loved and supported me.

When I came out to my bishop, it was a positive experience. He thought that my homosexual attraction was simply a phase I was going through, but he tried to build me up and provide healthy support. He wanted to make sure that I was loved and cared for, and not hated or hurt.

Mission and BYU

I served full-time in the Portugal, Lisbon mission. Those two years were truly some of the best years of my life. While on my mission, I came out to five of the twelve companions who I served with. They never batted an eye; they loved and cared for me just as they would anyone else. It didn't matter who I was attracted to.

When I was accepted to BYU-Provo, I was ecstatic. I had heard wonderful stories of outstanding men and women who were serving faithfully in the Church even though they were gay. I wanted to be a part of that community, a community of love and appreciation. After two months of finding new friends at BYU, I came out to them. They were all accepting and loving. Their opinion of Kyle the human being did not change when they found out that I was attracted to the same gender.

After a period of time, I decided I was ready to change and become attracted to women. I met with a BYU psychologist, which was extremely beneficial and uplifting. My psychologist was loving and accepting and didn't try to force me to change my feelings. I also met with a prominent LDS psychologist who specialized in helping gay men "change". We met for several sessions, but I found that my attraction to men did not decrease, and that as I tried to shut out those feelings, they only became stronger, and I became more estranged from my friends, family, and God. After a horrible time of trying to change, I decided to stop.

Focusing on "What" and not "Why"

Many people, gay and straight, religious and non-religious, have tried to find out the root cause of homosexuality. The current LDS position is that we simply do not know what causes this attraction. For me, that is enough. I do not have to know if I was born with it. Whether these feelings come from God, come from nature or come from nurture, I do not know. What I do know is that the Lord loves me and will accept me for who I am, and not for who I am attracted to. God and His Son love all their children.

Just recently, I have come to the conclusion that if I want to have a happy and meaningful life when it comes to expressing my sexuality and accepting who I am, I need to stop focusing on the "Why" or "How" and focus on the "What".

Instead of trying to figure out why God gives homosexual attractions to His children (if He does), I have decided to try and understand *what* God wants me to do with my life and who to become.

This simple change of attitude and change of thinking has eased the burden of "struggling" with homosexuality ten-fold. Instead of beating myself up over the unanswerable question of *how* or *why*, I simply am searching for my purpose.

Does this mean that God wants me to have a wife and children? Does this mean that God wants me to find a same-gender partner and live a monogamous, fulfilling life? Does this mean that God wants me to live alone for the rest of my life? I do not know. I am searching for the answer. I feel as if it may take years — or my entire life — to find out *what* God wants me to do.

God loveth His children

I have a firm belief, that as the Church increasingly shows love, care, and appreciation to the GLBT community, Church members will follow suit. It is interesting that in my experience, the members of the Church who are most accepting are the younger generation — the "chosen generation".

My friends continue to provide me peace and support through the rough times and challenges of life that I face. My friends are unmovable forces in a life that seems to constantly be in motion. I love them and they love me for me.

If you are a young person struggling with this as I was, know that being a homosexual and a member of the Church of Jesus Christ of Latter-day Saints is not a death sentence. You can find happiness, peace and joy in life as you learn to understand *what* God wants you to do. I personally believe that regardless of what your parents say, what your friends say, or what your ecclesiastical leaders say, what really matters is what God has to say. Lean on Him and His Son, and your life will be filled with goodness, happiness and peace.

We may not know the answer to all things, but we do know this: "God loveth His children" (1 Nephi 11:17).

And He does love you.

Resources

Books

- *Goodbye, I Love You*, by Carol Lynn Pearson, Random House, 1986. "The true story of a wife, her homosexual husband, and a love that transcended tragedy."

- *Peculiar People: Mormons and Same-Sex Orientation* by Ron Schow, Wayne Schow, and Marybeth Raynes, Signature Books, 1991. "In Peculiar People, a wealth of resources chronicles the successes and failures of contemporary LDS homosexuals ... These include the findings of biologists, therapists, and religious scholars."

- *Love Undetectable: Notes on Friendship, Sex, and Survival*, by Andrew Sullivan, Vintage, 1999. "Sullivan asks hard questions about his own life and others'. Can the practice of friendship ever compensate for a life without love? Is sex at war or at peace with spirituality? Can faith endure the randomness of death? Is homosexuality genetic or environmental?"

- *Same-Sex Dynamics Among 19th Century Americans: A Mormon Example*, by D. Michael Quinn, University of Illinois Press, 2001. "Using Mormonism as a case study of the extent of early America's acceptance of same-sex intimacy, Quinn examines several examples of long-term relationships among Mormon same-sex couples and the environment in which they flourished before the onset of homophobia in the late 1950s."

- *Prayers for Johnathan*, by Bridget Night, 1st Books, 2002. "As a Christian mother, [Bridget] is terrified when she discovers her son has a same-sex attraction ... He logs into gay youth web sites and connects with a twenty-year-old gay young man [Soren] ... This book presents the e-mail exchange between

Bridget and Soren over a one-year period. Bridget shares her Christian reparative therapy views and Soren shares his pro-gay views ... This book demonstrates that sincerity exists in both groups and that mutual respect can be accomplished."

- *Anything but Straight: Unmasking the Scandals and Lies Behind the Ex-Gay Myth*, by Wayne R. Besen, Harrington Park Press, 2003. "Nationally recognized activist Wayne Besen spent four years examining the phenomenon of 'ex-gay' ministries and reparative therapies — interviewing leaders, attending conferences, and visiting ministries undercover as he accumulated hundreds of hours of research. The result is this groundbreaking exposé of the controversial movement that's revered by independent religious groups and reviled by gay and lesbian organizations."

- *In Quiet Desperation: Understanding the Challenge of Same-Gender Attraction*, by Fred Matis, Marilyn Matis, and Ty Mansfield, Deseret Book, 2004. "A parent's spiritual journey toward understanding. A young adult's search for purpose and peace."

- *Ex-Gay Research: Analyzing the Spitzer Study and Its Relation to Science, Religion, Politics, and Culture*, edited by Jack Drescher and Kenneth J. Zucker, Harrington Park Press, 2006. "Is homosexual orientation immutable — or can it be changed?"

- *Ex-Gays?: A Longitudinal Study of Religiously Mediated Change in Sexual Orientation*, by Stanton L. Jones and Mark A. Yarhouse, IVP Academic, 2007. "Is it ever possible for people to change their sexual orientation? Is the attempt to change potentially harmful?"

- *No More Goodbyes: Circling the Wagons around Our Gay Loved Ones*, by Carol Lynn Pearson, Pivot Point Books, 2007. "In *No More Goodbyes*, Pearson revisits the challenging subject of religious people relating to their gay loved ones who are often condemned by their church and — many believe — by God. Through stories gathered from the microcosm of Mormonism, it becomes clear how this emotional earthquake affects families of all faiths. The choices are crucial. The stories are tragic and triumphant ..."

- *Sexual Fluidity: Understanding Women's Love and Desire*, by Lisa M. Diamond, Harvard University Press, 2008. "This unsettling and original book offers a radical new understanding of the context-dependent nature of female sexuality. Lisa Diamond argues that for some women, love and desire are not rigidly heterosexual or homosexual but fluid, changing as women move through the stages of life, various social groups, and, most important, different love relationships."

- *Understanding Same-Sex Attraction*, by Dennis V. Dahle, A. Dean Byrd, et al., Brigham Distributing, 2009. "What is the truth about same-sex attraction? Can people really change? In this groundbreaking work, the authors of Understanding Same-Sex Attraction reach beyond the hype to dispel many of the false notions abounding about same-sex attraction."

- *No Going Back*, by Jonathan Langford, Zarahemla Books, 2009. "A gay teenage Mormon growing up in western Oregon in 2003. His straight best friend. Their parents. A typical LDS ward, a high-school club about tolerance for gays, and a proposed anti-gay-marriage amendment to the state constitution. In NO GOING BACK, these elements combine in a coming-of-age story about faithfulness and friendship, temptation and redemption, tough choices and conflicting loyalties."

- *Dear Mr. Stephens: Letters of Love and of Hope*, by Andy Fernuik, 2010. "Homosexuality and Faith... the world holds troves of keys, ready to unlock the universal mysteries now dividing families and nations ... As a young, gay Latter-day Saint, Andy Fernuik shares his love, his hope, and his beautiful paradox of same-gender attraction and faith in a loving, eternal God."

- *Gay, Straight, and the Reason Why: The Science of Sexual Orientation*, by Simon LeVay, Oxford University Press, 2010. "What causes a child to grow up gay or straight? In this book, neuroscientist Simon LeVay summarizes a wealth of scientific evidence that points to one inescapable conclusion: Sexual orientation results primarily from an interaction between genes, sex hormones, and the cells of the developing body and brain."

- *Homosexuality: A Straight BYU Student's Perspective*, by Brad Carmack, 2010. "You may be touched and learn some things you had never considered about same-sex marriage and homosexuality in the LDS church."

Church articles and statements

- "God Loveth His Children", 2007. http://lds.org/manual/god-loveth-his-children

- "Helping Those Who Struggle with Same-Gender Attraction" by Jeffrey R. Holland, *Ensign*, Oct 2007, 42–45.

- "First Presidency Statement on Same-Gender Marriage", 20 Oct 2004. http://newsroom.lds.org/article/first-presidency-statement-on-same-gender-marriage

- "Same-Gender Attraction", Interview by Church Public Affairs with Elder Dallin H. Oaks and Elder Lance B. Wickman, 2006. http://newsroom.lds.org/official-statement/same-gender-attraction

- "Church Supports Nondiscrimination Ordinances", 10 Nov 2009. http://newsroom.lds.org/article/church-supports-nondiscrimination-ordinances

- "Church Responds to HRC Petition: Statement on Same-Sex Attraction", 12 Oct 2010. http://newsroom.lds.org/article/church-mormon-responds-to-human-rights-campaign-petition-same-sex-attraction

Websites and Organizations

- A Guide for Latter-day Saint Families Dealing with Homosexual Attraction: "This guide is designed to help LDS families in which a family member experiences homosexual attraction." (http://ldsresources.info/guide)

- MoHo Directory: "The Moho Directory is a listing of all MOHO related blogs out there." (http://mohodirectory.blogspot.com)

- Exodus International: "Mobilizing the body of Christ to minister grace and truth to a world impacted by homosexuality." (http://exodusinternational.org)

- North Star: "North Star is a place of community for Latter-day Saints dealing with issues surrounding homosexual attraction who desire to live in harmony with the teachings of Jesus Christ and the values and doctrines of The Church of Jesus Christ of Latter-day Saints." (http://northstarlds.org)

- Affirmation: Gay & Lesbian Mormons: "We are an organization of people who believe in the worth of every soul regardless of their sexual or gender orientation. We rejoice in life. We reject the tyranny that would have us believe that who we are — gay, lesbian, bisexual, transgender — is evil or wrong ... We are a family that consists of active members of the LDS faith, former members and non-members." (http://affirmation.org)

- Evergreen International: "Evergreen is a nonprofit organization that helps people who want to diminish same-sex attractions and overcome homosexual behavior. It is also a resource to their loved ones, professional counselors, religious leaders, and friends." (http://www.evergreeninternational.org)

- People Can Change: "Facing the reality that you have unwanted homosexual feelings can cause tremendous turmoil ... But there is another way out. A path that led us to resolve rather than fight homosexual feelings. A path to authentic brotherhood. And to our innate heterosexual masculinity." (http://peoplecanchange.com)

- Gay Mormon Forum: "The mission of the Gay Mormon Forum is to shed positive light on the dialogue which is currently taking place in the LDS community on the topic of homosexuality, while fostering Christ-like approaches which encourage and affirm both the spirituality and wholeness of all human beings." (http://gaymormonforum.org)

- LDS Family Services: "LDS Family Services has 57 offices throughout the United States and 12 international offices in Canada, Great Britain, Australia, New Zealand, Japan, Mexico, Chile, and Brazil available to provide counseling services to individuals, couples, and families ... To receive counseling services, members may be referred by their bishop or branch president, or they may contact the agency directly." (http://providentliving.org/ses/emotionalhealth/0,12283,2129-1,00.html)

- The National Organization for Marriage: "The National Organization for Marriage (NOM) is a nonprofit organization with a mission to protect marriage and the faith communities that sustain it. Founded in 2007 in response to the growing need for an organized opposition to same-sex marriage in state legislatures, NOM serves as a national resource for marriage-related initiatives at the state and local level." (http://www.nationformarriage.org)

- Mormons for Marriage: "Mormons for Marriage supports marriage equality for all, and stands in respectful opposition to California Proposition 8." (http://mormonsformarriage.com)

- The Asexuality Visibility and Education Network: "AVEN hosts the world's largest online asexual community as well as a large archive of resources on asexuality. AVEN strives to create open, honest discussion about asexuality among sexual and asexual people alike." (http://asexuality.org)

- LDS Reconciliation: "LDS Reconciliation affirms the spirituality of Gays and Lesbians and seeks to provide a safe haven for individuals with a Latter-day Saint background to discuss the gospel of Jesus Christ." (http://www.ldsreconciliation.org)

- Gay Mormon Fathers – Gamofites: "Men united in the joys and challenges of being fathers, Gay, and Mormon. We are dedicated to fostering and supporting the needs and individual growth of members in an environment of confidentiality, trust, and unconditional love." (http://www.gamofites.org)

- PFLAG: Parents, Families, & Friends of Lesbians and Gays: "PFLAG supports LGBT people, their families and friends locally and nationally by providing PFLAG chapter helplines, support group meetings and resources ... PFLAG also advocates for equal rights for lesbian, gay, bisexual and transgender people on local, state, and national levels." (http://www.pflag.org)

- The Trevor Project: "A national 24-hour, toll free confidential suicide hotline for gay and questioning youth ... The Trevor Project is determined to end suicide among LGBTQ youth by providing life-saving and life-affirming resources ...." (http://www.thetrevorproject.org)

- Cor Invictus, a social networking website for gay or same-gender-attracted Mormons: "Some may choose to stay close to the teachings of the church ... Many will desire to date and meet that one person to build a life together with. A few will be family members or friends looking for information and a better understanding of these sensitive subjects ... We value all opinions and welcome respectful discussion ..." (http://www.corinvictus.com)

- Family Fellowship: "Family Fellowship is a volunteer service organization, a diverse collection of Mormon families engaged in the cause of strengthening families with homosexual members. We share our witness that gay and lesbian Mormons can be great blessings in the lives of their families, and that families can be great blessings in the lives of their gay and lesbian members." (http://www.ldsfamilyfellowship.org)

- Family Acceptance Project: "The Family Acceptance Project is the only community research, intervention, education and policy initiative that works to decrease major health and related risks for lesbian, gay, bisexual and transgender (LGBT) youth, such as suicide, substance abuse, HIV and homelessness – in the context of their families. We use a research-based, culturally grounded approach to help ethnically, socially and religiously diverse families decrease rejection and increase support for their LGBT children." (http://familyproject.sfsu.edu)

Glossary

Achievement Days: Activities for Primary children, emphasizing service and physical fitness.

Aaronic Priesthood: The *lesser priesthood*. It contains the offices of deacon, teacher, priest, and bishop, and includes the authority to baptize and administer the sacrament. Mormons believe that this authority was restored to Joseph Smith in 1829 through the laying on of hands of the resurrected John the Baptist.

Alma: One of the books in the Book of Mormon.

AP (Assistant to the President): The highest position of responsibility that a missionary may hold. APs assist the mission president in administering the mission.

apostle: A special witness of Christ. Next to the First Presidency, The Quorum of the Twelve Apostles is the highest governing body of the Church.

Articles of Faith: A list of 13 core beliefs written by Joseph Smith in 1842. The Articles of Faith are part of the Pearl of Great Price, one of the four volumes of canonized LDS scripture.

Atonement: The sacrifice of Jesus Christ which enables people to overcome the effects of sin, be resurrected, and obtain eternal life.

baby blessing: A blessing given to newborn infants. Typically, at church the father stands in a circle with other relatives and friends, holding the child and giving it a name and blessing.

baptism: The ordinance of immersing a person in water in the name of Christ. Mormons believe that baptism is essential for a person's salvation. In LDS temples, individuals are "baptized for the dead" (1 Corinthians 15:29), serving as proxy for those who were not baptized during their lifetime.

Beehive: A 12–13 year old participant in Young Women.

bishop: The highest office in the Aaronic Priesthood. A bishop and his two counselors form a *bishopric*, holding the responsibility for leading a ward. Bishops are unpaid and typically serve for no more than five to seven years.

blessing: A provident circumstance or gift from God. For other specific uses, see *baby blessing, patriarchal blessing*, and *priesthood blessing*.

Book of Mormon: One of the four volumes of canonized LDS scripture. Mormons believe that the Book of Mormon originates from an ancient American record written on metal plates, translated by Joseph Smith and published in 1830.

branch: A small LDS congregation, led by a branch president. A branch president may have two counselors to assist him.

BYU (Brigham Young University): The largest Church-owned university, located in Provo, Utah. It has sister schools BYU-Idaho and BYU-Hawaii.

calling: An inspired assignment to serve in a particular function in the Church.

The Church of Jesus Christ of Latter-day Saints: The church founded by Joseph Smith in New York in 1830. It received its current name in 1838. Members of the Church are commonly known as "Mormons".

confirmation: The ordinance in which a person receives the gift of the Holy Ghost and formally becomes a member of the Church. Individuals are typically confirmed within a week of their baptism. In temples, individuals are confirmed for the dead.

covenant: A sacred agreement between God and an individual. Mormons make covenants when they are baptized, partake of the sacrament, and attend the temple. See also *sealing*.

CTR (Choose The Right): A motto that is taught to children in the Church. Some choose to wear a "CTR ring" as a reminder to choose the right, i.e., to do the right thing in everyday situations.

deacon: An office of the Aaronic Priesthood which young men may receive at age 12. Deacons may pass the sacrament and are organized into *deacons quorums* headed by a *deacons quorum president.*

D&C (Doctrine and Covenants): One of four volumes of canonized LDS scripture. It consists primarily of revelations received by Joseph Smith between 1828 and 1843.

EFY (Especially For Youth): An annual week-long summer camp for LDS youth, held at various locations worldwide, dedicated to helping participants come unto Christ.

elder: An office in the Melchizedek Priesthood which men may receive at age 18. Among other things, elders hold the authority to give priesthood blessings. Elders are organized into *elders quorums* headed by an *elders quorum president.* Even though most men in the Church have been ordained as elders, the title "Elder" is generally applied only to full-time missionaries and to General Authorities.

eternal marriage: See *sealing.*

family home evening: A night set aside to spend with family (typically each Monday night). Family home evenings may include prayers, spiritual lessons, activities, and food.

Fast Sunday: Typically held on the first Sunday of each month, Fast Sunday is an opportunity for Church members to abstain from two meals and give a *fast offering,* a financial donation for the benefit of those in need. On Fast Sunday, church services include a *testimony meeting,* in which members of the congregation may stand and publicly share their testimony.

First Presidency: The highest governing body of the Church, consisting of the President of the Church and his two counselors.

General Authorities: The men who serve at the highest levels of Church leadership, including the First Presidency, the Quorum of the Twelve Apostles, and others.

General Conference: A worldwide Church meeting held twice per year, broadcast from Salt Lake City. It consists primarily of talks from Church leaders addressed to all Church members.

Godhead: Heavenly Father, Jesus Christ, and the Holy Ghost, who in Mormon teaching are three distinct beings. Heavenly Father and Jesus Christ have a body of flesh and bones, but the Holy Ghost does not. The Holy Ghost, also known as *the Spirit*, testifies of Heavenly Father and Jesus Christ and reveals truth to individuals.

gospel: The basic teachings of the Church, including the teaching that all mankind may obtain eternal life through Jesus Christ by faith, repentance, baptism, and the gift of the Holy Ghost.

Heavenly Father: See *Godhead.*

high council: A group of twelve men in each stake who assist the stake presidency. Each ward is assigned a high council member who visits the ward periodically.

home teacher: Each member of the Church is assigned a pair of home teachers who have the responsibility of visiting the member at least monthly and providing spiritual support.

Honor Code: The BYU code of conduct, which among other things requires that students be honest, use clean language, abstain from alcohol, tobacco, coffee, and tea, and live a chaste and virtuous life. See also *law of chastity.*

Institute (of Religion): A religious educational program offered by the Church Educational System to university students and other young adults.

Joseph Smith: Founder of The Church of Jesus Christ of Latter-day Saints. Joseph Smith was born in Vermont in 1805, saw God the Father and Jesus Christ in a vision in 1820, established the Church in 1830, and was murdered by a mob in Illinois in 1844.

Laurel: A 16–17 year old participant in Young Women.

law of chastity: The requirement that Church members not have sexual relations except with their lawfully wedded husband or wife.

LDS (Latter-day Saint): Members of the Church are called Latter-day Saints.

the Lord: Jesus Christ. See *Godhead* and *Atonement.*

Melchizedek Priesthood: The *greater priesthood.* It contains the offices of elder, high priest, patriarch, and apostle and includes the authority to perform priesthood blessings and confirmations. Mormons believe that this authority was restored to Joseph Smith through the laying on of hands of the resurrected apostles Peter, James, and John.

Mia Maid: A 14–15 year old participant in Young Women.

mission: All able young men are strongly encouraged to serve a two-year full-time mission for the Church at age 19 or soon thereafter. Young women are permitted to serve an 18-month mission if they wish, once they reach the age of 21. Missionaries primarily spend their time finding and teaching people who are interested in learning about the Church. For young men, serving a mission is often considered a rite of passage in the Church.

Mormon: This term is commonly used to describe the Church and its members. It originates from the fact that Church members believe in the Book of Mormon. The word Mormon in the Book of Mormon refers to a specific prophet-historian who compiled the ancient American record.

Moroni: A book in the Book of Mormon, named after Moroni, the son of Mormon. Moroni is the last writer in the Book of Mormon. He sealed and buried the ancient metal plates and subsequently appeared to Joseph Smith as a resurrected being, showing him where the plates were buried.

Mosiah: A book in the Book of Mormon.

Mutual: A social activity for Young Men and Young Women held in the evening once per month.

Nephi: A prophet-historian in the Book of Mormon. In one challenging, well-known passage of the Book of Mormon, Nephi is commanded by the Spirit to kill a man Laban, in order to obtain the *brass plates*, a sacred record which was in Laban's possession. Laban had previously robbed Nephi and his brothers and had tried to kill them. Nephi at first hesitates to kill Laban, but then obeys the voice of the Spirit.

ordinance: A sacred, formal act performed by priesthood authority. See also *baptism, confirmation, sacrament,* and *sealing.*

patriarch: A person who is ordained to give patriarchal blessings.

patriarchal blessing: A blessing given by a patriarch, offering personal guidance for a person's life. Members of the Church typically receive a patriarchal blessing by the time they are young adults; their patriarchal blessing is recorded and printed so that they may refer to it throughout their life.

priest: An office of the Aaronic Priesthood which young men may receive at age 16. Priests may bless the sacrament, and are organized into *priests quorums* presided over by the bishop of the ward.

priesthood: The authority to act in God's name. Men first receive the Aaronic Priesthood and then later the Melchizedek Priesthood.

priesthood blessing: A type of blessing which elders may give, through the authority of the Melchizedek Priesthood, by laying their hands on the head of a person who is sick or in need of comfort.

Primary: The Church's organization for children up to 11 years old.

prophet: A person called to speak for God. Members of the First Presidency and Quorum of the Twelve Apostles are sustained by the Church as prophets. The President of the Church is often referred to as *the prophet.*

Quorum of the Twelve: See *apostle.*

Relief Society: The Church's organization for women.

revelation: Communication from God to mankind. The Doctrine and Covenants contains revelations received by the prophet Joseph Smith. Individual Church members may receive personal revelation for their own lives.

sacrament: An ordinance performed each Sunday during *sacrament meeting*, in which Church members partake of bread and water in remembrance of Jesus Christ's body and blood.

Savior: Jesus Christ. See *Godhead* and *Atonement.*

scriptures: The canonized LDS scriptures consist of the Bible, the Book of Mormon, the Doctrine and Covenants, and the Pearl of Great Price.

sealing: An ordinance performed in temples to unite families for eternity. Couples who are married in the temple are eternally *sealed* to each other as part of the ceremony. Children who are born to eternally married parents are automatically sealed to them and are said to be *born in the covenant.*

seminary: LDS religious education for high school students.

set apart: After an individual accepts a calling to serve in a particular function in the Church, a leader *sets* them *apart* for their calling. This is done by having the person sit in a chair while the leader stands behind them, rests his hands on their head, and offers a prayer, blessing them in their service.

Spirit: See *Godhead*.

stake: A group of about five to ten wards, presided over by a *stake president* and his two counselors. An annual *stake conference* is held for all members of the stake.

Sunbeam: The Primary class for three-year-old children. The term occurs in a popular Primary children's song, "Jesus wants me for a sunbeam".

Sunstone Symposium: An annual four-day event held in Salt Lake City, not sponsored by the Church, but hosting discussions on all aspects of Mormonism.

teacher: An office of the Aaronic Priesthood which young men may receive at age 14. Teachers may prepare the sacrament, may serve as home teachers, and are organized into *teachers quorums* headed by a *teachers quorum president*.

temples: Sacred buildings where Church members make covenants and receive ordinances, including sealings. In order to enter the temple, Church members must have a current *temple recommend* signed by their bishop and stake president. To obtain a temple recommend, members must pay tithing and obey the law of chastity and Word of Wisdom, among other requirements.

Temple Square: The location of the Salt Lake Tabernacle as well as the Salt Lake Temple. This historic site is the most popular tourist attraction in Utah.

testimony: A spiritual witness about the truthfulness of gospel principles. For *testimony meeting*, see *Fast Sunday*.

tithing: The practice of giving 10% of one's income to the Church. These funds are used to maintain and expand the Church.

ward: A Church congregation, typically containing a few hundred members.

Word of Wisdom: The requirement that Church members abstain from alcohol, tobacco, coffee, tea, and illegal or harmful drugs.

Young Men and Young Women: The Church organizations for young men and women aged 12 to 17.